INTERVIEW LIKE A BOSS

INTERVIEW LIKE A BOSS
(A complete guide for job hunters.)

HANS VAN NAS

An imprint of Simon & Schuberr publishers.

FIRST EDITION, REV. 1

Library of Congress Cataloging-in-Publication Data

Van Nas, Hans-
    Interview Like A Boss / Hans Van Nas. -1st ed.
        p. cm.
Includes notes.
ISBN 978-0-692-47156-2
    1. Success in interviewing. 2. Strategic plannning 3. Negotiating in business. I.Title

05   06   07   08   09   ▲▼▲▼ RRD   10   9   8   7

No time to explain, get in!

WHAT WOULD YOU LIKE HELP WITH?

THE BASICS

ONE

....

MAKE YOUR SOUND/S BITE

~~"She wouldn't even let me holla. I was like, 'please you ugly anyway.'"~~

The first 20-seconds can put you in the friendzone, especially at an interview! Hiring managers decide pretty quickly whether they're feeling you or not.

That's why they start the interview by popping the "tell me about yourself" question.

The "tell me about yourself" question is the most common ice breaker, or opener to job interviews, that hiring managers ask. But if you're like everyone else, you're not exactly sure what the question is, so you're not exactly sure what the answer should be. You're a bit worried that a rambling, go nowhere introduction can knock you off the list, just as you're about to make your debut.

Now whatever you do, avoid giving the 'what do you want to know?' response. Nothing is more irritating to hiring managers. This goes back to the time factor: remember, you have just 20 seconds to impress them and answering a question with a question disrupts the flow.

What the hiring manager wants is a quick overview of who you are, professionally speaking.

Instead of freestyling it, stick to responding with a crisp, clean **FIVE** point introduction—**1** your name **2** your status **3** what you did at school or work **4** the type of person you are **5** why you decided to apply.

Your introduction sets the tone for the rest of the interview. Blow the answer and out you go. Put some swagger in your answer and you'll look hotter than the center of a microwave burrito.

What you should do next...

Get your mitts on one of the 20+ second intro examples (for your particular job) that matches your personality.

At this point, you can decide to **1** leave the example bone stock or **2** rip sentences and stitch together your own ONE-OF-A-KIND introduction.

Build it any way you like, but make sure you cover all **FIVE** points or you'll have a chunk of your intro missing. Oh, and if you're bi-lingual, say so! The hiring manager might be bi-curious. Wait, bi-curious might not be the right word, but we'll stop there. You get the point.

When you're ready to practice it, just keep repeating your intro over and over to yourself. It will sink in. You're 100% ready when you can picture the hiring manager and think COME AT ME BRO.

(Still have a "wut" on your face? Then look at the next page! The kuleness is off the chart! This is game changing, history making stuff right here!!)

CHOOSE AN INTRO...

TOTAL NOOB INTRODUCTIONS

example | smooth personality

(1) Good morning, my name is Bad Mammajamma and **(2)** I'm looking to join an organization where I can practice teamwork and handle greater responsibility in the real world. **(3)** With that in mind, I'm a very focused individual who easily picks up new direction. I am flexible with change, comfortable in a fast-paced environment and can handle busy phone lines. I would say that one of my favorite experiences is being a problem solver. **(4)** In fact, I see problems as an opportunity to learn. I never complain about something without offering a solution and realize that if you want to be successful you must work well with others and make meaningful commitments. **(5)** What I'm looking for now is gaining real, valuable work experience and refining the 'people skills' that I believe are key to my future professional success.

example | happy personality

(1) Good afternoon, my name is Jack Squat, and **(2)** when I found out about this opening, I knew I had to apply. From what I've learned, you are very committed to finding someone who can handle a real-world environment. **(3)** With that in mind, I'm a confident presenter, able to focus on a variety of detail-oriented tasks, and comfortable with digital tools. I believe in good time management because if you're good at managing your time, you're good at managing stress. **(4)** About me, what I've learned is that if you're positive and highly passionate about your work, your enthusiasm rubs off on the rest of the team. I'm great with moods and people, and teamwork really energizes me and makes me want to come to work everyday. **(5)** That's why this opportunity is so much more to me than money. It's a way to learn from others and experience what the world has to offer. To me the real joy of life is working.

...MORE ▶

example | **online personality**
(1) Real pleasure meeting you, my name is Bayou Bob and **(2)** what brings me to apply here today is I'm looking to gain as much experience as possible from a proven team such as yours. **(3)** Some of my greatest strengths are my online social media skills. Computers and other digital tools have helped me build my problem solving abilities, make new contacts and learn to multitask. In fact, over the next two years I plan on taking online classes to give myself even more exposure to the digital world. **(4)** About me, what I'm most proud of is my work ethic. I work until the job gets done, regardless of the time clock and have a sense of urgency when completing a task. I am proficient working independently or as a productive team player. **(5)** However, I would say that experience is the thing I'd like to improve upon most. That's why when I found out about this opening, I applied at once. The way I see it, your real education begins here.

example | **everyday personality**
(1) Thank you for this opportunity, my name is Pimp Aderos and **(2)** I've applied for this position for the chance to work closely with an experienced team. **(3)** Thanks to some great opportunities, I've become a good problem solver who can think on my feet. I work well with a diverse group of people and would say that the most important skill I've learned is to apply common sense and take care of issues without having to wait for step-by-step instructions. **(4)** In fact, I consider myself the right arm support for a manager or team. I'm flexible with my schedule, to support staff or cover vacations, and would welcome the chance to be cross-trained with additional tasks. (I'm also Spanish-English bilingual.) **(5)** Looking at your company, my background seems particularly well suited to this role and I would welcome the chance to work with you!

TELL ME ABOUT YOURSELF

USE THIS SPACE TO CREATE YOUR OWN VERSION OF THIS INTRO.

ACCOUNTING & HR INTRODUCTIONS

example ⏐ accounting & financial services
(1) My name is Ken Spiracy, and **(2)** I'm a recent graduate of Manchesthair College earning a Business Management diploma. **(3)** Some of my technical know-how includes petty cash and credit card reconciliation, daily closing, invoicing adjustments, as well as check reimbursement. I'm proficient with Quickbooks® and pride myself on preparing clear and accurate reports. I've been responsible for checking documentation for accuracy and am comfortable using digital tools. **(4)** Although a strong point of mine is attention to detail, I consider myself more of a creative problem solver. I easily pick up new direction and can handle sensitive issues with diplomacy and even-handedness. I'm also open to being cross-trained to assist with additional responsibilities because that seems to be the way this industry is heading. **(5)** I've applied for this position because I excel in the kind of collaborative working environment you've built here. From what I've seen, you definitely have the capacity for me to grow my skills.

example ⏐ human resources
(1) I appreciate the opportunity to be here this morning, my name is Elemenopy, and **(2)** I've spent the last two years preparing myself to work in human resources. **(3)** Thanks to the day-to-day operations at my prior job, I've become proficient conducting compliance audits, developed working knowledge of HRIS and Payroll systems and even found ways to improve the pre-boarding, on-boarding, and off-boarding processes. I consider confidentiality a top priority and like to react quickly to identify and solve problems. I've also become quite familiar with compensation frameworks (and have experience with work visas and green card processes.) **(4)** What I'm most proud of is promoting an employee-oriented, high performance culture. We spend so much of our lives at work, and I like to make sure employees are happy here. **(5)** That's why when I found out about this opening, I knew I had to apply. I am quite interested to learn more about the needs of your department, and if we determine I'm a good fit for this role, ready to begin contributing.

9

ADMIN ASSISTANT · SALES · MANAGEMENT INTROS

example ı **administrative assistant**
(1) Good morning, my name is Paige Turner, and (2) I'm a recent Manchesthair College graduate (3) where I've received extensive training in administrative assisting and business management. My qualifications include strong calendar management skills and proficiency with Microsoft Office®, which seems exceptionally well suited to this role. I'm also comfortable coordinating meetings, conference calls and point-to-point travel, if needed. (4) About me, I'm a problem solver with the ability to handle very hectic situations. I'm great with moods and people and have the ability to "put-out fires" quickly and then move on. Good phone etiquette has always come easy to me and I think my internet savvy could be particularly valuable to you. I pride myself on being a forward thinker and am very detail oriented. (5) In fact, I see myself as the right arm support to a leader or team. That's why when I found out about this opening, I applied at once.

example ı **sales & marketing**
(1) My name is Sideshow Bob, and (2) I really wanted to learn every aspect of this business from the ground up, so I enrolled in Manchesthair College and recently graduated with a business diploma. (3) I worked hard to learn everything from promotional planning and advertising to using web collateral for growth and profitability. (4) What I'm most proud of is my ability to connect with people and talk directly to the client's needs. I am a persuasive communicator with well-developed presentation skills and love the challenge of working under pressure and facing deadlines. (I'm also bi-lingual.) (5) Your company's fast-paced, learning-rich environment caught my eye because, for people with a get things done attitude, this position has a lot of appeal.

...MORE ▶

example I management
(1) Thank you for this opportunity, I'm Trilobite, and (2) I am a graduate of Manchesthair College with a Business Management diploma. (3) I'm a really energetic person and a real self-starter. What I mean by self-starter is that I like to motivate teams and get them to deliver targets. I'm experienced in recruiting talent, locating and organizing resources, and can fill any gaps to improve performance without increasing COGS (cost of goods sold). I can also run a major change project. Thanks to some great opportunities, I've been able to refine my online social media skills which, frankly, can make many feel lost. (4) I would say that one of my best qualities is that I'm a hands-on person who enjoys maintaining a high level of work intensity. I love rallying team members together to meet the needs of the customer and giving employees a sense of worth and the feeling that they matter. I have a strong record of controlling expenditures and can think on my feet. (5) I know that your company is looking to connect with someone who can get off to a fast start, roll-up-their-sleeves and begin taking on responsibility. And that's what brought me to apply here today.

ADMINISTRATION INTRODUCTION

example
(1) Thank you for the chance to meet with you this morning, I'm Sofa King Happy and **(2)** I'm looking for the opportunity to advance my career with a large, diverse [financial, legal, regulatory, educational, security, IT, research...] group such as this. **(3)** Thanks to my most recent assignment, I developed a great rapport with our clients (to help foster a positive company and brand image). I also played a critical role performing budget reporting and forecasting, reviewing and analyzing reports in order to identify best practices. But I would say that my chief strength is that I'm a creative problem solver with the ability to balance multiple priorities and deadlines. (I can successfully implement position control and redeploy staffing lines to other units with greater needs.) And I have considerable proficiency with the MS Office Suite® [Quickbooks®]. A high-performance culture like this requires a deep, strategic knowledge of trends and contemporary developments. And I'm adept at preparing ad-hoc reports for center and institute leadership and can translate complex information to a non-technical audience. **(4)** Outside of my skills, I can work independently on self-guided projects or cooperatively as part of a team. (I am flexible with my schedule, available for extended travel, and willing to work regardless of the time clock to resolve any issues.) I can handle sensitive matters with diplomacy and even-handedness, and am happy to liaison between business units and support resources. I'm also open to being cross-trained to assist with additional responsibilities because that seems to be the way this industry is heading. **(5)** I realize that this is a very demanding role and you're looking for a candidate who will thrive in this position. If we determine I'm a good fit, I'm ready to roll-up-my-sleeves and begin taking on responsibility. Because the prospect of accessing the knowledge base that comes with an experienced group such as this is very exciting.

CHEF INTRODUCTIONS

If you have fast food experience, SAY SO. Fast food workers are the superheroes of the service industry. They've seen it all.

example | restaurant
(1) My name is Thrill Billy and (2) and even in culinary school, I knew I wanted to apply here. Everyone has a different style but I want to learn YOUR technique, and I'm prepared to roll up my sleeves, wash dishes and work my way up. (3) About me, I pride myself on my strong knife cuts and keep my knives super sharp. I'm also flexible with my schedule and can easily handle overnights. (4) I realize that if you want to be successful you have to make meaningful commitments and you also have to work well with others. That means tell me how you want your misenplace prepped and I'll have it done AND be consistent day-after-day. (5) From what I understand, you're looking for someone to get into your kitchen and bust their behind. I'd like to be a part of that. I want to learn how to cook and gain as much experience as possible which is why this job appeals to me so much. The way I see it, your real education begins here.

example | restaurant
(1) Good morning, I'm Carney Asada and (2) I recently graduated from Manchesthair Culinary Institute. (3) Thanks to my most recent experience (externship), I've become a great multitasker. Whether it's knife cuts or working until the job gets done, regardless of the time clock, I take pride in every detail. In fact, my misenplace is always ready when you need to fire it. (4) About me, I'm a really energetic person who's a real self-starter; what I mean by self-starter is that when I prepare or execute food items at a given kitchen station—grill, sauté, Garde Manger—I like to leave stations prepped and clean for the next shift. (5) Of course, I realize there are many ways of doing things, and

...MORE ▶

everyone does it differently, so I want to know: how do YOU want it done? I'm ready for you to tell me what product you stock and what you want me to do with it to make dinner, lunch and breakfast.

example | catering
(1) Good afternoon, my name is Kim Chee, (2) and I'm looking for a new opportunity to ~~ROCK~~ join a caterer where my 'get things done' attitude and skills can be put to use. (3) My most recent job (externship) played a big part in my decision to apply here. Much of my time was spent learning how to organize my misenplace and making sure my misenplace is consistent in size, something I understand you look for. That said, I'm ready to start from scratch everyday and not get one step up. The way I see it, the more techniques you learn, the more range you have—the more valuable you are. (4) While I'm a newcomer to catering, I will put in the time needed to get up to speed as quickly as I can. When it's time to hustle and they say run, you run, and that's why organization to me is HUGE. (5) When I found out about this opening, I applied at once. This is the place I've been looking for and I'm excited to learn in a high-volume, fast-paced kitchen.

COMPUTER SCIENCE INTRODUCTIONS

example ı graduate looking for work
(1) Good morning, my name is Xiaomao and **(2)** I'm a recent Manchesthair CS (computer science) graduate [Software Engineer | Software Developer | Computer Programmer] looking for a career opportunity to (advance my) work with high-performance software systems. **(3)** I really wanted to learn every aspect of CS (computer science) from the ground up, so I learned as much as I could while in school and during my internship was a lead developer on [an open VR SDK, genetic fuzzy tree, Monte-Carlo tree search with deep neural networks, natural language processing, the EM algorithm...]. In fact, I'm very involved with the developer community. And I would say that one of my favorite experiences is interacting and brainstorming with other CS engineers [developers | programmers] and debating the merits of different approaches. I've always been of the opinion that great engineers [developers | programmers] aren't linked to a specific language, and because I want systems to be as future-proof as possible I'm adept at [modifying existing software to optimize operational efficiency, correcting errors, performance-load testing, feature and system testing, designing the right interfaces, developing best practices for scaling an application] as well as [ENIAC, PHP, JavaScript, C++, SQL, Ruby, Java, C#, Python, Ruby, C...]. **(4)** About me, I consider Computer Science the business of learning. And when stepping into a new platform I love to teach myself anything I don't yet know. I pride myself on writing clean code and am ready to take on any one of multiple roles. I'm great with moods and people, and would say that the most important skill I've learned is to apply common sense and take care of issues without having to wait for step-by-step instructions. **(5)** What I'm looking for now is gaining real valuable work experience, and I believe that joining a company like this one will give me those opportunities. [Pootykat, Inc.] is my top choice employer. And I've applied for this position because I excel in the kind of collaborative work environment you've built here.

...MORE▶

example ı experienced

(1) It's a pleasure to be here, I'm Yuhr Daddy and (2) I'm a [Software Engineer | Software Developer | Computer Programmer] looking to help drive innovative software with a dynamic engineering company such as yours. (3) Thanks to some great opportunities, I've spent the last 5 years in various senior developer roles iterating robust, stable software solutions. Because our industry progresses at a rapid pace, I'm heavily involved with the developer community [attend-speak at numerous regional developer conferences, user groups...] and keep up-to-date with the latest trending technologies. I would say that one of my favorite experiences is interacting and brainstorming with other CS engineers [developers | programmers] and debating the merits of novel [frameworks]. (I enjoy creating mental models of how the parts of a system will work to anticipate problems and plan ahead in the design—models that help me refine my architecture.) I've always been of the opinion that great engineers [developers | programmers] aren't linked to a specific language, and because I want systems to be as future-proof as possible I'm adept at [modifying existing software to optimize operational efficiency, correcting errors, performance-load testing, feature and system testing, designing optimal interfaces, developing best practices for scaling applications...] as well as [PHP, JavaScript, C++, SQL, Ruby, Java, C#, Python, Ruby...]. (4) About me, I would say that my chief strength is that I'm a hands-on, creative problem solver. I easily pick up new direction, and like to react quickly to identify and solve unexpected issues, especially on tight timelines. I'm flexible with my schedule, and proficient working independently or as team-member [cooperatively with distributed teams throughout the globe]. (5) I know that your company is looking to connect with someone who can get off to a fast start, roll-up-their-sleeves and begin delivering targets. And that's what brings me to apply here today—the chance to work and grow in a high-performance culture such as yours.

DENTAL ASSISTANT INTRODUCTIONS

example ı **about to graduate**
(1) Thank you for the opportunity to be here, my name is Ginger Vitis and **(2)** I'm about to graduate Manchesthair College with a comprehensive education as a dental assistant. **(3)** This past summer I was able to extern with a busy practice and administered x-rays and set-up instrumentation for the doctor. During my "down" time, I restocked and escorted patients to their rooms. I would say that one of my favorite experiences was setting temporary crowns (and it's also the thing I'd like to really improve upon.) **(4)** What I'm most proud of are my excellent chairside manners and telephone etiquette. A trip to the dentist can be very stressful and patients need someone they can relate to...that they can feel comfortable with. I enjoy putting people at ease, especially children, and am proficient working independently or as a productive team player. (I am also bi-lingual.) **(5)** What I'm looking for now is gaining real, valuable work experience as a dental assistant. I'm very impressed with the setting you have here and if we determine I'm a good fit, I'm ready to start contributing.

example ı **recent graduate**
(1) My name is Drew A. Blanc, and **(2)** I'm a recent graduate of Manchesthair College earning a dental assistant diploma. **(3)** I've always loved science, so I learned as much as I could while in school and became especially skilled at instrumentation, x-rays and tray-setups. Filing and working with digital technology has always come easy to me and I'm at my best while working under pressure and faced with the challenges of a busy office. **(4)** About me, what I learned is that if you're positive and highly passionate about your job, your enthusiasm rubs off on the rest of the team. In fact, I chose this field because making connections with patients really energizes me and makes me want to come to work everyday. **(5)** That's what brings me to apply here. I'd love to work and learn alongside an experienced team such as yours.

...MORE ▶

example | graduate looking for work

(1) I'm Misty Waters, and **(2)** I am a graduate of Manchesthair Technical Institute accelerated dental assistant program with over 160 hours externship hours. **(3)** As a dental assistant, I've rotated through the back office administering x-rays, setting-up instrumentation and I became particularly good at coronal polishing. What greatly interests me is assisting with temporary crowns and insurance verification, which I see as the next logical step in my career. **(4)** I would say that one of my favorite experiences was appointment scheduling because I like to make people feel like they're being taken care of. I always treat people with a warm, caring attitude. I'm great with moods and people and flexible with my schedule to help support staff or cover vacations. **(5)** My internship made me realize how much I really wanted to be a dental assistant and that's what brings me to apply here today. From what I've seen, you definitely have the capacity for me to grow my skills.

BIOMEDICAL ENGINEER INTRODUCTION

example

(1) I appreciate the opportunity to be here this afternoon, my name is Trauma Momma and **(2)** I've applied for this position to help drive the development of [sensor systems, therapeutic devices, algorithms, imaging, prosthetics, nanoparticles, bioengineered organs...] with a leading-edge institution such as yours. **(3)** My most recent experience (internship) included participation in groundbreaking research on nanoparticles that could stop internal bleeding (special projects). I helped deploy analytics that detect and track disease states of patients and developed a strong familiarity with the NRTL certification process (CSA, UL, ETL). I would say that one of my favorite highlights was interacting with clinicians and patient advocacy groups. Being part of a multi-disciplinary team, I collaborated with key opinion leaders to advance a technological breakthrough in [nanotech]. **(4)** About me, I'm an instinctive self-starter and able to prioritize and reprioritize tasks. Technologies may be sensitive, so I like to react quickly to identify and solve problems, especially those on tight timelines. I consider myself a skilled problem solver, an advanced technical writer—I'm capable of translating complex information to a non-technical [lay] audience—and am a persuasive communicator with well-developed presentation skills. **(5)** One of the most rewarding aspects about this field is interacting and brainstorming with other BMEs (Biomedical Engineers) and technical teams on [science] that helps people live better lives. That's why when I discovered this opening, I applied at once. I would welcome the chance to contribute my clinical and biological knowledge in a high performance culture such as yours.

MASSAGE THERAPIST INTRODUCTIONS

C'mon you! Unleash your personality with a MAN-grip handshake that's sure to make a killer first impression on the hiring manager.

Massage therapy is a fascinating practice based on your awesomely powerful **phalanges**.

example ı graduate
(1) Real pleasure meeting you! My name is Chupa Cabra and (2) I'm a graduate of the Massage Therapy program at Manchesthair College. (3) I'm a really energetic person and a real self-starter. What I mean by self-starter is that I love putting new clients at ease by explaining every step of the way, including the benefits of massage. The more you go, the healthier you'll feel! (4) I'm especially skilled in cranial sacral, prenatal and triggerpoint and am comfortable working in a fast-paced environment. (I'm also English-Spanish bilingual.) (5) The way I see it, calm and stress relief begins here, with me, which is why this job appeals to me so much. To be honest, I'm looking at a few organizations at the moment, but your practice definitely has the capacity to grow my skills.

example ı recent graduate
(1) Great to meet you, my name is Neil Down, and (2) I'm recent graduate of Manchesthair Tech's massage-therapy program. (3) My specialties are deep tissue massage, to improve the breathing and enhance relaxation response, and sports massage, to help reduce pain. (4) I like going home at night knowing that my body work sessions promote relaxation and well-being. About me, I am in excellent health and can easily manage an abundant number of clients each week. (5) Because of my willingness to learn new skills, and desire to help people, I believe this might be the kind of office I'm looking for.

...MORE ▶

example ı self-employed but now wanting to get hired on.
(1) I'm Crocodile, and **(2)** I'm in private practice as a licensed in-home massage therapist. **(3)** By using the simple but powerful tool of touch, I have enjoyed seeing how my bodywork sessions help clients overcome stress and cruise through health obstacles with more confidence than they thought possible. It's rare in life to be able to say that you've made someone's life better. **(4)** Professionally speaking, my experience includes deep tissue, Swedish and reflexology. My favorite is working bits loose on larger people because it's challenging in terms of sheer tissue volume that needs to be worked over, but that's the fun part for me. **(5)** Thanks to some great opportunities I have had a chance to work in many different environments. But while traveling has its perks, I'm ready for the next step in my career.

CIVIL ENGINEER INTRODUCTION

example
(1) Thank you for this opportunity, my name is Dinosaur and (2) I'm an engineer-in-training [with a BS in Chemistry and] about to graduate Manchesthair's Bachelor's [Master's] of Science Civil Engineering program. (3) I've always loved engineering and material science so I learned as much as I could while in school, and during my training, was selected as team leader to coordinate multiple group projects. My chief strength was locating and organizing resources as project manager, and I advanced my drafting skills to include proficiency in Microstation®, Inroads®, as well as AutoCAD®. Professionally speaking, I'm flexible with change and can work independently conducting site visits, plot plans, and can manage designs and drafting with little instruction. I'm also a confident presenter. I'm ready to interface with structural engineers, soils engineers, City Building plan checkers, and clients. (I can also run a major change project and pride myself on reviewing structural analysis and calculations for accuracy.) (4) About me, I'm a creative problem solver with the ability to handle very hectic scenarios. I'm at my best when facing the challenges of a real-world setting and working under pressure. What I've learned is that if you're positive and highly passionate about your job, your enthusiasm rubs off on the rest of the team. (5) What I'm looking for now is gaining real, valuable work experience from a leader in this industry. [Toxic Toilet, Inc.] is my top choice employer. I'm very impressed with the setting you have here and I've applied for this position because I excel in this kind of collaborative work environment.

MEDICAL ASSISTANT INTRODUCTIONS

example | about to graduate
(1) I'm Supafly, and **(2)** I'm about to graduate Manchesthair College's medical assisting program and will be completing my 160 externship hours this month. **(3)** I've rotated through the back and front office, performing venipunctures, stocking treatment rooms and answering busy phones. I've also participated in taking 4-5 basic medical histories of patients. What greatly interests me is checking eligibility and insurance verification, which I see as the next logical step in my career. **(4)** About me, I like to make people feel like they're being taken care of and always treat patients with a warm and caring attitude. I'm great with moods and people and (am also English-Spanish bi-lingual.) **(5)** I'd love to gain as much experience as possible which is why this job appeals to me so much. I'm excited about the kind of fast-paced working environment you've built here.

example | just graduated
(1) My name is Max E. Pad, and **(2)** I recently graduated from an accelerated medical assisting program with over 160 externship hours. **(3)** I've always loved the medical field, so I learned as much as I could while in school and during my externship I administered 7-8 venipunctures, 5 injections, and performed basic labs. I would say that one of my favorite experiences is working the back office because of the one-on-one you get with patients. In the front office, I was responsible for answering busy phone lines, which has always come easy to me, and helped schedule appointments and greet patients. **(4)** About me, I'm at my best while working under pressure and faced with the challenges of a fast-paced office. What I've learned is that if you're positive and highly passionate about your job, your enthusiasm rubs off on the rest of the team. **(5)** What I'm looking for now is gaining real, valuable work experience as a health care professional. I'm very impressed with the setting you have here and if we determine I'm a good fit, ready to start contributing.

...MORE ▶

example | graduated a while ago but no job as of yet
(1) I'm Juju Beez, and **(2)** I've spent the last year completing my medical assisting diploma at Manchesthair college. **(3)** This past summer I was able to gain real valuable work experience by externing as an MA. Much of my time was spent in the front office as administrative support including scheduling appointments, explaining paperwork to new patients or walk-ins, and following up on appointment "no shows." During my "down" time, I restocked and escorted patients to rooms. I love the feeling I get when I make a patient feel comfortable and happy. **(4)** Outside of my skills, healthcare is a 24-hour a day system and I can manage any schedule to support staff or cover vacations. I am flexible with change and can easily pick up new direction. **(5)** That's why I'm excited to begin my work and learn from an experienced team such as yours. From what I've seen, you definitely have the capacity for me to grow my skills.

example | experienced
(1) Good morning, my name is Chulo, and **(2)** I'm a certified medical assistant with three years of experience looking to bring my skills to a busy practice such as yours. **(3)** Professionally speaking, my front office skills include scheduling, charting, and handling prescriptions. My back office qualifications include phlebotomy, administering injections, vitals and assisting the doctor with treatments **(4)** Though the patient load can get heavy at times, making connections with patients really energizes me and makes me want to come to work everyday. And the way I see it, if you're good at managing time, you're good at managing stress. I feel it's my duty to provide the best care at all times and be personable with a sense a humor. In fact, I see myself as the right arm support to the doctor and team. **(5)** That's why when I found out about this opening, I applied at once. This position fits well with my go-getter personality.

example ı **children oriented**

(1) Thank you for the opportunity to be here, my name is Pubert and **(2)** I just graduated Manchesthair College with a comprehensive education as a medical assistant. **(3)** Thanks to my most recent experience (externship), I was given the chance to work directly with patients in a fast-paced environment. My responsibilities included rooming patients, helping set up the treatment rooms in-between patients, as well as checking eligibility and basic insurance verification. The doctors and MA's were really great because anytime a patient needed treatment, they always invited me to participate or observe. **(4)** In general, I would say that one of my favorite experiences was putting nervous patients at ease, especially the younger patients and kids. I love this work and particularly enjoy interacting with children, which is just a great fit for my personality because I'm a big kid at heart. **(5)** When I found out about this wonderful opportunity to work with children, I knew I had to apply.

USE THIS SPACE TO CREATE YOUR OWN VERSION OF THIS INTRO.

MEDICAL BILLING INTRODUCTIONS

example

(1) Good morning, my name is Erma Gerd, and **(2)** I'm a recent graduate of Manchesthair College medical billing program. **(3)** Thanks to some great opportunities (externship), I've developed rapidly as a medical biller and have working knowledge of ICD9, CPT coding and am comfortable with MS Office® software modules like Excel®. I'm also HIPAA certified and can easily manage frequent interruptions. Good phone etiquette has always come easy to me and I think my ability to handle difficult accounts could be particularly valuable to you. What greatly interests me is appeals and pre-determination processes, and contracting with HMO, PPO, Medicare® and Medi-Cal®, which I see as the next logical step in my career. **(4)** About me, I like to make people feel like they're being taken care of and always treat patients with a warm and caring attitude. I'm great with moods and people (and am also English-Spanish bi-lingual.) **(5)** I'd like to learn more about the needs of your busy practice, and if we determine I'm a good fit for this role, ready to start contributing.

example

(1) Thank you for the opportunity to be here, my name is Terry Dactyl and **(2)** I'm a graduate from Manchesthair college where I earned by medical billing diploma and HIPAA certification. **(3)** I've always loved the medical field, so I learned as much as I could while in school and became especially proficient with direct billing functions and claim gear for HMO, Medi-Cal®, Medicare® and PPO's. My hands-on experience includes the MS Office® software modules, data entry and I always ensure proper coding compliance with CPT, ICD-9, UB-04 and HCPCS. **(4)** Although a strong point of mine is attention to detail, I consider myself more of a creative problem solver. I can handle sensitive billing issues with diplomacy and even-handedness and am comfortable contacting insurance companies and doctors' offices for answers to

...MORE ▶

31

billing and payment-related questions. **(5)** What I am looking for now is an office where I can use my abilities to create solid, long-term relationships with patients, and help the organization grow. I'm also open to being cross-trained to assist with additional responsibilities because that seems to be the way this industry is heading.

example

(1) My name is Pico de Gallo and **(2)** I'm a recent graduate from Manchesthair college where I earned by medical billing diploma and HIPAA certification. **(3)** Professionally speaking, much of my time has been spent performing real time billing and follow-ups with insurance carriers, which includes determining if accounts are billed properly, and that all payments and adjustments have been applied correctly. In order to handle a very high volume of billing and collections, I prioritize my workload and have become accustomed to the workings of a busy practice. My skills with claim gear, CMS-1500 and experience with Medisoft® have also been a big plus. **(4)** About me, I'm a problem solver with the ability to handle very hectic situations. I'm at my best while working under time pressure and have the ability to "put-out fires" quickly and then move on. What I learned is that if you're positive and highly passionate about your job, your enthusiasm rubs off on the rest of the team. **(5)** I've applied for this position because I excel in the kind of collaborative working environment you've built here.

ELECTRICAL ENGINEER INTRODUCTION

example

(1) Pleasure to be here and thank you for this opportunity. My name is Noneofthe Above and **(2)** I'm an Electrical Engineer looking for the chance to grow and innovate in a diverse, team-based environment such as yours. [ALTERNATIVE: I'm an Electrical Engineer with 8+ years producing results in the public and commercial sectors.] **(3)** [I really wanted to learn every aspect of this industry from the ground up, so] I spent the past year [the past 5 years...] applying theory and principles of electrical engineering to a diversity of projects—professional office spaces, mall and retail spaces, schools, hospitals...I can perform advanced load calculations. I'm experienced with CAD and (AutoCad®) REVIT® and can design, layout, and check electrical schematics to ensure the technical correctness of the drawings. [I also have good working knowledge of the Energy Code, National Electrical Code (NEC) and a general familiarity with the other NFPA codes that may apply to specific projects.] **(4)** Outside of my skills, I can interface with all levels of staff (coordinating with architects and engineers for compliance) to bring connectivity to built ecosystems. I'm comfortable with frequent deadlines and transitions, and pride myself on time management because if you're good at managing time, you're good at managing stress. **(5)** I know that your organization promotes a solutions-oriented, high-performance culture and that's what brings me to apply here today: the chance to work closely with a team of talented engineers.

NURSE · LVN · CNA INTRODUCTIONS

example | nurse

(1) My name is Debbie Downer and (2) I recently graduated from an accelerated nursing program with over 700 clinical hours. (3) I rotated through all clinical areas including cardiology, pediatrics, surgical, obstetrics, geriatrics, as well as the post-anesthesia care unit. During my clinicals, I directly cared for a group of 4-5 patients which included administrating their medications, monitoring vitals, and I inserted at least 20 foley catheters. I also administered over 35 flu shots at a local women's health clinic. (4) I would say that one of my favorite experiences was my last rotation; working in a level 1 trauma center, I conducted complete health evaluations and assisted with irrigating wounds, stitching, cardiac monitoring and IV setups. If presented with the opportunity, I'm particularly interested in pediatrics and would love to start in this area. (5) I know that your facility has a more fully developed pediatric nursing program and that's why I've applied here so that I can work and learn alongside an experienced team.

example | lvn

(1) Good morning, my name is Precious Snowflake and (2) I'm a licensed LVN looking to bring my skills into a facility such as yours. (3) This past summer, I was able to gain real valuable work experience by interning as an LVN. I directly cared for three patients and helped administer medication, performed blood glucose checks and monitored vitals. I took the opportunity to get to know our patients one by one and that really helped when it came to things like dressing, wound care and monitoring the response to medication. (4) In fact, I chose this field because making connections with patients really energizes me and makes me want to come to work everyday. Although my favorite types of patients are seniors, I enjoy working with a wide range of people. These are stressful times and they need someone they can relate to…that they can feel comfortable with. (5) My internship

...MORE ▶

35

made me realize how much I really wanted to be an LVN and that brings me to apply here today. What I'm looking for now is a position that will broaden the skills that I have with hands-on patient care.

example | cna

(1) Thank you for the opportunity to be here, my name is Nanaya Beesnus and **(2)** I recently graduated with my CNA license. **(3)** My most recent experience (externship) was in an extended care facility where I saw first hand how important CNA's are in an elderly person's life. I directly cared for 6-7 patients and assisted with feedings, bathing, ambulation and transferring residents. Much of my time was also spent changing linens and helping with dressing and grooming needs. **(4)** One of the most fulfilling aspects about the job is seeing a smile on their face and being someone they can lean on during a time of need. Little things, like speaking in a soft voice to respect privacy or helping with a small request, makes all the difference. Outside of my technical skills, healthcare is a 24-hour, 7 day a week system and I'm flexible with my schedule to help support staff or cover vacations. **(5)** Over the next two years I plan on taking EKG and CNA 2 to give myself a little more ability to actually treat patients, but for now I'd love to gain as much experience as possible which is why this job appeals to me so much.

ENVIRONMENTAL ENGINEER INTRO

example

(1) I appreciate the opportunity to be here this morning, my name is Bubba Mud and **(2)** I'm an Environmental Engineer looking to advance my skills and knowledge with a large, diverse [regulatory, educational, research...] group such as yours. **(3)** I've always had a passion for the outdoors, so I learned as much as I could while in school and during my most recent assignment (internship) assisted with multi-faceted Phase I Environmental Site Assessment studies. I developed basic knowledge of hydrology, soils [soil vapor sampling], wetlands, as well as sediment control. In addition to field assessment activities, I am fully prepared to assist with governmental permitting applications. I am also an advanced technical writer. My software proficiency includes AutoCAD Civil 3D® as well as the Microsoft Office Suite®. [I'm OSHA (40-hour HAZWOPER) certified, including my up-to-date 8-hour refresher and pursuing my OSHA 10-hour (Construction Safety) certification.] **(4)** About me, I'm an avid hiker and in good health, [In other words: physically able to walk around construction sites, occasionally climb slopes and berms, and cross uneven terrain], and have the ability to balance the needs of multiple concurrent projects. Although I'm outdoors-y (and like to promote environmental steward-ship), I enjoy a mix of field and office work and can travel overnight for field assignments in all weather conditions. **(5)** Your organization's unique concern for quality of life, safety and sustainability is what brings me to apply here today. You are a leader at site assessment studies and delivering innovate, creative solutions to protect human health. And that's why when I found out about this opening, I applied at once—for the chance to work and learn alongside a dynamic team of skilled engineers.

PARALEGAL INTRODUCTIONS

example
(1) Good morning, my name is Iguana, and (2) I'm a recent graduate from an accelerated paralegal program with over 400 externship hours. (3) The highlight of my externship entailed providing support for the top four lawyers of the firm. My role there included various aspects of discovery such as summarizing depositions, subpoenas, and cite checking. But it also involved completing key research like helping to define legal precedents, as well as reviewing legal documents for consistency. I learned the nuances of attorney settlement demand letters and developed advanced skills in E-Discovery®. (4) About me, I'm especially skilled in a fast-paced, learning-rich environment. I'm great with moods and people and can easily pick-up new direction. (5) What brings me to apply here is the opportunity to work closely with a highly experienced team. If we determine I'm a good fit for this role, I'd like to get up to speed quickly and help contribute to the growth of this reputable firm.

example
(1) I appreciate the opportunity to be here this morning, my name is Justin Case, and (2) I've spent the last two years preparing myself to work as a paralegal. (3) Some of my technical know-how includes the ability to draft and respond to discovery and motions, coordinate depositions, and assist with trial preparation. I have working knowledge of civil subpoenas, assembling trial notebooks, jury instructions, and motions in limine. (4) What I'm most proud of is my ability to connect with people and talk directly to the client's needs. I am a persuasive communicator with well-developed presentation skills and love the challenge of working under pressure and facing deadlines. I'm also flexible with my schedule and can manage a heavy workload. (5) In fact, I see myself as the right arm support to an attorney or a legal team.

...MORE ▶

That's why when I found out about this opening, I applied at once.

example
(1) Thank you for this opportunity, I'm Dweezil, and **(2)** I'm a NALA certified paralegal with extensive training in all aspects of discovery. **(3)** I chose this field because I'm a hands-on person and can easily prepare and file motions, draft responses to interrogatories, and navigate through court and government websites. I'm familiar with court systems and basic filing procedures, and am proficient with LexisNexis®, Westlaw®, and electronic filing (eFiling). **(4)** One reason I particularly enjoy being a paralegal, and the challenges that go along with it, is the opportunity to connect with people. I have a passion for interviewing witnesses, and corresponding with clients about case status and preparation. I know the importance of discretion and can handle highly confidential information. **(5)** What I'm looking for now is gaining real, valuable work experience and refining the 'people skills' that I believe are key to my future professional success. I've applied for this position because I excel in the kind of collaborative working environment you've built here.

MECHANICAL ENGINEER INTRODUCTION

example

(1) Good morning, my name is Buck Nasty and **(2)** I'm an engineer intern (working towards PE licensure) with a BSME looking for the opportunity to grow with a dynamic engineering company. [ALTERNATIVE: I'm a Mechanical Engineer with 8+ years producing results in Aerospace, Aviation, Defense, Energy...] **(3)** I've always loved the challenge of all aspects of design—modeling, prototyping, pilot builds—and whenever I have the chance to do a special project outside of work, I take it. I'm instinctive self-starter. What I mean by self-starter is that I like to think outside-the-box and discover novel solutions to challenging problems. [In fact, my team was recognized for a key advancement in...] I have substantial experience in [design work, research and development, manufacturing, installation, final commissioning] and can prioritize and reprioritize to balance the needs of multiple concurrent projects. I'm highly adept with [parametric modeling tools like] Solidworks® and ProE® and proficient [executing design projects] with Autodesk Inventor® [Revit®]. **(4)** About me, I've always had a passion for mechanics, and I'm an avid tinkerer and hobbyist with well-developed [creative] problem solving skills. Technologies may be sensitive, so I like to react quickly to identify and solve issues, especially on tight timelines. Although I'm successful working independently, teamwork really energizes me and makes me want to come to work everyday. I'm flexible with my schedule and ready to integrate with a Cross Functional Team (CFT). (I'm also an advanced technical writer.) **(5)** I realize that this is a very demanding role and you're looking for a candidate who will thrive in this position. And that's what brings me to apply here today—the opportunity to learn and grow with a diverse, innovative team of engineers.

PHARMACY TECH INTRODUCTIONS

example | retail
(1) Good morning, my name is Keano Worms, and (2) I've spent the last year preparing myself to work as a pharmacy technician. (3) I've always loved science and worked hard to learn everything from chemotherapies and IVIG's to tracking inventory with Etreby. Thanks to my most recent experience (externship), I was given the chance to verify TPN's, carefully double checking labels for accuracy, and I became especially skilled at tracking inventory and cart fill. (4) About me, I have a passion for taking the guesswork out of things and enjoy being a problem solver. I'm great with moods and people and can easily pick up direction. I can also manage any schedule to support staff or cover vacations. (5) That's why when I found out about this opening, I applied at once. For people with a get things done attitude, this job has a lot of appeal.

example | retail alternate
(1) I appreciate the opportunity to be here this morning, my name is Sharkasaurus Rex, and (2) I'm a graduate of Manchesthair College earning a pharmacy tech diploma. (3) Although a strong point of mine is dispensing and filling prescriptions, I'm also particularly good at logging and tracking inventory and can handle heavy call volume. I know my trades and generics by heart and what greatly interests me is checking eligibility and insurance verification, which I see as the next logical step in my career. (4) About me, I like to make people feel like they're being taken care of and always greet patients with a cheerful attitude. I'm flexible with scheduling, and can work independently or as a productive team player. (5)) That's why I'm excited to begin my work and learn from an experienced team. From what I've seen, you definitely have the capacity for me to grow my skills.

...MORE ▶

example | hospital

(1) I'm D. Shiznits, and **(2)** I'm looking to join an organization where I can practice teamwork and handle greater responsibility as a pharmacy tech. **(3)** Professionally speaking, what I'm most proud of is my compounding IV room experience; I've been told I have excellent compounding technique, accuracy, and speed. I've also become especially skilled at IV math calculations, flow rates and Pyxis procedures. **(4)** While technical know-how plays an important role in patient care, I consider myself more of a creative problem solver. Whether it's working longer hours or being cross-trained with additional tasks, I'm willing to do whatever is needed to support the team. I also enjoy putting patients at ease and am very kid friendly. **(5)** I'd like to learn more about the needs of your hospital, and if we determine I'm a good fit for this role, ready to start contributing.

IT ADMINISTRATION INTRO

example
(1) It's a pleasure to be here this morning and thank you for this opportunity, my name is SweaT-Rex and **(2)** I'm looking to advance my skills and experience [expertise] with a diverse group in the IT field. [ALTERNATIVE: I'm a Computer Systems Manager with 15+ years of producing results in the IT field.] **(3)** I'm an energetic person and an instinctive self-starter. What I mean by self-starter is that I like to perform hands-on fixes (and streamline work processes) to keep the technical infrastructure efficient and running. In fact, this past year I operated with zero downtime for over seven months. I provided direct technical support to 85+ local and remote users on all IT related matters including [workstations, laptops, printers, software applications, user account management...]. I monitored network operations and software applications, and performed routine server-to-cloud migrations. (I also filled gaps to increase performance and ensure the security of information assets, including mobile platforms.) What I'm most proud of is my ability to connect with people and talk directly to the clients needs. **(4)** I work well with a diverse group of people and am an excellent time-manager. I'm happy to field incoming help requests from business users. And I would say that the most important skill I've learned is to apply common sense and take care of issues without having to wait for step-by-step instructions. I'm flexible with my schedule, to support staff or cover vacations, and would welcome the chance to be cross-trained with additional tasks. (I'm also Spanish-English bilingual.) **(5)** You are my top choice employer—a company driven by technology with strong project expectations, and I've applied for this position because I excel in this kind of collaborate environment. I'm very impressed with the setting you have here, and if we determine I'm a good fit, ready to start contributing.

POLICE INTRODUCTIONS

example | military veteran

(1) Thank you for the opportunity to be here, my name is Lex Talionis, and **(2)** I'm a four-year veteran of the United States Marine Corps with substantial experience in infantry. **(3)** The Marine Corps provided exciting challenges throughout my enlistment and I really don't think I could have achieved the same success anywhere else. I led and supervised a team of 9 decorated soldiers, often in high pressure situations, and every step of the way I developed important skills like operating and maintaining computers and sensitive equipment, and the ability to put people at ease in tense situations. **(4)** As a career-minded person, I have a passion for taking the guesswork out of things and consider myself a problem solver. I'm at my best while working under pressure and faced with new challenges, and like to work until the job gets done regardless of the time clock. I am a persuasive communicator, (fluent in Spanish) and have solid foundation in report writing, which is why this career interests me so much. **(5)** What I am looking for now is an organization where I can join a diverse team and have a positive impact in the community. If we determine I'm a good fit for this role, I would like to bring my experience, training and proven accomplishments to this department and continue in my career path of dedicated service.

example | college grad

(1) Good morning, my name is Tim Buck II, and **(2)** I'm a recent graduate of Manchesthair College earning a Criminal Justice degree. **(3)** I spent the last two years preparing myself to work in the law enforcement field receiving extensive training in report writing and psychology, and I've developed into a confident presenter. My courses in Criminal Justice have built a strong foundation in investigative procedures and I am especially proficient with computers. **(4)** What I'm most proud of on a personal level is my background. By overcoming obstacles and

...MORE ▶

working my own way through school, I've become a role model in my family and in my community, which is why this job appeals to me so much. I realize that if you want to be successful you must set the example by working well with others and making meaningful commitments. **(5)** I consider this not just a job but a career, one that will enable me to grow a role model, earn a comfortable income and give back to the community that helped shape me into who I am.

example | universal

(1) Good morning sir, good morning ma'am, good morning sir, my name is Will Power. **(2)** For the past year-and-a-half, while preparing to become a peace officer, I've been a full-time restaurant shift leader. **(3)** I have done a lot of research and, although public safety is more involved, I've developed many of the same skills that police officers use on a day-to-day basis, like conflict resolution. My boss always tells me that I'm at my best when handling customer service complaints and in emergencies. I have a passion for taking the guesswork out of things, I'm great with moods and people and enjoy being a problem solver. **(4)** Outside of work, I an avid mixed martial artist. Although I'm not a violent person, I consider maintaining physical fitness at top priority because I realize that as a police officer there may be times when you'll have to use the minimum force necessary to affect an arrest. **(5)** While I have been successful as a shift leader, I am ready for the next step in my career where I can practice team work and handle greater responsibility. I intend to become very active in my community and that's why when I found out about this opening (during my ride along with Officer Popo Cuffs), I knew I had to apply.

TEACHER INTRODUCTION

example

(1) Good morning and thank you for this opportunity, my name is Custom Maid and **(2)** I'm presently [enrolled in a post-baccalaureate certification program] looking to join a school where I can guide the social process of learning in a dynamic classroom setting. **(3)** I've been influenced by so many great teachers, and thanks to some wonderful mentors, I'm experienced with both project-based and technology-based teaching methods. I love engaging and inciting inquisitive youth [adults] with tablets, laptops and other digital tools. I believe that the fundamental role as a teacher is to inspire, to challenge, to give students a sense of worth and the feeling that they matter. That's why I like to diversify the curriculum—to meet the needs of the individual. I'm adept at lesson planning. And I have an active interest in both student-centered and inquiry-based instruction styles. **(4)** About me, I'm a problem solver with the ability to handle very hectic situations. I'm great with moods and people and have the ability to "put-out fires" quickly and then move on. I like to take responsibility for the cleanliness of my classroom, personal workspace and shared environments and can handle sensitive issues with diplomacy and even-handedness. [I also have the flexibility to instruct (multiple grade levels, multiple subjects, special needs, ESL...).] Outside of teaching, I spend my time enjoying [arts, crafts, music], which as it turns out can be very useful in sparking ideas for school activities and projects. **(5)** You have a faculty rooted in honesty and respect who graduate courageous, committed, life-long learners. And that's what brings me to apply here today: to inspire even more students to love [math, English, history, science...] in a collaborative environment such as this.

X-RAY · MAMMO · ULTRASOUND INTRODUCTIONS

example ⏐ x-ray
(1) Thank you for this opportunity, my name is Miss Understood and (2) I'm a certified X-ray technician looking to bring my skills to a busy facility such as yours. (3) I've always loved science and technology so I learned as much as I could while in school and, during my externship, became especially skilled at preparing and disinfecting the procedure and exam rooms, as well as working with digital equipment. I would say that one of my favorite experiences was learning to position wounded patients. These can be stressful times, but by explaining the procedure and making careful adjustments, I enjoyed helping my patients relax and manage the pain. This in turn sped up my workflow by capturing a clear image on the first try. The way I see it, we are helping the doctor diagnose through our images, and picture quality can affect a patient's life (by pinpointing suspicious areas). (4) About me, I like to make people feel like they're being taken care of and always treat patients with a warm and caring attitude. I'm great with moods and people and I'm flexible with my schedule to help support staff or cover vacations. (5) What I'm looking for now is gaining real, valuable work experience and that's why I'm excited to begin my work and learn from an experienced team such as yours.

example ⏐ mammography
(1) My name is Ali Katt and (2) I'm a board certified mammography tech with two years of experience as a radiologic technologist. (3) I chose this field because making connections with patients really energizes me and makes me want to come to work everyday. I would say that one of my favorite experiences is putting nervous patients at ease. Even when schedules are packed tight, I always take the time to explain the procedure, where they need to go next and, most importantly, *when to expect results*. I'm also skilled at taking a quick exam to

...MORE ▶

minimize any discomfort that the patient might feel. **(4)** About me, I like to make people feel like they're being taken care of and always greet patients with a cheerful attitude. I understand that some patients can seem demanding, but it's not demanding, they're just nervous. By talking to them and explaining what is going to happen during the exam, you can form a good relationship based on trust and caring, especially with patients who come in year after year. **(5)** I know that your facility has a more fully developed mammography program and that's what brings me to apply here. I'm very impressed with this setting and excited by the prospect of a long-term career.

example ı ultrasound
(1) Good morning, my name is Giga Hertz and **(2)** I hold an ultrasound tech degree and am currently working towards my ARDMS credential. **(3)** My internship made me realize how much I really wanted to be an ultrasound tech and thanks to my most recent experience, I had the chance to track pregnancies, perform venous ultrasounds and scan for abnormalities like gallstones and tumors. My knowledge of anatomy was a big help during the ultrasound-guided biopsies. **(4)** Along with my technical skills, I'm great while working under pressure and faced with the challenges of a fast-paced environment. Even when schedules are packed tight, I can easily manage a heavy patient load and am great with moods and people. (I'm flexible with my schedule and easily pick up direction.) **(5)** What I'm looking for now is a position that will broaden my experience with ultrasound imaging. One of the most fulfilling aspects about ultrasound is seeing patients pull out of things and get better. Looking at your facility, I'm excited about playing an important role in the course of treatment alongside a veteran team.

TELL ME ABOUT YOURSELF

USE THIS SPACE TO CREATE YOUR OWN VERSION OF THIS INTRO.

TWO

....

MINI-ANSWERS TO GO!

Snappy answers that prove you're ready for prime time.

Let's start this puppy!

What's your best quality?
~~"I'm the marrying type. Well, I would like to get married, but I just want to do it once, and do it the right way with someone who will say, 'how was your day, honey? Let me fix you a bubble bath' and then put on a song that makes you cry when you listen to it. Aren't I the greatest?"~~

You: "I would say that my best quality is that I see problems as an opportunity to learn. I never complain about something without offering a solution and realize that if you want to be successful you must work well with others and make meaningful commitments."

How do you handle a high-pressure environment?
"~~I eat a whole box of donuts before shouting at everyone for judging me and then cry in the break room~~."

1 "I enjoy a fast-paced environment because it makes the day go by faster. I also believe in planning and time management to reduce panic deadlines and handle my workload."

2 "I'm great with moods and people, and though the work load can get heavy, if you're good at time management, you're good at managing stress."

Tell me about yourself.
"~~Oh super! I'm looking for a job so I don't starve or die from hypothermia. I guess you can say I'm living in the moment.~~"

Give the hiring manager a 20+ second **professional** overview of who you are. But if you're like everyone else and not sure exactly what that means, go to **page 1** and soak up all you can.

Where do you see yourself in 5 years?
"~~Not in this place…lol.~~"

In other words, how long are you going to stick around?

You: "I am interested in the opportunity for continued learning and professional development. Hopefully I will continue working with your organization and taking advantage of any growth potentials."

What kind of pay are you looking for?
"~~How much of my day will I actually spend…working?~~"

You: "What's your range?"
Hiring manager: "10-12 dollars an hour."
You: "I'm within your range."

When the decision is close between you and another applicant, some employers will try to put you on the spot to lock in a number. Their goal is to hire a qualified candidate for the least amount of money. Why take a pay cut? **Page 85** will teach you to how to negotiate like (you're) some sort of numbers wizard.

Why do you want to work here?
"~~I know, right?~~"

You: "What I've experienced here today, especially in terms of people and environment, impresses me. I'm also excited by the prospect of gaining real, valuable work experience from a reputable organization, as I believe yours is. That's why when I found out about this opening, I applied at once."

How much do you know about their organization?

HOMEWORK ASSIGNMENT: Spend at least five minutes+ on the company's website. Here is what to look for: **1** how old is the company **2** how large is the company **3** what's it proud of **4** who are its customers **5** what makes it great.

Add one or two of those points to spice up your answer.

What did you like least about your last job?
"~~That place was bad juju. I had to burn a candle and pray for protection every morning~~."

You: "Overall I've been very happy with my jobs. I've been able to work with some really interesting people, but now I am ready to handle greater responsibilities and build on what I have learned."

This is an old trick question. If you start bad-mouthing your present or previous employer, you will not get the job. As it turns out, employers hate backstabbers as much as backstabbers do.

Do you have any other interviews?
"I WISH!"

You: "I am currently scheduling my interviews to find a match between my qualifications and the needs of prospective employers."

An applicant with standards is attractive. An applicant who is choosy is attractive. Saying 'no' could signal that you're so desperate you'll take anything. And no employer particularly enjoys the feeling of being interchangeable with any other random employer that would have said 'yes.' The beauty about this short and sweet answer is that at no point are you pretending that you have interviews lined up. Tricky? Yes. But honest. Sketchy questions deserve slippery answers.

One more thing, do not pass on the name of any other employers you are interviewing with, but if asked...

You: "The organizations I'm interviewing with requested that I not disclose any open positions."

Do you have any children?
"Excuse you, but this ain't just a supersized chili burrito in my stomach."

Nearly right off the bat you're asked about kids. Being the self-righteous young stud or studette that you are, all hell breaks loose. You absolutely FLIP OUT and storm out of the interview feeling totally violated.

Whoa! Are you sure you want to go there? (Keep reading! It gets good.)

Twenty minutes later, you get home and listen to your voicemail message, "Hello there, didn't mean to catch you off guard with my question, it's just that we offer an on-site daycare and I was thinking, if you had kids, you might like to learn more about it."

Clearly, the concern here is over family obligations. This question might *seem* full of all kinds of wrong at first, but getting all uptight and pointing out that the question is illegal will be "off-putting." You probably won't get the job. Answering illegal questions, like this one, with a little diplomacy will avoid the risk of turning things sour.

1 "You know, I'm not quite there yet. But working with kids really energizes me!"

2 "I have experience with children and enjoy interacting with very young kids, which is just a great fit for my personality."

3 "Yes, I have two lovely children, and I am available to work overtime on short notice and can travel as needed."

Have you had difficulties getting along with supervisors or coworkers?

"~~Oh God, please no. Not this sh!t again. You're judging me because of the way I look. Yes you are, don't even try and pretend~~."

1 "Nothing major…I try to get along with everyone, and what I've learned is that if you're positive and highly passionate about your job, your enthusiasm rubs off on the rest of the team."

2 "Honestly, I try not to let little things bother me. Everyone has a bad day once in a while."

Why did you leave your last job?

"~~Well, they said if I didn't leave they would call the cops~~."

This is one of the most important questions that you may be asked. The worry is that, once hired, you'll quickly come to feel like you're "worth more than this" and jam. Your answer should scream reassurance.

1 "I wished to further my education by enrolling in school. I'll be forever thankful for the opportunity my previous employer gave me." (A little edjumacation never hurt!)

59

2 "I graduated and want to use my diploma, and broadened skill set, to meaningfully contribute to my career."

3 "I really enjoyed my last job and would still be working there, but my position was eliminated."

4 "I was one of many seasonal layoffs, and now I'm looking for a long-term opportunity."

5 "Despite being recognized as a top performer, my department wasn't producing as much as projected so they had to let people go."

6 "I was discharged during my six-month probationary period because I arrived late to work. This mistake cost me dearly and I've grown tremendously since then. I can say that I'll work all shift long, clock-in on time and if I'm delayed or am unable to make it, I'll contact you well ahead of schedule to make sure my shift gets covered." (Got fired? No biggs. You won't make the same mistake twice.)

Who was your most difficult boss and why?
"I asked 3 of my former bosses what they thought and they all came to the same conclusion; that if I let them go they promised to tell nobody."

Even if you personally can't stand your old boss, resist the temptation to throw her under the bus. You will instantly be red flagged for having a negative attitude towards your coworkers, and the hiring manager will not hire you.

You: "My former boss had an authoritarian style of managing and speaking to us. But, I learned that it is important to be patient and that constructive criticism is not an attack on me personally. I also learned how to handle stress and time management."

ANSWERS TO INTERVIEWING QUESTIONS

When would you be able to start work?
"~~Any time after 11:00am because this princess needs her beauty rest, ya feel me? Can I get an AH YEAH?!~~"

You: "I have availability beginning this week and can accommodate your schedule if necessary."

This carefully-worded reply let's them know you are available right away with poise and confidence.

Our last person was fired for being late. What are your thoughts?
"~~Move your meat or lose your seat!~~"

You: "I pride myself on being 15 minutes early to work. As a matter of fact, I always say, 'to be early is to be on time, and to be on time is to be late.'"

What outside-of-work activities do you enjoy?
"~~I do things naked! No really, I walk around the neighborhood naked when I'm alone. It makes me feel more confident and better about my body~~."

In other words, describe your "chill out" activity.

1 "I like to spend time gaming, reading and watching movies and I also enjoy solving riddles and puzzles." (Have at least one game-book-movie title to mention in case you are asked.)

2 "I love learning to how to cook and playing musical instruments. (Rock on!) It keeps me busy and I get to learn something new."

3 "I enjoy swimming at the YMCA and volunteering at my local community arts center in town."

4 "In my free time I read books, blogs, and try new technologies to improve myself."

5 "I enjoy volunteering with my church-mosque-synagogue-temple, and love reading and spending time with my family ~~and thinking bout life and stuff~~." (Use extreme caution when revealing any religious affiliation as it could trigger discrimination.)

How have you been keeping busy?
"~~None of your business, perv.~~"

Above and beyond anything else, the hiring manager wants to know how you are keeping up your skills while out of the workforce. Focus your answer on your professional development activities. Otherwise, it looks as if you don't really care about your career.

1 "I'm building my online social media skills (using digital tools), making new contacts, and reading books, articles and blogs outside my major to become more marketable."

2 "I'm taking online classes to further my education and broaden my skill set."

3 "I've been volunteering in a real-world environment to improve myself. I also attend refresher courses in college to ensure that my skills remain competitive while out of the workforce."

Why should we hire you over the other candidates?
"~~Because I got it like that!~~"

If you're invited to an interview, you're just as qualified for the position as anyone else who was invited. What separates you from the crowd is WHY.

By 'why' hiring managers mean **what inspires you?** Companies realize that if they hire someone that just needs a job, they'll work for a paycheck. But if they hire someone who believes in what the company stands for, that candidate will work for them with blood, sweat and tears.

The trick to answering this question is to shift gears, take their cause and make it your own. You are showing up to the interview because you believe what they believe; not just to start earning a salary or because you have to, but because *you want to.*

You: "I have no basis for comparing myself to the other candidates because I am not familiar with their profile. What I can speak to is what brings me to apply here today. To me the real joy of life is working. A career to me is so much more than money; it's a way to learn from others and experience what the world has to offer. Everything I do, I believe in learning. And that's why the prospect of working alongside an experienced team is so exciting. The way I see it, my real education begins here."

If someone walked in without an appointment, what would you do?
"~~I'd say, 'back of the line, buddy, back of the line~~.'"

You: "I would make every effort to accommodate them. If we have room on the schedule I will say, 'we have people currently scheduled, but we will try to squeeze you in as soon as possible. Thank you for your patience, please have a seat and make yourself comfortable.' If we are booked, I will schedule an appointment right away."

Now you're way beyond customer service. Now you're just being cool.

How would you describe yourself?
"~~I'm weird...I like the smell of gasoline. Sometimes I hear voices. I see~~ ~~dead people~~."

This question can really mess with your head because the hiring manager is asking, quite possibly, the fuzziest question imaginable. Most "describe yourself" questions boil down to 1 what qualities do possess that make you the best candidate for this job and 2 how will you make the company stronger?

But if you're like everyone else and not sure exactly what that means, go to **page 1** and soak up all you can.

Have you ever worked in this field before?
"~~I already told you NO...you monster~~."

YES: "Yes, my experiences include blah, blah, blah...with a solid background in blah, blah, blah. What brings me to apply here is the opportunity to work closely with a highly experienced team."

NO: "What I'm looking for now is gaining real, valuable work experience and refining the 'people skills' that I believe are key to my future professional success."

Fluff up a pillow and visit **page 211** if you have **never had a job** or have not worked in that particular field.

How do you deal with stress on the job?
"~~I find that if I cry myself to sleep, I usually feel better in the morning~~."

In other words, are you going to run out the door when things get stressful?

You: "I'm great with moods and people, and though the work load can get heavy at times, if you're good at time management, you're good at managing stress."

Emergency save.
"~~Haha, my mind just went blank, sorry~~."

It's easy to let your mind wander in a large group interview. Memorize this one-liner, just in case you get caught having a senior moment, and everything will be fine and dandy.

You: "I am afraid I didn't understand the question—can you reiterate—I do have a comment."

How do you deal with an upset customer?

"~~I would say, 'yeah, well, maybe we should kick back from each other for a while, man.~~"

In other words, can we count on your people skills?

You: "Clearly the customer needs to get something off their chest. I'll say calmly, 'I totally understand your concern and I'd be happy to look into that for you,' and find a solution. I'd finish by saying, 'Is there anything else that I can assist you with?' It's important that I give customers a sense of worth and the feeling that they matter." (In other words, "The customer isn't always right, but it's my job to make it right.")

Hiring manager: "What if the customer continues to raise a ruckus?"

You: "I will say, 'Hmm, let me give the manager a call and have him come look at this.'"

What are some of your strengths?

"~~I was born talinted but education ruiend me.~~"

1 "I'm a confident presenter, great with moods and people and have a passion for taking the guesswork out of things."

2 "I'm an effective problem solver who can think on my feet and like to make people feel like they're well taken care of."

3 "Some of my greatest strengths are my ability to prioritize, multitask and work until the job gets done, regardless of the time clock."

What is your greatest weakness?
"~~Kryptonite~~."

1 "I would say that my lack of experience is my biggest weakness and the thing I'd like to improve on most."

2 "I'm kind of OCD-ish...I prefer things to be really neat, clean and organized...I'm not a big fan of messy areas. I'm not really doing anything about it because it's just me. I guess it comes with the package, ha, ha, ha."

3 "I had trouble balancing the priorities in my life because I like being a people pleaser. Now I communicate what I can and can't help people with, and that has really helped me organize my time."

4 "~~I feel like no one is taking me seriously, and it hurts so much~~."

5 "I tend to make work my life and sometimes I feel like I'm missing out."

6 "I used to be the quiet type, but now if I ever feel I don't understand something, I immediately admit it and ask someone to explain things to me. This one step has seriously improved my life!"

Repackaging a strength into a weakness, like 'I work too hard,' looks phony and self-serving. Remember the purpose of this question is not to actually discover any weaknesses, it's to test your honesty and see if you are self-aware. You've been invited to interview. That means THEY WANT TO HIRE YOU!

Don't think of it as trying to be psychic and telling them what they want to hear. Pick a real weakness in your life but not something that is going to cost you the job.

What duties do you know how to do that fits with this job?
"~~Look guy, there's literally no where else I can go. Have some mercy,~~
~~you're ruining my life.~~"

It's okay to suck at word makin'. Stealth around **page 211**, especially
if you have never had a job or have not worked in that particular field,
and snag a few sentences.

Tell me about a problem you had in your life and how you solved it.
"~~It really worries me that so much of how people interact and treat me is~~
~~based on my good looks. This makes me feel a little bit ashamed. You~~
~~might disagree with me, but I think I should be treated just like any other~~
~~person.~~"

Asked another way, do you have the ability to "put-out fires" quickly and
move on?

You: "Five of us were assigned to work on a group project in school. We
hit some rough waters when two in my group didn't think their opinion
mattered. I told them that when I'm faced with an important decision,
I like to ask the advice of others. There are lots of possible answers
to questions and many ways to interpret a question. I loved seeing
how quickly that changed their attitude. From that point on, everyone
collaborated in the project, each bringing their bit of knowledge to the
scene."

What would you do if a client offered you money or a gift?
"~~I'd take the money. No, wait, the gift. Wait, is this a trick question?~~"

You: "I would explain to the client that I appreciate the gesture, but that
our company policy does not allow us to accept any gifts or gratuities."

EXCEPTION: Service jobs where tips are a given.

Do you have any questions for me?
"~~Am I your type? WOOP! WOOP!!~~"

Of course you have questions. You just can't think of any right now. Pick and choose from a list of thought-provoking questions on **page 79**.

Okay, we are done with the meeting. Thank you for interviewing.
"~~I shaved my goods for this?~~"

You: "Thank you for taking the time to speak with me about the open position. I was particularly struck by the impressive team you've built and would welcome the chance to work with you! If you need additional references or information to help make your decision, please let me know."

You've just earned yourself 1 bad@ss point!

If you get stuck on a question that you can't answer, say...
"~~Don't start with me~~."

"I don't know but to best answer your question I would like to research that a bit and follow up with you this afternoon."

It's okay to admit you don't know something as long as you follow with, "I'll get back to you on that."

(Go sneak around other chapters. It's fun!)

THREE

....

WUZ UP MA HOME SKILLY BISCUIT!

Guard your phone like a maniac. When it rings, answer it. Never ignore a "blocked" or "unknown" phone call. Not ever.

You say ur out wit ur boiz and she thinks ur out creepin' wit some other trick.
Not only does tone of voice determines how honest and persuasive you sound, people who voice their opinion in a direct, strong tone are perceived as truthful and having expertise. Monotone voices do not sound pleasing to the ear and can leave the impression that the speaker is being held *hostage*. (Eek!)

Would you enjoy giving the hiring manager an ear-gasm? Then put a bit more oomph behind it!

Convincing voices sound energetic, but not hyper. If you're hyper, try decaf and lay down with a cool wash cloth on your forehead for a couple of hours before the call. 'Energetic' means outgoing. Outgoing people sound vocally interesting by mixing their voice volume, changing up the tone from highs to lows while speaking and varying the sentence length.

Do the same and you'll burn with charm and personality.

By far, the biggest mistake is to sound too quiet, drab, and boring during a phone interview. It's okay to slow down your speech and speak LOUDER **when making a point**, or conversing with an elderly person who may suffer from hearing loss, otherwise, engage your listener with a phone voice that sings! The ear demands charisma.

Civilized discourse.

Dammit, you deserve to be heard! (But allow the hiring manager to finish speaking before you reply.) Speak clearly and directly into the phone or handsfree—with NO creepy mic breathing—so that the hiring manager can understand you. The clearest speakers are assumed to be the clearest thinkers. And do not put them on speaker.

You'll also need to cut down on saying 'like' so much and step up your vocabulary because a potty mouth or **s**treet **lang**uage will reduce your importance. (Besides strong language, please avoid using informal English such as 'ya know what I'm sayin,' and 'it ain't,' and 'real good,' and 'no problem' or any word that ends with 'shizzle.') You are a serious business contact for an employer looking to hire. Carefully listen to hiring managers on the phone and try to model their pace, tone, pitch, pauses and language and wrap up the conversation with a good final impression.

You: "Thank you for taking the time to speak with me about the open position. If you need additional references or information to help make your decision, please let me know."

Smile!

The meaning seems to be lost on so many people today. Smiling lights your fire when you speak and 'radiates' charm and personality from your voice. The hiring manager might not be able to look you in the eyes or see your facial expressions in a phone convo, but she'll "hear" your smile and pick up the lightened tone. She'll imagine your eyes squinting and a warm, glow-y smile.

Smiling affects the mind in powerful ways. Smiling taps into the emotional centers of the brain and elevates mood. Think of an unhappy thought (think of homework). Now smile. It's tough to hold on to an unhappy thought while smiling, isn't it? Smiling fills your brain with positive feelings and makes you sound **luminous** on the phone.

The best tool to use to help you smile during a phone interview is a mirror.

Call hating.
Please remove all unnecessary distractions, background sounds and noise pollution before dialing or picking up.

Wear interview-y clothes the day of the phone interview.
"But I hate getting all dressed up and *not* seeing anyone important that day." (Imagine how Gothic people feel!) Clothes can affect your confidence, self-esteem and, by extension, your tone of voice. Get out of your jammies, freshen-up and dress professionally if you are scheduled for a phone interview.

Confirm dates.
If a face interview is scheduled, repeat the date and time back to the hiring manager.

You: "Ok, that's Wednesday, May the 4th at 11:00 AM."

Thank you note.
No thank you note? Blasphemy! You are not a rude person. Don't allow an interview to change that. A phone interview is a really *real* interview. Be sure to send a thank you note to the hiring manager after the phone call (page 287).

FOUR

....

DON'T TALK TO ME LIKE YOU KNOW ME

Killer dialogue can create the impression that you're known. People who are known to hiring managers get put through by the receptionist.

When introducing yourself make sure your voice goes down at the end of sentences. Most job hunters have an upward inflection toward the ends of sentences. Upward inflections are perceived as questions and invites objections from the receptionist. Not only will that put her on the defensive, it also sounds very insecure—the opposite of authority—and more likely than not, reveals you as a nervous job caller.

You can transmit authority by speaking more s...l...o...w...l...y and by using a downward inflection in your phone voice. Just think, how would a serious business contact sound like? Practice making your voice sound deeper, while still sounding polite, and try to match your tone, pitch, pauses, and emphasis with the manager's, once the receptionist puts you through.

Script for randomly calling local businesses for any open position.
You: "Hello, if you can let the manager know that it's Conda, Anna Conda on the line for him, thank you. ["May I ask what's it about?"] Yes, of

73

course, I'm calling about recruitment. If you could just let him know that I'm on the line. [wait for manager] Hello Ms. Spelling, my name is Anna and I am wondering what positions are available at your office? [pause for manager's reply] I'd be happy to stop by, fax or e-mail my resume—whatever is easiest for you. [pause for manager's reply] Thank you for taking the time to speak with me about the open position. I am impressed by the team you've built and would welcome the chance to work with you!"

Script for randomly calling local businesses for any open position MAX ENERGY.
You: "Hello, Charlatan. I hope you're well today. Is the manager in the office, this is Mea Sammich on the line, thank you. [transferred to manager] Hello Mrs. Plurals, I am calling local employers this morning to see what positions you have available. [pause for manager's reply] I have an extensive knowledge of…blah and blah…and I am willing to do a working interview at your office as soon as of tomorrow to demonstrate my skills. How does that sound to you? [pause for manager's reply] It's a real pleasure meeting you over the phone and I look forward to seeing you this week."

Calling to get an update after your interview.
1 "Good morning Ms. Take, this is Illest Mamasita. I wanted to call and thank you for taking time to interview me last week for the opening. I'm very interested in the ▮▮▮▮▮▮ position and was wondering if you've made a decision?"

2 "Hi Mr. Bandito, you may recall that I interviewed three weeks ago for the ▮▮▮▮▮ opening. I was wondering if you're still working on a decision? [manager has not made a decision] Ok, thank you and if you need additional references or information to help make your decision, please let me know."

3 "Hello, I am calling to get an update on my status. [manager has not made a decision] When would be a good time to follow up with you? Sounds great, I'm really interested in this position and I'm willing to come in for a short trial period to see if there's a fit."

74

The hiring manager has apparently gone crazy. They hired SOMEONE ELSE.

At this point, play it cool. All kinds of things can happen: the noobie might not work out. You might get to be new hire #2 or #3. Larger organizations might hire you in the second or third round of openings because they're floating offers to other applicants to fill diversity quotas in the first. Smaller companies might experience a growth spurt. Leaving a SUPER-positive impression is the best way to boost your reputation while **keeping you on the list**.

1 "If the person that you've chosen somehow doesn't work out or another position opens, please call me. I'd love to come in for another meeting!"

2 "~~I'll accept that you are not going to hire me, but how did you get my girlfriend's phone number?~~"

3 "~~but...but....ok~~. :'("

4 "~~I ain't even mad~~. I appreciate the update and truly wish you success with your selection. Thank you for your time and consideration."

5 "~~Oh well whatever never mind~~."

6 "Ok, so you will be moving in a different direction then? Well, my best wishes for your success. I learned a lot about the job and your company during our conversations and would welcome the opportunity to join your company in the future."

You're HIRED!!

The manager just offered you a position. Get into your gargoyle stance and HOWL!

1 "This is fantastic! Have you decided on an actual start date of my employment?"

2 "~~I love you, man. Have your people contact my people~~."

3 "What wonderful news! I'm available to start this week. Should I bring anything with me?"

4 "Great! I'm really excited and look forward to working with you. Thank you! Has a start date been decided?"

5 "~~WHOOOHOOOooooooooooooOOOOooooooooooooooooooooooooooo~~
~~< breath > WHOOOHOOOooooooooooooOOOOooooooooooooooooooo~~
~~ooooooooooooOOOOOOOOOOOOooooooooooooooooooOOOOooooooo~~."

Should I leave a voicemail message for the hiring manager?
No. Censor yourself. Call back on private until you are able to speak to the hiring manager live.

On follow up calls to the assistant, politely ask, "What's the best time to call back?" Calling right outside normal business hours might help you get through to the hiring manager. For random job leads that are low priority, leave only one message. Otherwise, expect to make at least 15 calls before you get through to the hiring manger.

(If you get the feeling that the assistant is ****blocking you, please remain calm and visit **page 313**.)

FOUR+

....

BITE SIZE VOICEMAIL GREETINGS

Clamp your phone to your face because we're going to setup your voicemail box!

Please don't worry if you have a high, chipmunky (EEP!) voice. You'll get slack in the speech department as long as you don't record it in an echo-y restroom with a flush at the end.

This might seem like a no-brainer, but you're going to state your name in the greeting. A voicemail greeting without a name will confuse hiring managers and make them hesitant to leave a message. Many of them will worry they've reached the wrong person and hang up. And they won't always call back.

We'll also have to give your voicemail a reboot if you have a cutesy greeting. Cutesy voicemail greetings are *extremely* irritating to most people. No one knows for sure why. And you definitely don't want a voicemail filled with loud music, either. Our goal is to **encourage** hiring managers to leave a message, not traumatize them.

Choose one of the classy voicemail greetings on the next page, break loose your sexy 'phone' voice, and press record.

■ "Hi, this is Cray Cray. I can't answer the phone right now, but I do check my messages often. If you leave me your name and phone number, I will return your call as soon as possible. Thanks for calling!"

■ "Hello, you've reached Harry Sancho. I'm sorry I missed your call, but I'd like to get back to you as soon as I can. Please leave your name and telephone number after the beep."

■ "Hello. You've reached the voicemail box for Miss Creant. Unfortunately, I'm unable take your call at this moment, but if you leave your name and telephone number, I'll contact you back as soon as possible. Thanks!"

PHONE HARRASSMENT: Getting a new phone number can stop an annoying person from calling you, true. But if that phone number is listed on your resume, employers will not be able to get a hold of you either, and that can hurt your job prospects **big time**. Consider replacing their caller ID name with "Do Not Answer." When you receive a call from you-know-who, follow the instructions on the screen—do not answer. Problem solved.

FIVE

....

~~OBEY~~
QUESTION EVERYTHING

Questions prove that you really-REALLY want the job, not sorta-kinda want it.

Questions make your personality *pop* because it shows a confidence in your ability, a passion for work, and genuine interest and excitement at the prospect of joining that particular company. (It's not something you have to tell them. By asking questions, they'll know.)

Intelligent questions can put you in the "hire immediately!" category.

Asking questions is a mind trick where you reverse everything, so now the hiring manager is trying to impress you!

Oh boy, you're not getting the hint, are you? ASK QUESTIONS AT YOUR INTERVIEW. Kthxbye.

...SAMPLE QUESTIONS ▶

What you should do next...

Choose 2-3 questions from the list below that seem to jump out at you.

It is best to memorize those 2-3 questions before your interview, but it's also perfectly fine to write your questions on a notepad and pull out your notepad and pen during the interview. Feel free to ask something unscripted that's just on the top of your mind, as well. Jotting down the answers that the hiring manager gives you on your notepad will make the hiring manager feel important.

Questions.

- ~~Would you be upset if I promoted higher than you and then fired you?~~

- Why is this position open?

- How does the company measure my performance on my first key task?

- What would show that a job is being poorly performed?

- How can I help you get a stellar review next year?

- Given the opportunity, what goals should I achieve during the first 3 months and 6 months? (Shows you want a clear understanding of the job and the company before you commit.)

- ~~Does the company press charges?~~

- What has been key to *your* (the hiring manager's) success with this company? (Compliment sandwich. Now the hiring manager is trying to impress you!)

- ~~Do you think I'm pretty?~~

- What advice would you have given yourself a year ago?

■ How would you describe the work environment?

■ How would you describe a normal day on the job?

■ ~~Am I the only one in this building that hasn't got a clue what I am doing with my life?~~

■ If hired, what would I do in order to not just be good, but be *great* in the position? (Signaling you are interested in a career, not just a paycheck. Well played, job hunter. Well played.)

■ Is there a question you think I should ask but haven't? (Thought-provoking question, you mindfreak!)

■ What separates good employees from outstanding employees? (In other words, "School me, I'm a reasonable person. The mic is yours." Hiring managers LOVE this.)

■ Why did you originally want to work for this company?

■ ~~Are you feeling a little naughty right now?~~

■ Which skills would best help the company?

■ ~~What's it like to be extremely good looking?~~

■ How do you see this industry changing over the next 5-10 years?

■ ~~At first glance did you think I was crazy?~~

■ Will there be a mentor? Will there be on-the-job training?

■ ~~Is it difficult being an attractive employee in this office?~~

■ ~~Have you ever been boo'd?~~

■ ~~Is this company keeping its sizzle or starting to fizzle?~~

■ ~~What are the biggest lies your company puts out on the internet?~~

■ Will I be working individually or as part of a team? Will I be working in an office?

■ How would you describe the culture here?

■ ~~What kind of pay, bonuses, vacation benefits and stock options are you putting on the table?~~

■ ~~How much work will I have to do to make it seem like I'm actually working?~~

■ ~~Who wakes me up when I have to work?~~

■ I read on your website _____ and that sounded very interesting. Will my role be related to that? (Companies say a lot on their website, and someone who actually takes the time to read it immediately stands out.)

■ Can you tell me more about the career paths at your company?

■ ~~When did you give up on your dreams?~~

■ What challenges is the company facing in the next 3 months and what can I do to help achieve a successful outcome?

■ ~~Do you feel alive?~~

■ Will there be opportunities for overtime?

■ ~~Do you hate your work or just hate to work?~~

■ ~~Where do you wish you were right now?~~

■ ~~If you quit today, who would you tell to f-off first?~~

■ ~~Can I get a ride home?~~

- Do you have everything you need in order to make a decision or is there something we should spend more time on? (Stops things from turning sour **after you leave**. This question gives the hiring manager a chance to expose any bottled-up concerns about hiring you and gives you a chance to overcome any objections.)

- Is the company planning any streamlining? (Business buzzword also known as "downsizing" or "rightsizing"...means firing people.)

- ~~Now that you're older, and more wrinkly, does the young person inside you ever wonder what happened?~~

- ~~Are you worried about memory problems at your age?~~

- May I get a tour of your office? (Look at ease during the tour. Smile and nod to any associates that give you eye contact so you don't appear threatening. Throw a couple of flattering comments here and there. Don't get weirded out if the hiring manager doesn't allow an exclusive all-access backstage pass. Some companies have a policy that doesn't allow visitors to tour the building.)

- How did you feel that the interview went?

- ~~How often do y'all change stuff?~~

- What's the dress code?

- What are your top priorities for this position?

- ~~How much do you get paid?~~ (then follow with) ~~Is that a lot?~~

- ~~Do you drink blood at night?~~

- When can I expect a follow up from you?

- ~~Can I run my fingers through your weave?~~

SIX

....

DO NO EVIL
(~~UNLESS IT INVOLVES MONEY~~)

You are selling your precious life to employers. 40 hours a week is a TON of work. **If YOU don't value your time, you cannot expect the hiring manager to**. People mirror the worth you see in yourself.

As ironic as it seems, *not* negotiating can signal that you're "all about the money." If you're 'too shy' or 'too insecure' to negotiate, you'll seem so desperate you'll take anything. And no employer particularly enjoys the feeling of being interchangeable with any other random employer who would have said yes. An applicant with standards is attractive. An applicant who is choosy is attractive. Our culture associates "best" with most expensive.

If you tip-toe around the subject of money, the cost to you will be gargantuan.

BEFORE job offer.
At your very first interview, do not bring up the topic of money unless they bring it up first. Should the conversation turn to pay, however, the following dialogue will train you on how to correctly handle the situation.

Manager: "What kind of pay are you looking for?"

You: "What's your range?"

Manager: "12-14 dollars an hour."

You: "I'm within your range."

LEAVE IT AT THAT. During the interview stage, the hiring manager is looking to **screen out** candidates who want **more** money than the company is willing to pay. If you blurt out a number at this point, you'll most likely lowball yourself, or worse, be disqualified. The right time to negotiate is *after* you've received a job offer.

AFTER you receive a job offer.
The company just offered you a position. Hellz yeah!

You will now learn how to safely discuss money in a non-greedy manner, but be aware of the vibe you give off. Salary negotiations will go nowhere unless they get the feeling you're willing to walk away. Since you can't put a price on you, aim high and offer a justified discount. Nothing will increase their level of like-a-tude for you more.

You: "What's the salary range for this position?"

Manager: "About 12 an hour." (Yay. Dreams really can come true.)

You: "Twelve dollars an hour. [repeat his offer, pause for a moment and then continue] I appreciate your offer, but the amount is just a bit lower than I had expected...I'd like to ask, **what kind of flexibility is there?**"

SAY NOTHING ELSE. People will say anything to break the awkward silence, even if it is something they would rather not talk about ($). So silence instantly gives you control over a conversation (or a serial-killer vibe).

Manager: "Well, what amount did you have in mind?"

You: "I was thinking around 16." (Bump up his offer by at least 15-30%. Too little and he won't budge.)

Manager: "I can't do 16 an hour, but I can do 14."

You: "The work environment here really appeals to me and this is the kind of place where I can fit it. I'd be happy to reduce my hourly to 14, if necessary." (Aim high and offer a justified discount exactly as a shrewd negotiator would.)

$2 more buckaroos an hour = $4000 more a year. You win.

($4000 figure is based on a 40-hour work week for 50 weeks.)

The old double-switcharoo.
Negotiating is not a conflict. But if the hiring manager's reply to "what's your range" is some version of "I'm not telling you," you'll have to pull the old double-switcharoo to **figure out the maximum amount of money** the employer is willing to pay you.

Before we continue, understand that you may be unemployed, or right out of school, but you're not going to soften your stance. Do not feel as though you can't ask for anything. The hiring manager is looking for an applicant who will bring value to the organization, and by being a good negotiator, you prove exactly that, so stand your ground!

Returning back to our topic, the most important negotiating rule to remember is the person to say a number (salary amount) first sets the starting point. This means never shout out number first. Why not?

It's a game. If you blurt out a number first, lets say $14 an hour, you lose. Because he's not going to offer you MORE than $14. The hiring manager is going to negotiate you down, down, down and that means less money for you. But if HE blurts out a number first, lets say $14 an hour, you can negotiate up from there, all the way up to the maximum amount they're willing to pay, or have budgeted, for the position.

The dialogue below will enable you to outsmart the hiring manager like a mad samurai.

Manager: How much did you make at your last job?
You: "Although this position is similar, it's not quite identical to my last job. So let's talk about what my new role here would be and determine a fair salary around that."

Epic fliparoo. You know your worth and have standards with this response—no one's going to argue with someone asking for a realistic compensation range based on the actual job.

Manager: What are your salary expectations?
You: "I am more interested in professional development than a specific salary. I'm confident that whatever salary you've budgeted for this position, it's comparable to the rest of the market."

In other words, I value work experience, feel at peace with this bargain, and would like to think that I can trust this company.

Manager: Before making you an offer, I need to see what salary you would like. Can you give me a range?
You: "I'd seriously consider any offer that would be presented. Let's discuss the responsibilities for this position so I can get a sense of what you need. [after discussing] I would appreciate if you can provide the number that's typically budgeted for someone with these responsibilities?"

By being insistent and not caving in, you look like ~~a caffeinated superhuman~~ 1 you are good at what you do, 2 not begging for the job, and, most importantly, 3 giving subtle notice that you'll entertain other offers.

The message will be clear: you're on the auction block and going to the highest bidder.

"I cost the most because I'm the best there is." That's right!

(Extra Credit)

Are you getting ripped?!
Discover *roughly* how much your job pays per hour **in your area** (your city or county).

Cold-calling local employers is THE most accurate way to find out what salary the market is paying. Seek out a few businesses, glue the phone to your face and sound like a goody two-shoes.

You: "Hello, Citizen of Earth. I hope you're well today. I am doing career research for my school project and I'd love to talk with you about compensation. Would you be comfortable giving me a little guidance? Great! I was wondering how much dental assistants make at your office? What does the highest paid dental assistant make? And the lowest? Thanks!"

The numbers you're given is real-time data that you'll never find on the crowded web.

CONCENTRATED JOB LEADS
(JUST ADD WATER)

IF YOU HAVEN'T READ ALL THREE SECTIONS
BELOW, YOU'RE SUGGESTED TO DO SO
IMMEDIATELY

SEVEN

··

HEADHUNTERS

You are not going to believe this, but more and more companies and government agencies are giving total, unrivaled control of the hiring process to groups of headhunters…not Amazonian kind, but the **specialized** recruiter type.

Deep in connections to some of America's finest companies—both large and small—a headhunter is a job matchmaker. Good headhunters will capture job leads for you, coach you about the interviewing process and even work with you on building your resume.

Why do companies use headhunters? Mostly to avoid being blasted by emails, applications, resumes, and phone-calls from job hopefuls. It's faster and simpler to pay a third-party to fill a position than deal with this headache-y mess called 'the hiring process.'

That said, know that headhunter services are completely FREE of charge, as recruiters are paid by the companies who hire them (to find and screen qualified candidates). For you that typically means 1 NO minimum wage b.s. and 2 NO 100% commission and 3 thorough resume and even interviewing preparation (by reps who know precisely what the companies are looking for).

More importantly, these specialized headhunters are a part of the "inner-circle" and can make you a "connected" candidate, in with private industry businesses and civil service agencies.

> TEMP AGENCIES INFO: Don't be fooled. Temporary employment can turn into a permanent salaried position! Hiring you as a temp is a good way to fill the position without investing too much to see if you pan out. **Page 309** (volunteering) shows you how to 'get in good' and win the trust of a temporary employer.

Headhunters. What an idea! What's the catch?

Headhunters cost money. Well, technically all headhunter services are completely free of charge to you, but headhunters do charge companies around 12-30% of your hourly wage or bill companies for a one-time fee (usually 12-30% of one year's income) for the service of finding you for the company.

To help you understand how it works, let's say the company offers you $15/hour for the position, the company will actually be paying about $20/hour because a $5/hour cut gets kicked back to the headhunter as a finder's fee. You are not in any way involved in the behind-the-scenes negotiations. All you are told is 'welcome, your hourly wage is $15.' Most headhunters only get paid if you stay on the job for at least 3 months.

Working with a headhunter comes with a price, but it's a price you'll gladly pay.

> Some headhunting agencies will pay you an hourly wage *directly* and bill the company. This set up is called "contracting" and contract work generally does not come with a nice healthcare or retirement package.

How do I find a headhunter? (...and how do I become a headhunter?)
Your generation has access to job leads like never before in history thanks to the civilization-altering technological revolution known as "The Internet." The three options below will explain how to use the internet to create a list of local headhunters that specialize in your particular field.

Be aware that most headhunters specialize in industries such as administration, financial services, information technology, medical, engineering, security, manufacturing, culinary service, and so on.

Option A
To build a list of headhunters, Google® search using any of the following keywords and see what comes up: staffing services, consulting services, placement services, staffing solutions, employment services, staffing consultation, recruiting services, hire talent, placement firm.

The search results will mostly likely be links to recruiters from all over the map, from IT staffing, to military staffing, to culinary staffing. You'll have to filter through the staffing companies yourself or narrow down your search parameters.

For example, to find recruiters who specialize in medical-field jobs, take your internet machine and type these keywords: medical resources staffing services, medical staffing, healthcare staffing solutions, medical employment services, healthcare staffing consultation, nurse staffing agency, medical staffing agency, nursing agency, registry, medical healthcare services.

For recruiters who specialize in all other fields, simply add the name of your trade (administration, financial services, information technology or IT, executive protection, manufacturing, military, culinary service...) to these basic keywords: XXXXXXX staffing services, XXXXXXX consulting services, XXXXXXX placement services, XXXXXXX staffing solutions, XXXXXXX employment services, XXXXXXX staffing consultation, XXXXXXX recruiting services, XXXXXXX hire talent, XXXXXXX placement firm.

Then write or print out a list and begin making calls and introducing yourself to the friendly staffing reps who pick up. Be open and honest with what you are looking for and use the phone to find out instantly if they can be of help, whenever possible. **Ask for a referral** if that particular recruiter cannot assist you!

You: "Ok, thanks anyway...so who would you suggest I call?"

Option B
Go online and visit any of the employment agency websites listed here. Find a local office, call the office and make an appointment to introduce yourself. To avoid confusion, begin with Appleone.com and see what they offer first. Then clicky clicky on next website on this list.

www.Appleone.com
www.Bammusa.com (medical, financial, IT)
www.CareerGroupInc.com (administrative staffing)
www.Hudson.com
www.Insightglobal.net (IT staffing)
www.KellyServices.com
www.Manpower.com
www.Olsten.com
www.Olystaffing.com
www.RandstadUSA.com (IT staffing)
www.Roberthalf.com (finance, management, legal)
www.SelectStaffing.com
www.Techusa.net (IT, science, defense, engineering)
www.Vereduscorp.com (IT staffing)

Some of the specialized, independent headhunters you'll stumble across may work from a home office. This is perfectly normal and they probably enjoy relationships with a small but important group of employers, but please use caution when preparing to meet a total stranger in a private home for business! Trust your powerful instincts. Cancel anytime you get that eerie sense something isn't right.

Option C
Use these specialized headhunter-search websites to find a headhunter for the job you want.

> www.Aesc.org
> www.i-recruit.com
> www.NpaWorldwide.com
> www.OnlineRecruitersDirectory.com
> www.RileyGuide.com

Okay, I have a list of headhunters. Now what?
~~We must infiltrate their ranks and destroy them from within~~.

Select at least 2-4 offices in your area and schedule appointments to walk-in and introduce yourself. (Wear your interviewing clothes. This is a face-to-face meeting with a serious business contact.) Good headhunters will want to talk and meet with you. If a headhunter does not ask to meet with you, it might be a bad sign. Reconsider investing too much time with them and focus your attention on the others.

Fast forward, during your office visit with the recruiter, you are expected to take notes, be respectful, and follow their directions EXACTLY to the letter. Headhunters are motivated to place you in a job by the second greatest power in the known universe (greed), so they know their stuff (but some more than others). That means be open-minded to their advice ~~but not so open-minded that your brains fall out~~. The headhunter may test your skills and give you important interviewing and resume tips.

97

After your meeting, stay on top of the game by writing down each and every company your headhunters send your resume to. Some lower-quality headhunters will just spam your resume to anywhere, and you want to lock on to the recruiters with strong leads.

ADVANCED JOB HUNTER TACTICS: Creating the illusion that other headhunters are frantically trying to place you bumps you to the top of every recruiter's short list. When you begin getting replies from headhunters who are interested in you, start playing the recruiters off on each other by explaining that you are also working with another office. This strategy can trick different agencies-recruiters-headhunters into competing with each other to place you as **quickly** as possible. (Subtle manipulation will only work if you're completely prepared to interview, look spiffy and sound confident! See **page 169** to cover the basics.)

Trolling headhunters.

Calling or emailing your headhunters every two to four weeks for updates will NOT be held against you but do not let your voice sound desperate or mumbly on the phone. And don't push too much. You don't want to get flagged as difficult.

"When should I give up calling a particular headhunter for updates? I don't want to come off like a bugaboo." (Please note: a bugaboo is someone who bugs a lot...like a bugaboo.) Stop calling the moment you become employed or when they tell you to stop ~~or when you receive a restraining order~~. Otherwise, keep calling or emailing your list of headhunters until the end of time or the collapse of human civilization, whichever comes first.

As long as you left a good impression and stay in touch, you should eventually receive a call from a headhunter notifying you about an interview. At that point, **be 100% flexible with their schedule**, and NEVER cancel an interview. Flaking out will make the headhunter look bad in the eyes of the company that's hired them (to find candidates like you) and will damage the headhunter's hard-earned reputation.

Calling-off a scheduled interview is an unforgivable sin in the world of headhunters.

Scam-Hunters.

A legitimate headhunter will not charge you for connecting you to a job, **ever**. Headhunters are paid by the company that hires you. However, during your job search, you might encounter fraudsters that pretend to be headhunters to lure you into a scam. The scam is simple: give us $5000 (more or less) and we will "represent" you in your job search or promise—pinky promise—to get you a job. Provided they don't just run off with your money, the "service" is beyond weaksauce. It *might* include an offer to write a resume, some interview coaching, but basically it's just online resume blasting. This is a case where you don't get what you pay for.

But if this "service" floats your boat and makes you happy, no one is going to argue with you.

SEVEN

....

GOOGLE YOUR PROBLEM

The timid among us just go with the flow—we click, click, and click some more, wasting time and valuable energy. The savvy job hunters know about ways to get around the clicks. When it's a virtual ghost town online, they switch gears and use Google® maps to find local job openings that are completely 'off-the-grid' (not posted online).

Not all companies work with headhunters or post 'help wanted' ads. In fact, huge numbers of employers work **exclusively** with walk-ins or referrals because that 1 avoids having to screen hundreds of calls-emails and 2 attracts only those job hunters who *are willing to walk through the door and introduce themselves*.

In fact, many hiring managers get a raging semi just thinking about a job hunter walking-in and introducing themselves for a good reason—one personal encounter will reveal you more than a thousand words in an email. 'Footing it' shows a type of eagerness, a "go getter mentality" that companies sit up and notice. Not only that, it's a small but CRITICAL indicator of your true personality: an applicant who's happy with who she or he is, who will not feel shame or fear for stepping up their game, who is filled with life-energy and a resume in hand, with the confidence to back it up. If you are willing to dress up and greet the hiring manager in person, they will assume you will make the same effort as an associate of their company.

Every time you read this keep that in mind no matter how good your resume is, an in-person impression is always going to be bigger and more powerful than a paper or email impression.

To begin mapping out the "hidden job market" in your area, use the *exact* same technique headhunters rely on when they're prowling for hot job leads: Google® maps.

step 1
Go to www.google.com

step 2
Click on the "Maps" tab at the top of the page.

step 3
Type in your address. (example: 123 Sesame Street, Silent Hill, CA 90210)

step 4
Click on "Search Nearby"

step 5
Type in "medical," or "pharmacy," or "medical billing," or "manufacturing," or "security," or "mechanic," or "nurse," or whichever keyword describes the type work you are interested or specialize in.

Now Google® will return a listing of all related businesses near your home. If you click page 2, 3, 4 it will list these potential employers further and further away from your home.

step 6
Click the "print" button at the top right corner, then a new pop-up window will make you press print again. That will print ten (10) locations for you. Close the pop-up window. Now go to 'Page 2' and again, print and so on...

Grab a writing utensil such as a pen or scented marker and write down the locations if you don't have a printer handy. ("Go here, visit these guys. Now these guys. What about these guys? Sure, why the f@&* not?") If you do not own a mystery fun box (a computer) go to a library (it's a big building with books inside).

A rough guesstimate is that about 1-5% of these locations will be hot leads, most will be cold or warm leads. This is how the world works, if you want to generate some hot leads, you have to wade through the duds. Hey, even a great job hunter such as yourself can't win them all! (Hot, warm and cold leads are defined somewhere towards the end of this section to force you to keep reading...MUWHAHAHA!!!)

Once you've created your list of leads, you'll be ready to make contact.

step 7
Call to see if they are hiring. (Do you know how to cold call? Then learn! Pay a friendly visit to the "Phone Script" section on **page 73** to learn how to speak with total confidence.) Now print ONE resume and attach ONE thank you note (**page 283**) for each and every company that indicates that they are or will be hiring pretty soon.

Grab your interviewing clothes, plan your route to these organizations, book your first class flight on the bus, subway or express train and introduce yourself with that stunning smile everyone's so jealous about.

step 8
During your visit, pick up a business card and always follow this card RITUAL:

When handed a business card, don't just grab it and stuff it in your pocket. Make the person feel important by taking a good 3-5 second look at their card—you might see something that could spark a conversation. Hand-write notes on the back of the card such as date, location and what they offer. These comments will be worth gold when following up with the new contact. Then PLACE the card in your wallet to signal their importance to you.

SEVEN

....

ONLINE JOB ADS

The whole online job search thing is getting a lot of love at the moment.

It's still good if you filter out all of the noise. Applying online is basically a throw-the-noodles-against-the-wall-and-lets-see-what-sticks strategy. You can score interviews, but only if you post *fast* enough. (Often the first few qualified candidates to respond to a job ad **are the only ones** invited to interview.) On the average, most job hunters are getting mixed results: a few winners, some duds. But mixed results are always better than no results.

That said, some job hunters limit their ENTIRE job search to fingers hovering above the letters on the keyboard. That's probably the least effective thing you can do. Let's bring to your attention what may be the most glaring and amazing fact about applying online: it barely registers. It's a blip. How is the hiring manager supposed to notice your "I CAN WORK TOO" application submission over the other 283? The cold hard truth is they probably won't.

But some job hunters live in a warm, serene place called lala land. Calling for an update, or even going in person, is not in the game plan. (What they're usually trying to avoid is the human-beings part, the uncomfortable waits, stares and attention that comes with asking for the hiring manager.)

You can't just click away at everything in life, *including* your job problems. Online job ads function as great leads, but the human-beings part is what gets you jobs. This bears repeating, a phone or in-person impression is always going to be bigger and more powerful than an email impression. If you're not getting the results you want from the internet—then enough bellyaching online!—it's time to switch from wishful-based thinking to reality-based thinking and get your name out.

Skip the lonely online stuff, muster up some courage, call or take a stroll and drop by the actual companies who post 'help wanted' ads online. Handing your resume to a real person is a MUCH better experience than emailing it to somewhere in time and space. A smile and handshake will give the hiring manager something to start with. It will make her want to know more about what kind of person you are. You might even discover what a dump a few of them are or that the job leads might be located in neighborhoods too far for a commute, things the job posting *never* mentions. You may just drop the online thing altogether.

www.Careerbuilder.com
www.Careeronestop.org
www.Craigslist.org
www.Caljobs.ca.gov (Shout out to Cali!)
www.Engineerjobs.com
www.Federaljobs.net
www.GlassDoor.com
www.Indeed.com
www.Job-Hunt.org
www.Jobbankinfo.org (state employment agency)
www.Linkedin.com
www.Monster.com
www.Newslink.org (old-school "want ads")
www.TheLadders.com
www.USAjobs.gov

Definition of hot, warm and cold leads...

Hot lead
An immediate opening that you are qualified for.

Warm lead
A warm lead is only warm until it turns hot. (Usually a few weeks, sometimes months upon months...or years for sought-after civil service, tech or law enforcement jobs.)

Cold lead
A cold lead stays cold until the end of time. Either they never have any openings, or you do not like them, or they do not like you. Wash your hands of them and move on.

(Extra Credit)

A sneaky person's guide to figuring out who posted that anonyMOUSE job ad.

The shortest route to a new job is **direct contact**. When you find a job posting, apply online, and then make every attempt to get in touch with the hiring manager directly (for a glow-y phone or face introduction).

But what happens very often is that you'll see an ad for a job you want with the contact information completely missing. What do you do in this situation? Become a computer hacker, of course!

Sneaky example #1
"Chef Position Available. $18/Hour.
Reply to: humanresources@infusegreen.com"

The email to reply to in this example is *humanresources@infusegreen. com*. This is most likely a private, company email account (this means NOT a free to the public, anonymous Gmail®, Yahoo®, or Hotmail® email account) because Infuse® only grants its employees a company email address.

You can spot that this is an official email because of the name that comes after the "@" symbol, called the 'domain name,' which is bold in this example: *humanresources@**infusegreen.com***. The trick is to change the "*humanresources@*" part to "*www*". Go online and in the address bar on your web browser type in this: www.infusegreen.com

Doing so should take you to the company website, if they host one online. Most reputable companies will have an address and phone number listed on their website. Drop a line.

Sneaky example #2
Chef Position Available. $18/Hour.
Reply to: wutzadleeyo-catering@yahoo.com

This case is a little trickier. The company posting the job is using a public, free, anonymous email account (in our example it is Yahoo® Mail). BUT…the name of the account gives a clue. In this case, we read "wutzadleeyo-catering@yahoo.com."

Go online to Google® Maps (see the instructions above) and type in "wutza dleeyo catering" and see what comes up in your area. Call and find out if they're the ones hiring.

Sneaky example #3
Chef Position Available. $18/Hour.
Reply to: job-peuh7-25438274@craigslist.org

The email address in this example *job-peuh7-25438274@craigslist.org* is actually a temporary email that Craigslist.com offers to people who wish to remain TOTALLY invisible.

Unless there is a company name, phone number, fax number, you will have to reply to the anonymous Craigslist email address and hope to capture more clues IF the company decides to respond. Not all companies will.

Sneaky example #4
Chef Position Available. $18/Hour.
Reply to: Fax resume to (212) 555-2368.

Do a reverse search on the fax number. Go online to Google® and type in *(212) 555-2368* and hit *'enter.'*

Sneaky example #5
Chef Position Available. $18/Hour. Reply to: Call (212) 555-2368.

Tricked YOU! Hello, hello! When there's a phone number you ALWAYS call to prove that you are human-being with feelings and thoughts, and not just a payroll entry.

You: "Hello, I am responding to your job posting for ███████, which I understand may report to you. Since I happen to be in the area on Tuesday, I thought I would to drop off my resume and learn a little more about your company."

(Extra Extra Credit)

This thing is amazeballs!

Any smart, eager-to-believe job hunter can get hustled into scams that pretend to be real job postings.

It's better to learn how to identify and handle these scammers now then trying to deal with it later, when it's too late. It could stay with you for life as the scariest, most time wasting, brain scarring thing ever.

(in)famous scheme #1—WORK FROM HOME.
"I kept telling myself things would get better. Now I work from home and make thousands." You are then asked to pay money for online access to this "secret" job opportunity. These ~~slimy hustlers~~ disreputable people might try to sell a training "kit" to get you hooked in.

See no evil (do not read). Hear no evil (do not listen). Speak no evil (do not respond).

(in)famous scheme #2—PRINCE AND THE REVOLUTION.
"Could this be?" Should any overseas "prince" or member of a royal family email you, it is a scam that people fall victim to everyday. The storyline goes something like this: "I am a prince. I have millions of dollars. For sure. Honest. This time f'reals. Please help me. Oh yeah… and…he, he…don't tell anyone about this…we cool? Now I'll need a copy of your driver's license and wire me some cash."

Those pesky royal families and their investment opportunities!

(Do not even *think* about trying to hook up the "prince" with the other "princess" that emailed you a week earlier, you sick puppy!)

(in)famous scheme #3—MULTI-LEVEL MARKETING.
A multi-level marketing scheme (also know as a pyramid scheme) pretends to be a job but you are asked to sign up to "the program." Typically that means you go to a seminar, pay money to enroll—friendly reminder: jobs are supposed to pay YOU!!—then, as you become a minion, try to recruit other people into the scheme.

Clearly something's up and you'll know it's an MLM situation by the very first big clue: the "hiring manager" contacts you AFTER normal business hours (9am-5pm, Monday-Friday). You'll receive a call on a Sunday or at 10:00pm on a Tuesday or on a holiday, like New Years. The second clue is that caller will sound like a sales person and try a get a kind of bromance going. They'll call and call 24/7 until you're just burnt out on it. Offer no excuse, just keep repeating that you are not interested and politely hang up.

You: "Thank you, but I am not interested. Can you do me a favor and remove my name from your list. Buh byee!"

EIGHT

....

CHECK YOU OUT!

It sounds deceptively simple, but it works. Take in a deep breath and as you exhale, say the words '**I am prepared**.' Oxygen in. Bad energy out. This technique has helped countless applicants calm their nerves before interviews and tests.

three days before the interview.
- visit their website to get a feel for who they are
- practice pronouncing the name of the hiring manager (so you don't get tongue-tied)
- if any forms are needed, complete them neatly in advance
- print out 2 copies of your resume
- choose 2-3 questions that you'll ask the hiring manager and write the questions on paper (**page 79**)
- get a haircut and style appropriate to the job (the hiring manager wants to picture you in the role. **Page 225** or **page 237**)
- plan a bus route or figure out where you or your ride will park (it's okay to ask about parking…it will not be held against you)

day before the interview.
- check fingernails
- shine shoes, organize your interviewing clothes or scrubs, and iron out wrinkles
- match accessories-jewelry, but be very conservative…'less is more'
- use Google® maps to plan your route and identify the correct building entrance

things to take with you to the interview.
- phone (turn off before interview)
- 2 copies of your resume (one for manager, one extra copy just in case)
- notebook or sheets of blank paper, and two pens (pick up fancy ballpoint pens at the 99-cent store)
- breath mints or spray (no chewing gum during interview)
- your personal calendar

evening or night before the interview.
- talk to a bestie or close confidant for a last-minute jolt of confidence
- sleep early get a good night's rest (reverse psychology: turn off the lights and concentrate on staying awake to knock out)
- do not bend, fold, crinkle, crush, stain or mutilate your resume…in fact, don't even breathe on it

morning of your interview.
- stretch your bones in the morning as it will help improve your alertness and relax you
- check the weather and traffic report just in case you need to leave a bit sooner
- open up your email to check for any last-minute rescheduling
- go wee wee in the poo poo box
- boost brainpower by eating a powerbar or piece of fruit beforehand

just before your meeting.

- ~~let out a silent one~~
- do a 'once-over' in the mirror for hair and clothing
- pay attention to your posture and remember to pull shoulders up, then back, then relaxed down
- step through the door precisely *15 minutes* before the scheduled appointment, but not earlier
- get ready to deliver your 20+ second 'tell me about yourself' intro and put on a warm, relaxed smile
- prepare for a dry, firm handshake with good eye contact
- do not lock your keys in the car

seriously, what happened.

- write down the questions they asked you just in case of a second interview
- send a thank-you note (**page 287**)
- show a little love by thanking the person who connected you with this hot job lead

DANGERZONE

NINE

....

LET THEM HATE SO LONG AS THEY FEAR?

People only hate upwards. People only hate on those who they think are more successful or *are going to be* more successful than they are.

People do not hate downwards.

What to do with haters.
Haters are not the problem. "Haters gonna hate." It's your OPINION about haters that is the problem.

But the solution is simple—**embrace the haters.**

Because the more haters you have, the more successful you are.

TEN

....

RACE MATTERS

Racism is so dumb it hurts.

As a child, Earth's entire population is divided into two groups, kids and grown-ups. It's a mental shortcut; not so much a faster way of thinking, but rather a way of skipping the thinking altogether.

All people, you included, belong to the *same* race called *homo sapiens*. Scientists have crushed to pieces the argument that skin tone, or any other physical trait, bundles people into different "races." But trying to explain science to a **racist** is like playing against that annoying kid in the neighborhood who wants to make up rules as he goes along. Sorry, but you're not going to win.

Remarkably, by accident or by design, the whole subject of racism *at interviews* is completely culturally off-limits. No one wants to talk about it and very few will openly declare themselves a racist because it's so vulgar. Yet the cold, uncomfortable possibility that skin color or a last name could move your resume halfway, or all the way, to the trash bin is the world we live in.

Typically what plays out is you are invited to a face-to-face interview. People act all introverted as you enter into the building. The secretary does the classic double-take followed by a look of sheer disbelief. "Excuse me, but I think your skin color owes my eyes an apology." For no apparent reason the interviewer treats you hostilely from the get go, telling you before you've even settled into your chair how you are not a right fit for the job. A whole 5 minutes later you are *escorted* off premises, as if you're going to run out to the grassy area, pull out clumps of grass and throw them at the windows. Not quite the welcome you were expecting.

Yet that scene plays out everyday and it's enough to make anyone, young or old, dude or dudette, cry into a pillow.

Racists see you as a member of a group, not as an individual. And the labels white, yellow, red, brown, black have all sorts of unspoken stereotypes about work habits and intelligence and sexuality and other things baked into it. But it's not supposed to be like this. Skin color has no impact on how well you complete a job.

So why the hate?

Not so fast! Paranoia meets reality about half the time, not all the time. What if it was something less diabolical, like competition. "Compa-wuh?" You know, other peeps with resumes selling similar stuff. Maybe the interviewer was already sold on another candidate and just wanted to see who's behind that sexy voice as possible back-up. Maybe he didn't want to be responsible for sucking you into a bad scene; a total dive ran by a spasmodic owner. Hell, he might have been dumped by a high school sweetheart that looked like you 10 years ago and was flashing back, or having a bad day, or a world of other random things that had little to do with you.

Categorizing another person as a **racist** without any evidence of that person's actual character is a mental shortcut; not so much a faster way of thinking, but rather a way of skipping the thinking altogether.

Some people, especially those who lived through some dark patches with schoolyard bullies or bigoted teachers, tend to see racism in places where it may not exist. Any person can be considered racist if you try hard enough. You can see racism on TV, in movies, online, in advertisements and everywhere, but mostly in your own mind.

The most courageous step you can take is to check out of this exhausting game, this self-imposed prison of your heart and mind.

For racism will have no power over you, or affect you in self-generated ways, as long as you remember one thing: **not everyone is like that**.

With a crisp and clean introduction, great handshake and smile you'll find they will either get over it or if they don't, kick 'em to the curb and take your talents elsewhere because *not everyone is like that.*

"You can never be on top of the world if you're carrying it on your shoulders." (Anonymous, 2013)

ELEVEN

....

21 YEARS OF MYSTERY FINALLY SOLVED

How to get your ~~lazy, disorganized slacker who hates~~ others ~~and is a compulsive liar~~ ex back so you can concentrate on JOB HUNTING.

First, make sure no one controls your mind.
The greatest trick cheaters pull is making you believe it's YOUR fault.
(Blaming you...the victim!)

In a cheater's own words, what typically plays out is, "'Yeah I'm flirting with this new friend...it's FUN! As the night goes by it becomes, 'Well, one kiss isn't going to kill anybody.' After the kiss, nothing matters. 'We're both into it and, hell, no one will know...The consequences part does not happen until the next day. The next day is the worst, the lowest of lows. NO one is sympathetic to a cheater; not that they should be. So there is this internal guilt of 'Oh f***, this is so f****d.' Seeing you [or thinking about you] the next day is what makes me feel dirty and worthless."
('give_me_the_child', 2012)

When that happens, the cheater's mind instantly links all those negative feelings to you. **"Yes, I *might* be cheating, but you're the one making me feel bad about it."** (Makes cheating sound almost *positive*, doesn't it?) There's a bit of insanity in this logic, but it is how a person tries to emotionally deal with self-disgust.

This 'deviant' logic is used in many everyday situations: "Yes, I might be a cruel parent, but you're the one making me feel bad about it. Yes, I might spread rumors about you, but you're the one making me feel bad about it. Yes, I might hit you, but you're the one making me feel bad about it."

The way a cheater treats you is not a reflection of your self-worth, but rather how they think about their own self-worth. (Tilt back your chair, gaze at the ceiling and meditate on this for a moment.)

What you know may be wrong.
"It drives me crazy! Things could've been perfect. Then we got together and everything went downhill. WTF?!"

No one else will tell you, but the 'thing' that stops a person from actually *committing* to a relationship is the same 'thing' that causes cheating, break-up's and hit & runs. **BOREDOM**.

Boredom fizzles out *all* relationships.

Excuses like, "it's not you, it's me…I need space…things are moving too quickly…I love you but I'm not *in love* with you," are never the real reasons. The real reason is deep down inside the idea of being bored to death for the rest of their life is FRIGHTENING. First they get bored, *then* they get scared to commit (to a life of boredom).

I don't know how to say this to you, but…
Boredom isn't triggered some random, mysterious spasm of the universe, as some would like you to believe. The "mystery" that triggers boredom is (their) low self-esteem. Pay attention.

As the initial excitement wears off, the low self-esteem part of the mind kicks in, "HELLO, I never do anything great. So obviously this can't be great."

Low self-esteem minds **look down on *everything* they've accomplished.**

Most people can't spot low self-esteem because people with low self-esteem often act stuck-up. This might sound surprising to a skeptical reader but acting conceited is a dead giveaway that a person suffers from low self-esteem. It's not that complicated to understand.

Healthy self-esteem minds think, "I have no reason to act superior or inferior. We're all born naked and equal. I contribute as much as the next person, *in my own way.*"

Now compare this to how low self-esteem rolls: "I'm not worthy…I'm not worthy…I'm not worthy." People with low self-esteem have a low estimation of their VALUE.

Girlfriends-boyfriends who think "I'm not worthy" naturally question the intelligence of anyone fascinated by them. "Why would you be all into me? I'm not worthy, duh! That must mean you're an idiot. And I'm going to treat you like the idiot that you are."

When that happens, the game changes. They begin to 1 look down on you 2 begin feeling bored and begin to 3 emotionally disconnect.

You see, acting stuck-up literally means looking down on people. People with healthy self-esteem do not look down on *anyone*, and therefore never act stuck-up.

Watch what you say around a boyfriend or girlfriend with low self-esteem.
Whether they're aware of it or not, saying 'I love you. I want to be with you forever. I'll do anything for you' triggers a low self-esteem personality

HANS VAN NAS

to back-off, look down on you and think, "OMG what an idiot."

Stuck-up minds want a challenge NOT slavish love and devotion. Loyalty gets on their nerves. It's a sign of weakness. "But...but...will she still love me?" YES! Assuming someone with troubled past relationships would want reassurance or emotional stability is unwise. Any a person who is constantly surrounded by drama is typically the one who is causing the drama. Being cold-hearted makes you ~~more mysterious and more fascinating~~ sooooooooo hot(!) to a stuck-up, low self-esteem mind because you're saying 'back off, I am not fully conquered.'

Oh, man. I have never seen an adult cry baby tears.
But the sad, sad truth is that most people will try to put on a happy face—suffer in silence—and agonize over how to "fix" the problem. "Everything seemed cool. What went wrong?! I NEED TO KNOW."

(How many times do you have to be told? It's boredom.)

"I met a new friend but nothing happened."

(Told you.)

Let's get something straight. **To low self-esteem personalities, there's a sexiness associated with being ruthless.** They're only happy when things are complicated. That's why dating others and making them jealous can stop the rejection because low self-esteem personalities need fireworks. Relationships without struggle feel boring. 'Dating' doesn't mean you have to do anything physical. Just going out with a fresh face to the park or Micky D's is good enough to start their imagination running wild.

Sometimes you just have to give people what they want.

Jealousy.
"Hans is this super hot guy who is going to be a rockstar person

1 2 8

someday, but he says he doesn't want to!! He's dating this girl named Rebecca and I'm like super jealous of her because Hans is the hottest guy in the world!!!!" (hansissohot, 2009)

That's not the kind of jealousy we are talking about.

Real jealousy will make your blood boil to the point you want to incite a riot and set the world on fire. Jealousy is a backstabbing—"I've got the devil in me"—emotion that convinces you to do all the things that SCARE GIRLFRIENDS-BOYFRIENDS AWAY, things like trying to put them on lockdown. (No one causes you to feel jealous. It's self-administered.)

Worst of all, with jealousy **you're putting yourself down** because you're basically saying **'there's something missing inside me that only your love can cure.'** (Not true! There's nothing wrong with you. The world's full of people with who can give you affection and butterflies in your stomach. He's not your salvation.)

Jealousy turns relationships sour because jealousy comes off as clingy, or in extreme cases stalker-ish and pervy, to a person pulling away. "But I'm only jealous of *every single person* he talks to because I don't want anyone other than →me← realizing how amazing he is!!" Yes, but jealousy causes low self-esteem and turns the relationship into a negative crowding experience. Is it worth the price?

As long as you refuse to budge from JEALOUS RAGE-mode, get ready to play hide 'n' seek. (They hide while you seek.)

The law of attraction.
Whether they're aware of it or not, when people associate you with positive feelings, people find a way to be **physically** near you. When people associate you with negative feelings, they avoid you.

With positive feelings, people sitting down lean-in towards you, people stand closer to you, and people reply quickly to calls or messages so they can feel a connection to you. People also walk close by, sit nearby you or "just happen" to be in the area where you are, all without realizing it.

With negative feelings, you become radioactive. People sitting down lean back and away from you, people fold their arms when speaking to you, and people turn their face away from you, avoiding eye contact. People also tend to flake out on you and do not pick up (or reluctantly answer) calls or messages, as if you're bothering them or interrupting something important.

That's why acting complain-y kills-off any chances you might have to win your love interest back, especially when combined with jealousy, because it adds negativity to your personality. Acting depressed might work in the moment, but it only adds all-the-more negativity to your personality which gives *even more* reason to leave. Intimidations or ultimatums (do this or else!) never work because, again, negativity is an anti-fun thing that makes people want to get the heck away from you.

Being negative or positive is not a personality type or chronic condition, it's a choice. You can switch sides any time.

The naked truth.
Have you considered the possibility that the entire relationship is devoted to a delusion?

No doubt, it's love. **But maybe it's sick love**, just like feeling hurt is a sick pleasure.

Understanding why people get hooked on sick love can be extremely helpful. Sick love is pain combined with love. Pain is a signal something's wrong. People naturally avoid pain, but when a person decides to put a low value on them self (the definition of low self-esteem), they crave the reward that comes *after* enduring pain—a chance to feel high & mighty.

Here is how. First the part of the brain that wants to feel sorry for itself thinks, "poor, poor miserable me. Look at heartache I'm putting up with! Look at the sacrifice." The pain is the set-up. Now comes the reward, "I would *never* treat you like this." In other words, "I'm better than you."

Healthy self-esteem minds do not think they're better than anyone else, they just **realize when there isn't a match**. "Yes, you held my heart, but you skipped the not-being-a-jerk-about-it part. Good bye."

The problem with sick love is the dependence on destructive people for feeling good about our self.

Sick love and sick pleasure drowns out healthy love and healthy pleasures—especially important when children are involved. (Being around destructive partners can be very traumatizing to children. Children pick up a lot of the tension parents feel.)

Fixing crazy.
The world is filled with mixture of great people, so-and-so people and crazies. There are shortcuts to happiness and the shortcut is—are you seated?—STOP DATING CRAZY.

But you want to fix crazy. You consider it a *challenge*. (CHOO CHOO! All aboard the crazy train.) Really? The message you send when trying to fix someone is, "I am right and you are wrong." People love to be heard, but can you think of anyone who likes being preached to?

Relationships sometimes create over-dependency and we feel frustrated when we don't have supreme powers to control the other person into doing things our way.

I just want to be loved. Is that so wrong???
"I'm a helpless romantic that *needs* to be loved and *needs* to be understood." It is nice to be loved. It is nice to be understood. But, it's only a DESIRE. Know the difference. A real life need is clean drinking water, something a billion people who got stuck drinking ice-cold cup of WTF know all too well. (1 billion+ people go without clean drinking water every day.)

We're all being mass-manipulated by movies, music and flashing, seizure-inducing advertisements into believing there's something broken inside that only romantic love can fix. (It's an incredible con job when you think about it.)

The belief that you need is what causes your pain. Change this belief and you'll never ~~act like an aggressive mutant~~ be anxious or mad when something doesn't go your way. You'll feel disappointed and frustrated, but you won't find yourself curled-up in a ball, devastated by hurt and anger, wondering if you'll make it.

Independence.
Everybody seems to want this thing called "independence" really-really bad. But **people can't define what independence means, so they wrongly define independence as rebelliousness**. It's so far out of control that even many grown adults act like maladjusted children and sit in the back of the room with their "deal with it" shades on! Of course, it's to prove just how ~~hostile~~ INDEPENDENT they are. This "independence" craze is at an all-time high and it just seems to be getting worse.

Is your special someone rebelling against you?

Hey, here's a thought: why don't you ease up off the "serious talk."

Explaining yourself about what you want and why you did what you did is known as "serious talk." "Serious talk" uses pressure and confrontation to ask for *more* than what you're being given—that looks clingy, whiny and makes people feel like you're trying to control them. Yet another (yes, another) problem with "serious talk" is your ~~special someone~~ rebel-without-a-cause is probably not aware that boredom is causing her to pull away. Acting bossy (serious talk) plants a poison pill in her head, "Oh, it's because you're controlling, that's why! I've discovered why! Now I'm aware of a real, concrete reason why I should leave you. Thanks!"

"Serious talk" is old and busted. The new hotness is *totally giving up*.

Totally giving up means stop resisting. Stop playing tug-of-war (let go of the rope and they'll fall on their booty). Allow them to be negative, jealous, self-destructive, threaten to leave, or whatever floats their boat. If a fight is brewing about trust issues, be friendly and just go with it, "Yes, you will never be able to trust me," and ~~laugh like a super villain~~ shut up. You see, agreeing is not a sign a weakness, it's giving a rebellious person a ring made of kryptonite.

Your rebel is secretly in love with her negative feelings and when you try to reason with her, you are telling her that her negative feelings are wrong. That's an attack on her pride.

By totally giving up, or acting unfazed, you are rejecting the rebellious part of the personality and frustrating their ego; a must if you want a rebellious person to respect you. Rebels need something in you to fight with. Once he or she notices that you're no longer interested in fixing them; that you've checked out of the game; that you're learning to be happy and giving yourself value WITHOUT *a her or a him,* you become (independent!) irresistibly attractive—the only way to be these days.

You can't just use this strategy for a few days or a week, think the relationship is "cured" and then slip back to high pressure, confrontational tactics. They'll rapidly lose respect (and piranha-bite you) the moment you come-off clingy or complain-y. And the tougher it is for you to stick to this strategy, the more you actually need to because it shows how overly-dependent you are.

> The real definition of *independence*? Being happy and giving yourself value without a her or a him.

I have low self-esteem. No one told me.
Self-esteem is how you value yourself.

Low self-esteem means you are putting yourself down and lying to yourself; valuing yourself lower than some (put down), yet higher than others (lie). Healthy self-esteem means that you realize the truth: we humans are all on a level playing field. The two are fighting a battle for your soul. Both are two sides of the same coin: Two beliefs trying to take on the world and make it in their image.

To change your self-esteem, change your opinion about your value.

"I'm worthy. I am worthy. **I AM WORTHY**. Other people's happiness doesn't take away mine. I'm responsible for my own happiness and will keep my options open. And if I can't find happiness with you, I'll find happiness with someone else. Every fairytale has to have a happy ending, including mine."

Hands up if you think you're worthy. \o/ Your personality is now *sparkling* more than those bullring piercings!

This is usually the part when (surprise!), guess who shows up at the door with a 'this time is going to be different' promise? They'll try and convince you that the relationship isn't toast, the edges are just burnt a little bit. You'll ponder—as though it were some agonizing, complex dilemma— whether to fall for the excuses and lies…again.

It's your self-esteem. You're in charge. You call the shots.

(Extra Credit)

No more Mr. Nice Girl. No more Ms. Nice Guy.
Everybody knows you're being played but you absolutely refuse to believe it. You need hard proof. Until then, ~~you'll be content banging your head against a wall~~ rather than being left to walk in the dark, let's rebalance the power in the relationship.

You're trying to get from point A to point B but there's a road block: low self-esteem.

Provided your ex is not 100% emotionally unplugged, these steps will restore the ~~allure and mystery~~ sexy demon hunter back in your personality—the quality that made you so tantalizing in the first place:

Act happy ALL of the time, even after long periods of silence. Reconnect with your friends. Date others to make them jealous. (Yes, you really have to get out of the house. Do you have an escape plan?) Send mixed signals. Do not defend yourself or explain your thoughts-feelings. Ever. No *'after all I've done for you'* guilt trips. **Accept that crazy comes with the package**. Look passionate about life—choose a hobby and really get INTO it. Texts and conversations should be ~~scandalous~~ short, positive with you ending the conversation first. Ignore some calls. Deliver slicing glares and icy shoulders instead of a lovey-dovey vibe.

The more love-attention you give (e.g. "I love you lil puppet for forever xoxoxoxo frown misty") the more your ex is able to let go. The less love-attention you give, the more your ex will cling.

(Well, now that a life-mystery as been answered for you, visit **page 147**.)

TWELVE

....

·SHOUTS· MOTHER OF GOD, YES! THANK YOU FOR THE INTERVIEW

The hiring manager's first thought WILL NOT BE, "oh, you must have a family to feed."

The hiring manager's first thought will be, "Umm, how bad did you screw up at your last job?"

You may be desperate for the job, but your **vibe** should NEVER show it.

You'll scare them. They'll think something is wrong. They'll wonder why you're having so many problems landing a job.

In case you didn't notice…
Every single example that you're encouraged to rip from this book showcases **1** a confidence in your ability **2** a passion for a certain type of work, and **3** genuine interest and excitement at the prospect of working with that particular company. Isn't that interesting? That's on purpose, silly!

Everyone naturally thinks they're going out of their mind with frustration and self-doubt during a job hunt. Feel free to act like a Chihuahua and curse humanity in the privacy of your home, but don't act desperate at the interview. Don't even *think* about it.

WARNING will register on their radar.

You will signal that you're so desperate you'll take anything. And no employer particularly enjoys the feeling of being interchangeable with any other random employer that would have said 'yes.' An applicant with standards is attractive. An applicant who is choosy is attractive.

Right now you have a lot of negative self-talk going through your head. Your brain is replaying painful scenes over and over. Do not trust your brain. **You are not destined to become a jobless hobo**. And the best thing you can do for yourself is realize that. Until then, act cool...they can smell fear.

(If you've always dreamed of being more confident, keep on dreaming...Just kidding! Today is your lucky day. Flip to **page 147**.)

THIRTEEN

······································

PIMP-SLAPPING THE DEVIL

You might visualize yourself jumping up from the chair, knocking him down on the floor and chocking him until everyone pulls you off. "Hold my coffee while I do this…"

"Every one of us has a fighting spirit, a confidence that allows us to wake up in the morning, and take on the world. [Evil bosses] want to take this power away from you." (Morrissey, 2008) And they will not rest until they have you sucking your thumb in the corner. ~~LEAVE WHILE YOU STILL HAVE TIME!!!~~

Never stick your application in crazy.
There is a serious epidemic occurring and it must be addressed, once and for all: stressful jobs that pay terribly. It may sound odd, but what should tip you off to these type of openings is **extreme friendliness** during the application-interview stage for no apparent reason. You can compare it to Hansel & Gretel getting lured into the witch's lair with sugary treats. What child would refuse a treat? And how many applicants wouldn't want to sign up with a company that treats you super, super nice?

139

Watch out! It's probably a trap. And one you can easily avoid as long as you catch on early and walk away from the whole thing. Trust your powerful instincts. Why would a company in a down economy be on the constant lookout for fresh meat? The answer is disturbingly clear: **they're going to use you up and toss you out**, and this is what forces the company to keep posting new 'help wanted' ads every week, ones that most likely contain statements about what you COULD earn instead of what you WILL earn.

High turn-over is a humungous **RED FLAG** that a company is under terrible management.

So call in and cancel the interview any time you sense a distressed organization, a creeper vibe, or just find yourself extremely uncomfortable in that person's presence. The hiring manager won't hold it against you because now he'll have more time to play with his headless doll collection.

Evil Boss.
How do awful human beings become bosses? Not so fast! Perhaps he's not an evil boss but a disappointed one; or a serious businessman who *fears* respect into everyone. Challenge yourself and find out if *you* are the problem. Are you a boss-hater? Do you despise authority just because? If the answer is 'yes' then the boss is probably just reflecting back your bad energy.

But—and this is an important BUT—if your attitude or performance is not the concern, then it's your boss. Evil bosses are in their 20's, 30's, and 40's and think it's okay to act like a child. They shout down employees to feel like GODS in the workplace. (It's the only time they feel a sense of power.) The schizo mood swings, humiliation, secrecy, taking credit for things you do, intimidation, split personality, playing favorites, breaking promises, arrogance, mean streak humor, sarcasm, vapid accusatory tone, and hooliganism is **designed** to make you nervous, doubt yourself, and even stutter.

Anyone who tears your face off at a moment's notice can totally destroy your confidence. It can also leave you breaking out into fits of tears for no reason and make you feel like you're full-blown CRAZY.

Do not allow this to happen to you. We must to disarm your tormentor, professionally, before it's too late. (If you allow yourself to get ghetto, or be yelled at, you will damage your own reputation and the attacker will walk away victoriously. Never give your power away.)

Be 100% sure that it's a hard-hitting insult and not just workplace playfulness.
Blogger Jay Morrisey deserves an award for his astonishingly compelling written work on handling bullies at work. According to Morrisey, evil bosses use insults for dominance, laughs and respect. That's why most insults are delivered in front of others, not one-on-one in private. He advises that whatever you decide, *do not ignore* the insult because they'll just continue to abuse you throughout your relationship. Instead, **turn the audience against the evil boss** with the kind of verbal intimidation used by lawyers, corporate rivals, and police officers. These brilliant one-liners will leave the evil boss with teeth clenched, hands shaking, and whole body boiling in liquid hate.

1 "Did you just insult me?" ~Jay Morrisey
(As the tension in the room rises, the answer will most likely be 'no' because a 'yes' response by an evil boss means unprofessional conduct, a possible visit from human resources, plus grounds for lawsuit.)

2 "Are you trying to be funny at my expense?" ~Jay Morrisey
(This needs to be said in a calm and emotionless tone. Do not be scared to respond in this manner. Your aim is to take the power away from the instigator. Although an evil boss likes attention, they don't like *this* kind of attention—exposure as a bully.)

3 "That's what our world needs, another bully." ~Jay Morrisey
(In certain older cultures—75,000-100,000 years ago—when people behaved as bullies, we killed them. People HATE bullies.)

4 "I will talk to you but I will not let you shout at me. You are my boss and I respect you. But you are not my mother." ~Jay Morrisey
(Nice touch! In effect, you are humiliating your attacker by remaining calm and making them look like a drama queen. Now the little weeny has to come up with another plan.)

5 "I'm sorry you feel that way, and..."
(If you fear losing your job, respond softly with this quote to play it safe. Repeating "I'm sorry you feel that way, and..." fizzles out the attack, reduces the impact of the insult in front of others, and sets the example in the face of stupidity.)

Evil coworkers. (Demonoids.)
Being trained by a douchey coworker, who carries the kind of smirk on their face that makes you want to scream, is not evil. They might not be supervisors, but they've been there a while so "respect" their seniority. In time, they will cozy up to you.

But if you're dealing with a coworker circlejerking to score some high-school popularity points, the gloves come off, beeches. THIS MEANS WAR. Drop the maturity and enter beast mode. Do NOT allow **anyone**, including a "friend," to dog you out and possibly bad-mouth you out of a job. (Respect is far more important than friendship. With respect, you can continue being a kind, giving person but others will be afraid to treat you like a chump.)

Again, know your (fr)enemy. Serial verbal attackers want to make you upset and get you to make a fool of yourself. Deny anyone this control over you. **DO NOT APPEAR SENSITIVE**. Do not just sit there silently raging on the inside. We can easily squash this bug by using a few potent one-liners.

1 "Not today, [insert name of troll]. Any other day, it's cool. But NOT today!"
(Do not give eye contact and put them on BLAST. Sound loud but matter of fact-ly. The instigator, who desperately wanted to appear dominant, now looks stupid with every-body watching.)

2 "I'm not laughing with you, I'm laughing at you."
(Laugh to show you are not easily offended and then bust up louder with your own maniacal

laugh. They'll lose all power in this conversation.)

3 "Normally I think your jokes are funny, but I'm starting to understand why people don't like you."
(Subtle humiliation. Leaves the aggressor reduced and filled with FUD—fear, uncertainty and doubt.)

(Extra Credit)

Under different circumstances you would probably be good friends if it wasn't for the whole raving maniac boss thing they have going on. But since **no one** is entitled to run around and bully and intimidate in the workplace, you are going to professionally annihilate this villain, because for some, there can be no redemption.

First, document and report ALL abuse.
Your tormentor sits in an office built on lies. Remember that. People raised on compulsive honesty have a difficult time coming to terms with cold-hearted, deceitful people. So here is how you can protect yourself: when your boss (or coworker) crosses the line of professional conduct, write down what happened, who witnessed it and put a date and time of the incident. Not only is writing a GREAT stress reliever, should human resources, the department of labor, lawyers, or even the police begin investigating, you will possess an incredibly detailed report of every single incident, complete with any harassing emails, audio-video recordings, and texts as supporting evidence. If you cannot recall the conversation word-for-word, do your best to recreate it.

Evil bosses lie about everything, especially when facing disciplinary action, an epic legal smack-down in court or other nasty entanglements. Documenting abuse will prevent your attacker from spinning statements around to make you look like the bad gal-guy. Always keep in mind that when it comes time to **1** file an official complaint (with human resources or state Department of Labor) or **2** lawyer-up and sue the bejesus out of them, the person with the most paper wins. (Paper means evidence.)

To find your state's Department of Labor, go online and visit
www.dol.gov/whd/contacts/state_of.htm

Second, do not expect a company to fire an evil boss that profits the company.
You have to understand the dynamics at play. The organization can always hire a fresh, ambitious candidate ready to work, but finding a boss who can actually show results ($cashola) is FAR more difficult.

Third, avoid complaining to your boss's boss.
Higher-ups are typically people who don't think their little boo boo (evil boss) is guilty of anything particularly serious. They'll suggest if you have a problem with your boss to ask them nicely to stop. Yep, see that abusive hostile carnival freak in the big corner office, go talk to her about how you don't like her being an abusive hostile carnival freak. Yeah, tell her how much she sucks. Why didn't you think of that before?! (Going over your boss's head will backfire and turn a terrible boss into a maniac boss.)

Fourth, quietly transfer to a different section, division or company.
Since you can't really go on a hunger strike, physically avoid being around this filthy beast of meat and hair as much as possible. (And when you get home, take a long shower to wash off the stink.) In the comfort of your surroundings, sit down and plan out your exit strategy. For a small mom & pop business, consider quietly applying to other jobs and turn in your resignation letter once hired. (It's much easier to find employment when you are already employed, if you can stick it out.) If you can't handle the scene, take a job that pays less just so you don't have a job you hate. Not a job you like, just a job you don't hate, for now, to keep your sanity. If you're with a larger organization and prefer not to abandon ship, consider submitting a request to transfer to a new section, department, division or shift and ride it out until you're approved.

Fifth, exit without moaning "they screwed me!"
If this tyrant believes that tactics like this are going to intimidate or block you in any way from continuing your rise to success, this person is beyond deluded. If anything, it will only have the opposite effect and embolden you even FURTHER. You are damn well sure not a pawn in this circus show. But drumming up sympathy or trying to get coworkers to gang-up on a toxic boss will only downgrade your stature. ~~DESTROY HIM BEFORE HE GROWS STRONGER AND DECIMATES ALL OF HUMANITY~~. Leaving gracefully, with a cool head, proves how effective you are in a group and dealing with higher-ups who are a little low on brain cells...in this case, one with an instinct of how to bring someone down, but too paranoid and threatened to give even the most deserving associate one step up. ~~SOMEONE HOLD HIM DOWN AND DRIVE A SHARP STAKE THROUGH HIS HEART~~.

FOURTEEN

....

CONFIDENCE—I'M ON MY LEVEL

For a long time now self-help gurus have been telling the public a story that is not quite true. This not-quite-true story is that you can, somehow, trick yourself into confidence. Psych yourself out. Often this involves attending pricey seminars, or self-hypnosis, or listening to a charismatic, deep, manly voice over speakers.

But confidence is absolutely NOT something you need to pay anyone, like a self-help guru, to teach you. You learn as you go.

To help move things along, however, just ponder and imagine what would happen if you decided to...

Accept yourself.
The kryptonite of confidence is *pressure*.

Pressure drowns out your own inner voice and let's the noise of other people in. "You've failed before, so why even try? You're only going to fail again. You should be so much further in life by now." Whose voice are you hearing? Is it yours?

Imagine waking up tomorrow morning with ZERO expectations. Zer0. How would you feel? No, really, how would you feel?

Confidence simply means **being happy with who you are**—nothing to prove, no unrealistic image to live up to, and comfortable in your own skin. Every time you look at yourself in the bathroom mirror what you're seeing is this rather beautiful, afraid person feeling pressured into silence or aggression or shyness or all kinds of other things. That's the worst type of prison to live in, a mental prison where you live your life fulfilling the wishes and dreams of other people.

Only once you begin to let go of the expectation to be perfect AND this ridiculous notion of what and where you "should" be in your life, can you realize a Universal Truth—that very few things in life really matter, no one gets out alive anyway, so do whatever you want.

Think outside-in.
People see OK as a word. You see OK as a sideways stickman.

Confidence means happily doing the **opposite** of what everyone else thinks and does. ˙ʇuǝɹǝɟɟᴉp ǝq oʇ pooƃ s,ʇI Trouble sleeping? Turn off the lights and concentrate on staying awake. The internet getting crowded? Go offline and hand-deliver your resume. Everyone else wants perfection? Do the opposite and decide to like who you are. Uh oh. Your significant other wants to leave you?

Everybody's primal instincts, the first thoughts that will race through the dumpee's mind is 'must stop rejection, chase after her, reassure her, say baby I freakin MISS you, track whereabouts, use pressure, reason with her, use guilt, PUT HER ON LOCKDOWN.'

Is that what a confident person would do? Let's try the opposite. "You are right, totally right! Things will never work out. Let me help you pack. But, can we get you out by 4pm because I have a date tonight?"

Will your girlfriend come back? The answer is obvious.

Drop the baggage.

"Before you diagnose yourself with depression or low self esteem, first make sure that you are not, in fact, just surrounding yourself with a[$$]holes." ~ Steven Winterburn

A toxic person is anyone who lowers your self-esteem or emotionally drains you with their *negativity* issues. Toxic people can be anyone—boyfriends, girlfriends, parents, teachers, an ex or even a best friend. So here is what to do: ELIMINATE them completely from your circle. Never see them. They do not exist.

People change and not always for the better. Sometimes there are just some things that will never be the same, no matter how badly we want to relive those moments. Everything has a life cycle, including friendships and relationships.

Appreciate the good times together and what you had, and ACCEPT that you may never be there again.

Just go with it.

Fun fact: people don't want to hear your opinion. They want to hear their own opinion from your voice. That's the reason why arguments can never be won (and often explode into two people trying to out-crazy each other). Regardless of how factual, correct, or logical you opinion might be, disagreeing attacks the other person's pride because—no matter what—you are communicating 'YOU'RE WRONG!'

To *win someone over*, always agree with their feelings. Confident people have **nothing to prove**.

A boyfriend says, "This relationship will never work out. Things are moving too quickly." Listen to his doubts and reply, "You are right. We do need more space. Things are moving too quickly." It's fascinating to watch, but all of the talk about breakup will not only end, he will slowly back out of the issue all together. (Until next time ☺.)

Similarly, should a hiring manager criticize your experience, resume or answer during an interview (this is important), your brain will want to switch to defense mode. Turn OFF the auto-pilot and do the opposite of your first instincts! Smile and respond with, "I appreciate the feedback. Is there anything else I should be aware of?"

It's most likely a test to see if you have a DON'T FUXING TELL ME WHAT TO DO!!! personality.

Become situationally aware.
Never ignore the feeling that something's off.

Those little questions or doubts left "in the dark" always grow into fear inside the minds of hiring managers and others. Being misunderstood has its place (Hot Topic®), but definitely not at an interview. If you sense that the hiring manager, or even a friend or random stranger, is confused about your response, ALWAYS address it just like in these two examples:

1 *"I noticed some hesitation, would you like for me to explain further?"*

2 *"Would you like an example of what I mean? I would be happy to help clarify…"*

On the flipside, it's not SHAMEFUL if *you* don't understand an idea, word or instructions, either. Who cares if you stutter? Who cares if you don't say a word perfectly? You don't "get it" when everyone else in the room does. And?

The pressure to be perfect comes from only one place—**you**. No one can intimidate you. You can only intimidate yourself. (Put on a robe, grab your wizard hat and take a minute to think about this.) Let other people, who value themselves so poorly, shake in their boots around celebrities, politicians and hiring managers. We are all born naked and equal. You contribute as much as the next human, *in your own way*. Start acting like it.

CONFIDENCE

(Extra Credit)

"I spent most of my life being overweight, and the fat-girl treatment really affected me. What affected me even more was *losing weight* because one night I had a sudden realization... I am the same person I was when I was fat, but now everyone wants to talk to me and pay attention to me. Guys hit on me, and other (pretty) girls are waaaaaaay nicer to me. It felt like I was living someone else's life. At that moment I realized I relied on their opinions for TOO DAMN LONG, what they think doesn't matter, and I'm awesome, and that's all there is to it. Haven't had any confidence problems since that night. Just be patient with yourself. It'll come to you."

~Anonymous, 2010

I have low self-esteem. No one told me.
Self-esteem is how you value yourself.

Low self-esteem means you are putting yourself down and lying to yourself—valuing yourself lower than some (put down), yet higher than others (lie). Healthy self-esteem means that you realize the truth: we humans are all on a level playing field. The two are fighting a battle for your soul. Both are two sides of the same coin: two beliefs trying to take on the world and make it in their image.

To change your self-esteem, change your opinion about your value. You are what you think.

"I'm worthy. I am worthy. **I AM WORTHY**. The way a person treats me is not a reflection of my self-worth, but rather how they think about their own self-worth. My value is not how much money I have in the bank. I am not a job title. I don't need to impress people I don't like. We are all born naked and equal and I contribute as much as the next human, *in my own way*."

Hands up if you think you're worthy. \o/ Your personality is now *sparkling* more than those bullring piercings!

It's your self-esteem. You're in charge. You call the shots.

FIFTEEN

....

WAITING IN LIMBO

All it takes is 5 seconds to call or email you with a polite PGA message.

> *"Dear Dude or Dudette,*
>
> *Thank you for your interest. However, we've decided to hire another associate. Please Go Away.*
>
> *Sincerely,*
> *[blank]."*

But no, companies would rather douche it up and put your application or status "under review" for an eternity—weeks, months, sometimes years. (How lovely!)

Not only is it physically nerve-wracking to wait for a callback that may never come, job cliffhangers switch the brain to OCD mode: *Should I jump on the low pay, far away, not-so-nice job for now? Yeah, no...I'll be forced to bounce when the better job picks me up...Damn. Not cool.*

Ok, ok…The interviewer seemed very hopeful. Maybe I should just put in my two weeks notice on Monday. But what if I'm being passed up because NOTHING seems to be happening…NOTHING!!!!!

Oh lawdy, lawdy, lawdy. To anyone frustrated about not getting a callback, companies didn't decide one morning to douche it up, blame it on the rest of the applicants who did. You would be absolutely astonished how many applicants just lose it and threaten to sue for discrimination, even threatening to beat some *ss, when given a polite PGA call back or "courtesy" letter. So from the hiring side, calling back with a pass is just asking for it—giving ammo to people who might use it in court to sue for discrimination or start bad tripping.

Smaller companies game this out and figure no one is going to sue a little office; however, biz owners are people too—with feelings and thoughts—and just think it would be rude to turn you down. People are 1 socialized to never be rude and 2 uncomfortable breaking bad news, so they try to avoid hurting your feelings by not responding.

At this point, play it cool. While keeping you in the dark might *appear* as an obvious signal the position has been filled, **you in fact have no clue**. Look at it this way: if you are the successful applicant, are they going to forget to offer you the job? No. No, they are not.

Larger organizations might hire you in the second or third round of openings because they're floating offers to other applicants to fill diversity quotas in the first. Smaller companies might experience a sudden hiring freeze. Regardless, hiring managers work on their own timetable and by not officially rejecting you, they can (and often do) consider your application again at a later date. For now, the best way to boost your reputation *without invading their space* is to send a 'thank you' note after the interview (**page 28 1**).

Leave it at that. For two weeks.

Provided they said a decision would be made in "a week or two" or "should hear within 10 days," checking-in two weeks after your phone-face interview is well within your rights and will NOT be held against you.

When calling for an update, use an open-ended message like this:

"I wanted to express thanks for taking the time to speak with me about the open position. I was particularly struck by the impressive team you've built and would welcome the chance to work with you! If you need additional references or information to help make your decision, please let me know."

Now enough with all of the seriousness and go visit **page 225** or **page 237** to make sure your clothes don't have more jam than Bob Marley...for your next interview, helloooooooooooooo!

SIXTEEN

....

I'VE COMPLETELY WASTED MY LIFE

Dr. David Viscott knows exactly what's up.

As a former professor of psychiatry at UCLA and Pulitzer Prize-nominated author, he was one of *the* world-recognized experts on **motivation**. In his own words, Dr. David Viscott will explain what causes your mind block and how to fix it.

Every time you read this, keep that in mind no matter how far into crazy town you feel, your life can be radically, permanently changed. Dr. Viscott will take it from here.

(Emphasis added.)

Did you know that most people don't know how feelings work? And the truth is if you don't understand how feelings work, you don't understand the world around you. The truth is, the way you see the world is in large part distorted by the feelings that you have not expressed and you've held in and are causing you to see those unexpressed feelings in the world.

For example, if you've been hurt, hurt turns into anger after a while.
And you walk in the world as an angry person, eventually seeing anger in places where it doesn't exist. And the tendency is to react to comments that other people make with anger. And that's why you sound inappropriate.

Each of us has a goal in life. And the basic goal of mental health is to tell how you feel to the person who caused you to feel that way, when they caused you to feel that way.

The idea is to keep your feelings current.
Keep your feelings of the moment. And keep them real.

If you think about it this way, a person who is not living in the feelings of the moment, is living in a world that has already past and they're trying to catch up with what's going on. If you're holding feelings in, you hold feelings in at a great cost to you.

And the cost is the cost of energy.
Because to hold anger in place, to hold hurt in place, uses up your emotions, uses up your energy and causes you, more than anything else, to have less energy to invest in the moment now.

When that happens, something strange happens to you. You make less of an investment of yourself in the world around you, and because less is given, you get less coming back.

So, if you've been hurt, and you're not expressing that hurt,
you end up carrying the grudge, going into the world unable to commit to anything, you don't take responsibility for yourself and the worse thing that happens is you begin to believe that the world is a place where you're not going to get your share of the good things in life.

That sounds sad. It is sad. The reason it's sad is because it becomes a self-fulfilling prophecy.

Often when children come from a home in which the parents have been either alcoholics, or addicted or otherwise not present for them, they grow up feeling something is owed them. They try to be perfect, they try to please. But then when they get to a place in life when they're about to have success, something strange happens to them.

The thing that happens to them is they hold back on their success.
Because to them, with angry parents and feelings from the past that they have not expressed, to be successful to them is a dangerous thing. Why? It's very easy to understand. If they succeed, where is the evidence that they would have for blaming their parents for the way their life turned out. If they succeed, how can they say, 'look what *YOU* did to me.'

The problem is that most people struggle with this one way or another.
Do you know, a way of looking at this is, adolescence is said to be over when you can do what's right for you even though it pleases your parents.

When you've had a childhood which has been a lot of anger, a lot of hurt, and where you've had to hold your feelings in, one of the most difficult things you can do is succeed and feel good about it.

What does this require?
It requires to feel good about yourself, that you have to begin to forgive your parents. How do you forgive someone who was terrible to you, who was never there, who was never the parent

that you needed? Well, the answer is: you have to forgive them anyhow. Look at it this way...

The essence of forgiving is to let go of the hurt.
Think of it this way—if someone called you up on the phone. (I want you to think of someone right now who you've hurt, someone you've did something really awful to in your life, shouldn't be hard to find out. Someone you've really hurt. Got that person? Alright.)

Imagine the phone rings, you pick it up and that person's on the phone. And they say, 'you know, when you hurt me years ago, I just wanted you to know that the pain no longer bothers me.' How would you feel? No, how would you feel? You'd feel relieved, wouldn't you? Well, that relief comes because the other person has let go of the hurt.

Letting go of the hurt is the beginning of forgiveness. If you forgive your parents, it means you let your parents off the hook. That is true. But, one of the things you've got to understand:

When you let your parents off the hook, you let yourself off the hook of having to be a failure.
Because now you can succeed and take pleasure in it.

~Dr. David Viscott, MD

SEVENTEEN

....

PLEASE. SOMEONE. UNFUGG MY BRAIN.

People fake being okay for a long time. You'll never know by looking at them. They grow up making their way through life not talking about it, smiling, like everything is picture perfect. They put on a happy face because that's what you're supposed to do. But underneath the calm surface they're hiding a dark secret.

Stress, crippling anxiety, severe depression, even suicidal thoughts hundreds of times a day, every day.

Clearly something is pushing them into an altered state, this emotional corner. Something is putting an overcast shadow over everything, making the world around them cold. What could it be?

Before we find out, let's do a thought-experiment. Imagine if a random person walked-up and told you that you're in an abusive relationship with a serial manipulator; that this someone is intentionally trying to screw things up in your life just because they can, all while pretending "I'm just trying to help you!" Would you want to know who it was, even if it was someone very close to you?

Okay.

It's your own brain. People are so invested in believing that their thoughts are real, that they've lost the ability to step back, look at things from the outside and see what their own brain is doing to them.

So there you are, sitting in front of the monitor job hunting, awake and alert. Are you thinking to yourself, "Woooo yaaaa, today it's ON like donkey kong!" Or are you're going to be listening to *this* voice: "I f'd up in school and now I'm paying the price. I have no idea what I am doing but it sure seems like everybody else does. I'm a waste. A total loser."

That voice isn't you. **The voice** is depression talking. But depression lies. Depression is a liar.

During episodes of depression, you will feel like you've never been happy in your entire life. This is NOT true, regardless of how "real" it may seem at the moment. Depression tricks you by 1 feeling more "real" than happiness and 2 making optimism and happiness seem delusional. In fact, if you're severely depressed, you'll feel like you're at THE most rational point of your life. This is why you can't simply cheer a depressed person up—"Just be happy!"—or tell them to snap out of it, "it's going to be okay!" OUR INTERNAL LIE-DETECTOR GOES OFF. How can you be happy if the best things in life don't faze you? Said differently, you're not depressed because you're not aware of all these amazing opportunities and people zooming by. You're depressed because you are, and yet, unable to feel happy about it.

Somewhere deep inside your brain, depression is pushing you into a hypnotic trance. And it doesn't matter where you go. You're in an abusive relationship *with your own brain* and you cannot escape out from your brain. Depression will use **the voice** to drag you into a terrible, dark void regardless of your surroundings.

The voice will repeat familiar-yet-painful scenes from your past and tell you that you're a piece of garbage with nothing to live for. **The voice** will talk you to the edge of the cliff, and try to push you over. **The voice**

will steal interviews from you, job opportunities, countless friends and relationships, your home, your money, your precious dreams and every ounce of rational thought you possess. Don't trust **the voice**. **THE VOICE** is a silver-tongue demon. **THE VOICE** will kill you. **THE VOICE** is your only enemy because it's the only thing coming for your life.*

No one's going to tell you that your thoughts are "crazy." YOU must consciously control the speed and direction your mind takes and learn to stop **the voice** as soon as it starts.

But the one thing that will help you the most is at the same time the hardest to do and that is to accept that *sometimes your brain lies to you*. Your brain is being hacked like a computer, and depression is rewriting your thoughts.

Until you're willing, at the very least, to entertain the possibility that your inner-monologue is really screwed up, your brain will take you places it doesn't need to. That's the real hell of it: you'll wake up thinking of something positive, like a cool new book, an exciting job prospect, a sweet and flirty girlfriend and then slowly, without even realizing it, **the voice** will make you take a strange turn. You'll begin to question people's motives and intentions, question their true feelings, assume everyone's sinister or lying, and end up deeply isolated in loneliness for no reason whatsoever. Just watch. Settle into your couch and let your brain do 'it's thing.' Shhhh, listen carefully.

No sign of it, yet.

Not a whisper.

All is quiet. Maybe it's asleep.

Perhaps **the voice** will leave you alone today.

Is it here or isn't—*this is bullsh*t...why am I even reading this...so I can get a meaningless job and hate my life even more...for what, I'm nothing* *but a lazy emotional wreck...I am useless...I will never amount to anything...my mind is a wasteland and I'm not getting better and I'm not going to get better...my health sucks and I'll probably die of some horrible disease not too long from now...I'm just an empty prop filling up space and dragging things out so my friends won't wonder about me...what the hell do people see in a loser piece of sh*t like me, anyway...I know they don't really like me...they're just trying to be polite...it's true, I'm the only one who sees how things really are...and there's no way anything good will work or last...I'm completely lost...deteriorating...everything in my life is just a distraction until I can sleep...the most merciful thing would be to end it all quickly and sleep forever...*(Brought to you by **the voice**.)

With depression, everything feels too real. But nothing is what it seems. Depression is a puppet master, an illusionist, and while your brain is under its spell, your thinking is distorted, and **the voice**—the negative self-talk—is a symptom of depression rather than reality. (Some people spend their whole lives figuring this out.)

Fighting your thoughts is the only way to stop the insidious voice from wreaking havoc with your psyche. ("Oh! Shut up, stop whining." Telling **the voice** to F off is a necessary and healthy act. Never allow **the voice** to bounce around in your skull unchallenged because recovery is not about 'learning how to live with depression.' It's about psychological warfare and you must kick depression's useless 'behind' if you want to get out of it.)

At some point we all become awakened and learn: don't trust politicians, don't trust the media, don't trust big business. One day, not too long from now, it'll dawn on you, "don't trust **the voice**!" And you'll always remember it, the moment you saw daylight. You'll wish that someone had told you not to believe in your thoughts ages ago. You will awe at the extraordinary way **the voice** manipulates information. You'll accept that the way you feel right now is *not* the way you'll feel next week, next month or next year.

Until then, monitor your thoughts very closely because the second you drop your guard **the voice** will be there, hungry and vicious, and ready to pull you back into the ashes.

*Slightly alarmist perhaps, but then again depression convinces 105 people to commit suicide and talks another 2500 into attempting to kill themselves EVERY SINGLE DAY in the United States alone, so maybe not.

FOR THE WIN

EIGHTEEN

....

YOU'RE SOOOOO CLOSE!

> *"I've pictured my phone ringing off the hook, discussing multiple job offers, negotiating salaries because I think my funny easy-going friendly personality could truly shine once I'm in. The part that freaks me out is that all of those thoughts and excitements get shut down immediately when my head says, 'ummm...where do we even start with that?!' So the freaking out part is WILL I EVEN MAKE IT ANYWHERE???"*
>
> ~Nicolas Prado

It hurts to watch revved-up job hunters put off a glittering career just because they don't know where to start. If you yourself have not already learned the fastest ways to get hired, now would be an excellent time to do so. Have a seat over there.

Ok, let's begin with some shortcuts. You want shortcuts? You want some razor-sharp, incredibly intense shortcuts?! **THEN THIS SECTION IS YOUR BEST FRIEND**. Let's do this!

GET STARTED EMPLOYMENT KIT

Remember when they said "all you need is a resume." Yeah, about that.

A resume is a great conversation piece at the interview, but you'll need to back it up. It's kind of hard to tell you're a bad mammajamma from a sheet of paper. Yet amazingly, so many job seekers just blindly fill out the "I CAN WORK TOO" application, submit a resume, cross their fingers and hope for some random act of magic at the interview.

Despite your high intelligence, even you might be tempted to just walk into the interview and wing it. That is risky. People make a big deal out of things. They'll wonder why you didn't prepare. They'll assume you will be equally unprepared for the job.

Let's fill you in on the secret 'behind-the-scenes' work for a SUCCESSFUL interview, step-by-step. 1 A resume is your ticket in. Create one first. 2 Practice a crisp 20-second+ introduction to sound snappy. 3 Scan the mini-answers to interview questions section so you don't get tongue-tied. Finally, 4 choose two to three questions that you will ask the hiring manager. Questions show you really *really* want the job. *Now you are prepared!* Now you will *SCREAM* reassurance to the hiring manager who is worried that you might pose a flight risk (get frustrated and just quit). You will look like the best candidate they can choose.

Remember, hiring managers read between the lines and **can spot a prepared candidate from space.**

▣ Resume	**261**
▣ Cover letter (paper introduction, in case a face or phone introduction is not possible)	**255**
▣ 20+ second introduction	**1**
▣ Mini-answers to interview questions	**55**
▣ Questions you should ask	**79**
▣ Thank you note	**281**

WE'RE IN LOCKDOWN MODE!
Enough is ENOUGH! One does not simply 'get a job.'

Unless you're waking up at 7 or 8am and spending 8 hours a day getting connected, sending resumes, and filling out applications, you are living inside a box you have locked yourself into.

Right now finding a job **is your job.** Live it, breathe it. Resumes and applications can get you interviews, but only if you respond *fast* enough! (Often the first few qualified candidates to post a resume to a job ad are *the only ones* invited to interview.)

This last point is so important that we're going to stop for a second and see if there's anything going on (inside your cranium) that might be affecting your motivation or draining your life energy. Check the box that applies to you and continue on if there is no page listed or flip to the listed page and then circle back.

- ~~Stop balling my busts!!! I'm audie~~.
- Ah, I getcha. Applying for only one or two jobs is a waste.
- 4 out of the 5 voices in my head say that applying for only a couple of jobs is a waste.
- My priorities are wack. I want to do everything else BUT look for job leads. **Go to p.157**
- Waking up feels like a deep injury I have to spend the next two hours healing from. **Go to p.161**

MAN THE F☺☺☺ UP!
"We require 2-3+ years of experience. Otherwise, do not apply."

Apply anyway. (DO IT YOU WUSS!!)

Hiring managers put in the ads what kind of candidate they would "ideally" like. Think of it like top goals for a candidate. But if such a candidate is out-of-reach, they'll usually at least consider an applicant with less. Throwing in your application gives *the hiring manager* a chance to decide if there is a fit. Perhaps you know a second language that the organization would die for. Maybe "2-3+ years experience" actually means people skills, not technical skills. And let's not forget those lovely employers that want EVERYTHING and ask the impossible.

Either way, **apply to ALL job postings** you are interested in as long as you have MOST of the qualifications, consequences be damned!

The worst that can happen is they say no.

(Keep in mind that companies often include some specific instructions in job ads just to see if you'll make an effort to follow them. If you get instructions, follow them!)

WIGGLE IN BY VOLUNTEERING.
Why do you wait 15 minutes before replying to a text from your new man-woman crush?

Because texting back right away leaves the impression you're not busy. And "busy" is the universal code-word for success, duh! It's true! Just ask ~~mindless drones~~ society. The ~~busyness~~ business world is the world of success. Being unemployed is kind of like an unexcused absence.

That makes people living outside feel isolated, disconnected. So sad.

As if life isn't difficult enough, many companies greet excited job seekers with "MUST BE CURRENTLY EMPLOYED, NO EXCEPTIONS." How encouraging! Guess companies want to see that you can get up in the morning and show up. Now most organizations won't advertise 'unemployed need not apply' because it's kind of clueless and evil—cluelessly evil—so they ~~kick you while you're down~~ discriminate against the unemployed on the down low.

Instead of throwing up one well-deserved middle finger...request to *volunteer*. POOF! You're in. In no time, you're working and establishing a reputation. And what better way to prove yourself than working with your dream company before they're able to hire you? Lucky for you, companies open their arms to volunteers because they figure if you're willing to work for free, hey, why not?

What's important here is that **a volunteer job is a job**. In fact, businesses must provide insurance coverage for volunteers and some volunteers even go through a formal interview process. Volunteerism fills up a resume very quickly and no one will know about the pay, perks or benefits. Some fear that down the road companies looking to hire will discover it was an unpaid position and hold it against them. That is eye rolling-ly ridiculous. Volunteering looks just as good (if not BETTER) than a paid position because instead of using empty buzz words like "I'm a dedicated employee" you're actually practicing what you preach.

The best part about volunteering is that *you* get to decide which company is most deserving of your time and *you* set your own schedule. And what's the worst that can happen: someone likes you and you don't like them. Oh, gee, how horrible is that?

Let's step back for a moment and forget that volunteerism fills up all of the empty space on your resume. Forget that volunteering keeps your skills razor sharp. Forget that volunteering connects you to people with the power to hire you. Let's even ignore the fact that a volunteer job can turn into a permanent, salaried position.

When you volunteer, you are an OUTSTANDING person without any further explanation.

REALITY CHECK: Most job hunters are in a situation where every single penny counts. Of course, you are not expected to work for free forever, as free trials come with an expiration date. But if volunteering is not a possibility because you're low on ends, focus all of your energy on the first three important shortcuts.

(Extra Credit)

Do not call 1-800-BUTT-HURT.
Before you shed big manly tears or baby tears—not receiving a job offer, or even an invitation to interview, does not mean someone else is better than you. Look at the interview as one of several paths that can lead to many possibilities rather than as a career success or failure test.

Opportunities have a mysterious way of sneaking up on us. Have faith that things happen for a reason.

Close your eyes and try to imagine what would happen to your ~~career~~ mental stability working at a place where it was not meant to be. There, you see. Be careful what you wish for! Seriously. You hold in your hands the most powerful book on interviewing ever written and if you put in your share, you **will** taste victory. And it will be glorious.

Now get it together. You've got stuff to do. Go do it!

NINETEEN

···

HEY YOU, NOT YOU...YOU.

People (with the power to hire you) do favors for people they like.

Yet amazingly, so many job seekers just blindly fire off their "I CAN WORK TOO" resume, cross their fingers and hope for some random act of magic. Worse yet, some live in a technology bubble and use texts or emails to avoid all human interaction, as if to protect themselves from employers who might want to get to know them.

They wait for a response...and wait...and wait...and slowly start to realize...NOTHING is happening...NOTHING!!!!!!!!!!!

Nothing happens because the most important thing about a resume is not what's in it. The most important thing about a resume is **how it gets to the hiring manager**.

Whoa!! What was that?! Look closely...closer...closer....there! Do you see it? It appears to be your first-of-three networking lessons to help find you an "in."

Friends with benefits.

To get connected YOU have to be a connection and leave no-buddy behind. Be on the lookout for your BestFriendForever or anyone else in your circle and when you spot an opportunity, "talk up" your friend. Getting connected is not a selfish quest! Don't think about whether you'll "get anything" in return. When you give only to receive—quid pro quo—people can tell. It looks shady.

Understand that the more *other* people believe that they'll be taken care—well taken care of, the more opportunities they'll throw right back at you. And nothing gets a hiring manager's juices flowing more than, "My friend Ryan is a rock star…man, Ryan ROCKS! You ROCK! TOGETHER YOU COULD ROCK!!! and I've heard that several companies are practically fighting over Ryan, wink, wink."

With a ton of employees, projects and clients, hiring managers can't just sit there and read the email of every single job hopeful. At the same time, the fear of hiring a bad apple from a random of group strangers (applicants) can keep some hiring managers awake at night because that's THEIR reputation on the line. "It's better to pass on a good applicant than hire a bad one." Companies try to solve this dilemma by offering their own employees a nice little $1000 to $5000 bonus for helping to bring in a "known" talent. (YOU!! YOU ARE THE CHOSEN ONE!)

Vouching for a proven performer not only quickly sways the hiring decision, the recommended friend earn instant credibility BEFORE they've even submitted an application or resume. Applications, resumes and cover letters might get you interviews, but networking gets you jobs.

> CAUTION: Adjust your expectations back to real world levels, for even a bestie can disappoint sometimes.

Schedule lightning-fast 'information' interviews.
What is an information interview, you ask? In a job interview, your target is to get hired, but in an information interview, your target is information. Picture yourself as an investigative journalist: you ask the questions, you're in control. (Whooosh to **page 79** for a complete list of questions.)

Seek out a business, or government organization, find an insider who is on the career path you aspire to (preferably a manager with the ability to hook you up), and reach out to them by phone, social media or email. A faster alternative is to simply walk-in to the premises and ask the receptionist who she would recommend speaking to about careers in [blank]. Once you're put through to the right individual, make it clear that their advice will shape and inspire you for years to come and could have a tremendous impact on your life. Rest assured, you're *not* invading their space. Even if they seem all booked up and carry a busy vibe, a 15-minute ego-boosting moment is great reason to schedule you in because even people starved for time like to talk about themselves.

Use this outstanding example to request a meeting, quoted from Kelly Giles' blog "Grads In Transit":

"Hi [Ms. Escúchame],

[I'm a recent graduate from Manchesthair College] interested in a career in [medical assisting]. I'm looking [into furthering my education], but I'm not sure which program is best for me. I'd love to talk with you about your career and experience in this field. The kinds of questions I have are:

• What is a typical day like for you?
• Are there multiple paths to get to a career like yours?
• [What part of your job do you personally find most satisfying?]

If you'd be comfortable [giving me a little guidance], please let me know, and we can figure out a time to get together. I'd be happy to meet in person, or talk by phone or e-mail—whatever is easiest for you. Thanks for your time!"

Being that you're fresh out of school, jumping back into work or looking to switch jobs, a 15-minute information interview is a ridiculously easy way to get connected with referrals, 'buzz words' to include in your resume, and insider advice you'll never find on the crowded web.

Don't be surprised if the conversation even leads to a job opportunity. However, **it's critical not to flake out on your new contact**.

Reach out to anyone the interviewee refers you to. If you don't, you'll make yourself look bad, embarrass the interviewer who recommended you as a reliable person, and ruin it for every future job hunter.

As an investigative journalist, you're going in slightly undercover, so follow these three important 'information interview rules' to prevent you from experiencing a 15-minute-long awkward moment: **1** don't mention that you are job hunting because you're pretending that you might not even go into that field **2** bring a resume but don't force it on them **3** focus on the person you are interviewing, not the company or yourself.

Pocket a stack of 'mini-resume' cards.
You already know that making the right job contacts is THE key factor in getting an "in." Living near an urban area, you won't have any trouble finding those with influence and power…people with 'something real' to offer you. But a mere 'contact' won't help you unless you can leave the right impression, one that enables your job connection to feel confident enough to work with you or recommend you—that's where mini-resume cards come in.

Mini-resume cards are the currency of networking.

What's a mini-resume card, you ask? Imagine a resume shrunk down to a bite-size 2 x 3.5-inch business card. Printed on the front side is your name, email and phone number and on the back side three or four key accomplishments or qualifications (not past job titles or duties).

From the contact's perspective, any job hunter who takes the time to print a mini-resume card is a put together individual, someone who can help to solve THEIR problems and help them to reach their goals (if hired). As excited as you may feel about that, you know there's a catch…a big one. A mere 'contact' is not worth anything unless you actually make a move, introduce yourself and get your name out. Business contacts need to become meaningful job connections.

Let's walk you through an everyday, typical scenario you may find yourself in to demonstrate how you should present a mini-resume card to a new contact.

Imagine you're at a party where this cougar is gazing deeply in your eyes. Do you know how to handle a cougar? Then learn! Stand facing her, look dreamily back in her eyes, draw her gently towards you, tilt your head and whisper softly in her ear, "I need a job." Now bust out your mini-resume card! Do not move in for the kill. Just exchange digits for now. She might be a cougar, but you are a shark after dark. (Substitute "cougar" for "sugar daddy," if that's how you roll.)

Joking aside, always follow this card RITUAL with cougars or *any other random potentials*:

> Anytime you give a card, ask for a card. When handed a business card, don't just grab it and stuff it in your sexy, tear-away pants. Make the person feel important by taking a good 3-5 second look at their card—you might see something that could spark a conversation. Hand-write notes on the back of the card such as date, location and what they offer. These comments will be worth gold when following up with the new contact. Then PLACE the card in your wallet to signal their importance to you.

Don't be picky. Circulate your mini-resume cards *everywhere*—neighbors, friends, haters, toddlers. And ask for **favors** NOT open position so you don't put people on the spot (unless you're into that kind of thing).

TWENTY

....

LET YOUR BODY ROCK!

"Hmm, I can tell from your body language you'd like to..."

Speak friggin LOUDER!!
You are part of a species called 'human beings' with feelings and thoughts. Why do you sound like a baby mouse?! And where's the personality? Do they have to look for it?

If you find yourself center stage suffering from a major case of deadness, pump up the volume, step up your game and say it like you've got a pair. Job hunters who voice their opinion in a direct, strong tone **are perceived as having expertise**.

And smile. Smile a lot. Show-off those pearly yellows! Don't be embarrassed if your teeth aren't straight, or perfect, and if you're wearing braces, OMG who the hell cares?! Smile wide and flash those grills. Hiring managers are put at ease with your attractive, hypnotic, vampire-like smile. A person who smiles can get away with almost anything.

Real eyes, realize, real lies.
What are you blinking about? Heyo, she's right there. Look the hiring manager in the eyes! Constantly looking around the room while you are talking gives the impression you're either uncomfortable or hiding something. For a hiring manager who wants to make eye contact, it's a distraction.

And when it's the hiring manager's turn to speak, give an occasional nod to signal you are following along. If you sense that you are staring into the hiring manager's eyes a bit too long, hold it for a split-second longer and break away. Every-so-often, casually glance at the hiring manager's hands as she speaks.

For panel and group interviews, acknowledge **everybody** in the room with eye contact and a nod. In panel interviews, give each and every panelist equal 'eye contact time' while speaking, even if one or two of them absolutely refuses to look at you during the ENTIRE interview. The panel could be testing your situational awareness, a common trick in law enforcement interviews to see if you're equipped for the job. ("Situational awareness" means being mindful of what's happening around you under stress.)

With group interviews, give the participants equal eye contact while speaking, not just the company representatives. The purpose of a group interview is twofold: **1** to see just how outgoing you are compared to the group of applicants and **2** save time-money on interviewing.

THE SCIENCE OF GOING EYEBALL-TO-EYEBALL: strangers who stare at you for 1+ second want to fight you or mate with you.

Handshake: you're doing it wrong.
Are you a princess? Maybe you are. But not at your interview!

Do not shake a hand like a princess. Give a businesslike-firm handshake to both WOMEN and men using the whole hand (while looking the hiring manager in the eyes).

A proper handshake means palm-to-palm with a firm grip, but not so firm that you end up relocating the bones in their hand. It's half-way between a MAN-GRIP and princess shake. Place pressure at your fingertips if you encounter someone with a delicate hand, pump two to three times, then snap your hand open for a crisp and clean release. Don't hold on to their hand and drag it down with you as you let go. Should you accidentally grip the hand like a princess, quickly (as in a split-second) open up your grip, push forward and grab that hand before the hiring manager gets a chance to kiss it!

It's your first encounter with the hiring manager and a limp 'princess' handshake signals you cannot commit to anything. On the flip side, too strong of a handshake with a machismo rearranging of the finger bones is considered a display of dominance or thinly veiled hostility.

Practice the handshake with friends or anywhere, even if only in your head, to find the perfect balance.

Handshake awareness.
A handshake speaks a language of its own.

Do not use your left hand to sandwich the manager's hand while shaking hands, and do not place your left hand on their shoulder while shaking hands like you see the president do with other international leaders. Such hand gestures do not communicate warmth, affection or trust. These gestures communicate POWER. "I'm allowed to touch you, but you can't touch me." It's a display of **dominance**.

Avoid shaking with your left hand, even if you're left-handed, because in some cultures it is highly offensive and in the American culture it's just plain weird. (Injuries or disabilities that affect the right hand are exceptions to the rule, of course.)

Timing the handshake.
YOU are expected to initiate the handshake at an interview. As soon as

you see the hiring manager, it's showtime. Smile, get up off your booty, walk up and extend your hand. Keep your hand outstretched until the manager shakes it, and even if your hand floats for 4+ seconds, remain cool and in control.

In the extremely rare case that your hand is totally ignored by the hiring manager, just go with it. Lower your hand and continue on completely unfazed. It could be a secret way of testing your people skills and seeing if you can maintain composure when dealing with something entirely unexpected.

Don't get up all in my mug.
The correct handshaking distance is close enough so that your arm can bend at the elbow when shaking hands. If your arm is stretched-out and locked at the elbow, you're standing too far from the hiring manager. Whether you're aware of it or not, standing too far signals that you don't like the person you are shaking hands with.

Hands.
It's okay to let words move your hands when MAKING A POINT. Otherwise keep your hands on your lap or on the table. Unless you or the hiring manager has an actual hearing disability, do not "speak" with your hands.

Legs.
Keep both feet planted on the floor, but crossing your legs is fine if you're wearing a skirt.

Posture.
Appearance is more than just clothes.

Every time you sit down, square your shoulders—pull your shoulders up towards the rainbows and unicorns in the sky, then all the way back, then slightly relaxed. Rolling back your shoulders causes your chest to slightly flex out. Posture is a not-so-obvious trick that actors use to signal confidence and look more attractive by using the poetry of body language. You're doing it *correctly* if it feels slightly weird, like your chest is sticking out too far. (You'll have to get over the giggle-factor.) All it takes is to convince your mind to move your chest a little further out than usual. Let's try it right now. Stick your chest out...a little further...a little further...there you go. Never be ashamed to ROCK.

Now suck in your jigglers! When you tighten your stomach, it helps maintain good seating posture and takes pressure off of your back. Don't forget to breathe or you will pass out and wake up to a scraggly-bearded man giving you mouth-to-mouth. (Pardon the unpleasant imagery.)

Chairs & slouching.
Don't plomp down on a chair like a dead fish. Control your descent for a nice soft landing.

> DEFINITION: "Plomp" is onomatopoeic and describes both the action of dropping down into a chair and the sound a chair makes when you drop down on it. Please note: 'dead fish' is typically a problem affecting the you-know-what in a relationship, not interviewing.

Use your hands to steady yourself and scoot your curvaceous booty all the way to the back of the chair. Lean all the way back pimpaderos-style for a split-second, now pull your back off the chair 2-3 inches forward aaaand hold. Whoa, you look offensively attractive!

> DEFINITION: "offensively attractive" *adjective* uh-fen-siv-lee uh-trak-tiv is characterized as an individual that's so hot that they are not even hot anymore because everyone knows she's-he's impossible to get, causing resentful displeasure. See mirror.

Fidgeting.
CGI, video game characters and robots have that creepy ability to sit perfectly still. Humans, with all of our little movements like hand tapping, breathing, foot motions and shifting, aren't still. Not until we take our final dirt nap (die). So relax and be natural. As a good listener, lean in slightly when the hiring manager speaks but avoid playing with your curls, folding your arms, cracking knuckles, putting your hands in your pockets or shaking.

Look comfortable in your own skin, especially around an INSANELY HOT PERSON, and you're body will naturally signal, "look what a great catch I am!"

(Now run over to the clothing section to see if the outfit you picked last week makes you look fat. **Page 225** or **page 237**.)

TWENTY ONE

....

MASTER OF PUPPETS

The following section contains exclusive *psychological* tricks for pursuit of celebrity and status at work. What this section does not contain are mind games that cause pain, anger or anything that can be categorized as hurtful to other human beings. It's literally just you getting in tune with what people think and running the show at work by ~~manipulating~~ "influencing" your teammates. If you're cool with that, please continue reading, and have an awesome day.

How to get along with people you don't like.
For a long time, you thought you were very devious. "Oh yeah, let me help you with that because I'm a good guy-gal." But you were actually only helping out to score points so that you can pull favors from them in the future! Life was beautiful. That is, until you encountered this coworker with the kind of twisted and rude personality that made you want to crawl under a couch. Their attitude stank! Their evil-eye stank! Man, the stank was so bad you had to fart to *freshen* the air.

As a master-manipulator, you constantly have to learn new mind tricks. Quite possibly the greatest career challenge you'll face is how to handle ~~antagonistic~~ nasty coworkers, especially being a noobie.

187

As unlikely as it sounds, to break the ice with a new coworker who's always staring you down with these, like, knife-dagger eyes—ask to borrow their pencil. "Hey, do you mind if I borrow your pencil for a bit? Thanks!" Coworkers almost never refuse. Amazingly, this simple gesture tricks people into convincing *themselves* they like you. "I did her a favor. I guess I like her. That's the only reason I would have done that." (Psychologists call this *post-hoc rationalization*.)

Moving to up to management, do you need to make a cold boss melt? Then admit that she knows more about a subject than you do. Remember, when selling something (in this case your likeability), try to do more listening than speaking.

> PRO-TIP: You'll see that it doesn't take much to make someone's day and win love at work, but flattery is a double edged sword. Be careful when using flattery. Always sound sincere or you will look shady. Then no one will trust you and you will die lonely.

Want to turn the coldest coworkers into mush? Ask about their **kids**.

Coworkers sometimes feel threatened by 'the new guy-gal,' especially if they perceive you as the ambitious type. As a "go getter" you must resist the natural urge to show off. You can be as ambitious as you want, but balance it out by appearing modest at all times and praising good work, regardless of who completed it.

Silent but deadly.
One of the best conversational skills to master is creating an awkward silence.

People will say anything to break the awkward silence, even if it is something they would rather not talk about. So silence instantly gives you control of a conversation.

Silence is a trick used by all manners of professionals. The police use silence to get suspects to admit to a crime or incriminate themselves, and to elicit eyewitness testimony. Shrewd job hunters take advantage of awkward silences during pay negotiations with the hiring manager. (Negotiators intentionally create awkward silences to get the other side into giving away more than they intended.) Silence is used by medical doctors to get details about a patient's condition. Even psychologists occasionally zip their lips during counseling sessions, as silence is therapeutic.

People love ~~to talk~~ flapping their gums and will fill the silence with something, anything, even if what they talk about lands them in serious trouble. Become an expert at out-waiting people because ~~eventually they'll crack~~ it's not about how smart you are. It's about how smart you are twirling people around your finger like a cowboy.

How to criticize your coworker or boss.
A colleague or supervisor made a mistake that could spill over and affect *your* reputation. Now you are FORCED to point it out. Instead of spending time in crippling anxiety thinking about a possibly tense situation, memorize savvy one-liners. Silky smooth responses will help prevent hard feelings, or being placed on the sh!t list, for simply pointing out an error. (You never want to look like you're throwing a mistake in their face.)

1 "Do you have a sec? We need to make some adjustments (avoid saying "corrections") here and here. How would you like to handle that?" Before the moment of silence turns awkward, say this: "You mind if I give a suggestion?" (Now proceed to correct your coworker's mess.)

2 "I've haven't seen someone do it like that before. It's kind of interesting, but have you considered this approach? I find that it's faster and simpler."

3 "~~This is terrible! What's wrong with you?! Do it again and don't waste my time.~~"

4 "Hey Mr. Mangina, these numbers seem a bit 'off.' Could you go

189

over them really quickly or perhaps check to see if you emailed me the right file? The newest copy may have gotten lost in my inbox somewhere." (Giving your coworker a way to save face prevents friction.)

5 Let's say you and your coworker just flat out disagree, period, and the all the mindfreak stuff does not work: "Well, we both agree that this is a problem that going to need a good solution, which is what really matters." (Again, always give your coworker a way out of a disagreement!)

6 Instead of naming names or singling out individuals, act as if the problem arose from some mysterious supernatural jinxing force that "obviously" cannot be blamed on any one particular coworker.

"Go away" signals.
Most coworkers will not straight-up tell you 'go away' because that's impolite and unprofessional. What they will do is give off a number of signals to indicate that they're uncomfortable or don't want to talk to you. Learn to pick up on these cues.

- no response to messages
- one-word replies
- avoids eye contact
- crosses arms or turns face away from you
- answers questions but never asks any (being polite but not trying to keep the conversation going)
- one-way contact (with you always initiating)
- keeps conversations shallow and changes the subject when you try to go deeper
- attempting to "escape" the conversation by speaking with other coworkers, texting, or looking around the room

If a coworker is not interested in talking to you, that's perfectly fine. There's no need to push. Gracefully exit and go jibber jabber with some other dude or dudette. Making an insulting remark to make yourself feel better or starting explaining why you'd like to have a conversation is perceived as an attack on the coworker's pride because you're not respecting them as a person or their boundaries.

Understand that human beings aren't born with social skills, so don't feel bad if you've crossed the line on occasion—the line is blurry and socialization is a life-long learning process. The fact is people are surprisingly terrible at detecting feelings of deadpan faces or sensing chemistry. It can take years of experience to judge the difference between "serious" looking relaxed face and anger or a shy person and someone not interested. (Introverts might not start a conversation, but will be happy when you do!) Even the so-called "experts" can't always tell the difference because there is no magic formula. Be patient with your self, keep testing boundaries and just pay attention to how people react to you, especially when you enter a room. While on the topic, here's a little science-y trinket for you…watch/learn.

Men, if you want to appear sexy, don't smile when you enter a room. Either look tough or troubled and stick out your chest and suck in. Whatever you do, don't smile. (BONUS: Don't look directly into the camera for profile pictures.)

Women, if you want to look sexy, then smile. THAT'S SO SEXY. (Go look in the mirror, it works!)

(Extra Credit)

What makes people tick?
Every generation of scientists tries to figure out what this madness that we call the human brain is all about. The human brain is the most complex machine in our universe, but it's an understandable complexity.

The human brain seeks security, stimulation and an identity.

The human brain seeks to AVOID shame and death.

That is all.

NOOBIES

TWENTY TWO

....

THE FIRST TIME

*"For some reason this scares the living crap out of me!!!!!!
All these thoughts swirl around in my head, 'what do I say,
what don't I say...oh crap did I say something I shouldn't
have?' My head gets bombarded with "what IF's" and I think
it is because this is the industry that I love, and I haven't
had a big interview in this line of work yet, and I will have so
much pressure on myself I'll end up scaring myself into not
being who I really am. I kinda put a lot of pressure on myself
when it is something I really love. I think I just need to be put
through a mock interview so I have a rough idea of how it is
going to go down..."*

~Nicolas Prado

Mock interview.
Let's take a sneak peak into what goes down at a typical interview to help
you get rid of the interviewing jitters. Settle into your chair and if you have
any questions *at any point*, please raise your hand.

Chit Brix goes to interview.

It's 10:00 a.m. and Chit Brix arrives at ███████ a half hour early. He finds a parking spot in the shade and then takes a few moments in the car by himself.

> *You've been invited to interview. That means the organization already has a positive impression. You don't need to stress. The hiring manager is probably hoping that you're an all-around down-to-earth, likeable person. Remember, the best interviews are conversations, so be relaxed and allow your "real self" to come out.*

Chit does one last-minute check to see that he has a ballpoint pen, notepad, and two copies of his resume. He puts his phone on silent, takes a deep breath and exhales saying the words 'I am prepared.' Chit wipes his hands on a paper napkin to keep them dry, gets excited in his chest, puts on his 'incredibly happy to see you' face and exits the car.

> *The interview starts well before you greet the receptionist—the organization begins to evaluate you the moment you are identified. Put on a warm, glowy smile in case they are watching.....they always are.*

Chit enters the building at about 10:15 a.m. and introduces himself to the receptionist seated at the front desk. He uses his *full name* and says he has a 10:30 appointment with Ms. Chieveous, with a relaxed confidence. Fifteen minutes later, a woman comes out to greet him. "Chit?" she asks.

> *As soon as you see the hiring manager, everything falls back to you. It's showtime. Smile, get up off your booty, walk up and shake the hiring manager's hand. YOU are expected to initiate the handshake at an interview. (Do you want to fine-tune your handshake, voice and body language? Hit up page 181.)*

"Yes, Ms. Chieveous," replies Chit, as his smile lights up the room. "My name is Chit Brix. Thank you for inviting me today." *SHAKES HAND* "You're welcome, it's nice to meet you," she replies, sharing a smile. As they walk into a small conference room, the innocent-sounding small talk begins.

> *Chit's walk to the interview room is the most important walk of his working life. He is being evaluated. Ms. Chieveous wants to see if Chit's **personality** clicks with her team. In other words, is this someone she might enjoy working with? While escorting candidates to the back, hiring managers typically begin the interview with some small talk about the weather or a joke. It's okay to laugh at jokes, but don't make any, and it helps to think of something safe, sensible and interesting-ish to say in response, as long as it's not stupidly revealing or fake. Aware of such good business etiquette (page 201), Chit doesn't just nervously smile and nod, he's a part of the conversation and laughs at Ms. Chieveous' lighthearted humor. Of course, they're not buddies (quite) yet and Chit's still addressing a company, so he's respectful.*

Chit remains standing until Ms. Chieveous asks him to be seated. "I've brought a fresh copy of my resume if you'd like to see it," says Chit.

"I would, thanks. Please have a seat," replies Ms. Chieveous in a light, upbeat tone. Chit hands her the resume being sure not to place anything else on the conference table. The first 20 seconds have passed and he's done it! He is still alive.

> *Ms. Chieveous has the floor.*

"So, tell me about yourself," says Ms. Chieveous, breaking the ice. Chit goes on auto-pilot and recites his memorized 20+ second introduction (page 1), "Thank you for this opportunity, my name is Chit Brix and... blah, blah, blah...what I'm looking for now is gaining real, valuable work experience which I believe is key to my future professional success."

Ms. Chieveous nods her head as if in agreement and says, "OK." She's obviously impressed but has to play it cool. "Why are you interested in working with us?"

> *Chit continues answering this and several other common interview questions for another 15 minutes to an hour. Chit carefully avoids "I really need a job"-type wording because no employer particularly enjoys the feeling of being interchangeable with any other random employer that would have said 'yes.' An applicant with standards is attractive. An applicant who is choosy is attractive.* (Want a cool intro to sound like Chit? Visit **page** 1. Want to practice snappy answers? Go to **page** 55.)

Ms. Chieveous prepares to wrap things up, "Do you have any questions for me?"

> *Ms. Chieveous turns the tables on Chit to see if he's down for the cause. She wants to find out whether Chit truly cares about the job, or just the paycheck. In other words, does Chit have a self-absorbed "what's-in-it-for-me" type of personality or is he here to ~~ride or die for life~~ contribute to the relationship? The fact is without asking questions at the interview, you will look like you're only interested in being a payroll entry.* (Would you like to ask thought-provoking questions? Swing by **page** 79 on your way out.)

Chit picks up his notepad and reads the first of his three questions out loud, "What separates good employees from outstanding employees?" As a good listener, Chit leans in slightly and takes notes as Ms. Chieveous answers.

> *The last 5 minutes count, too. A good last impression will have as much of an impact as a good first impression. During this time, the hiring manager is answering your questions and assessing your overall performance. Typically the interview is finished when the hiring manager stands up. However, if you get the vibe that the interview has reached its conclusion, it is okay to stand up first.*

Chit gives Ms. Chieveous a firm, dry handshake and concludes by saying, "Thank you for taking the time to speak with me about the open position. I was particularly struck by the impressive team you've built and would welcome the chance to work with you! If you need additional references or information to help make your decision, please let me know."

> Remember, the walk back to the front desk is the second most important walk in your work life. Be on guard. You are still under evaluation.

The interview isn't over *over* until Chit walks out the building, and gets in the car, ~~and shouts 'IN YOUR FACE!! IN YOUR FACE!!'~~

Chit heads home to have himself a juice, snuggle with his blankie and go nap-nap.

> SKILLS TEST: At some point before, during, or after the interview you *might* be skills-tested. It's not as bad as it sounds. The skills test is usually a 'situation simulation' where they put you in the role of the position and see how you do or a type of written exam specific to that job. Most employers give advance notice of any such testing, but some random employers might not.

...EXTRA CREDIT ▶

(Extra Credit)

You had your 15 minutes, now GTFO!
Of course, the hiring manager will be observing and evaluating you throughout the interview, but behind-the-scenes, some basic evaluations are made by hiring managers.

- Mental alertness, is the candidate lost in space? (Hello, hello…it's not the caffeine that should wake you up, it's the interview!)
- Strong introduction. (Many hiring managers decide whether they're feeling you or not in the first twenty seconds **page 1**.)
- Good eye contact, firm handshake and confident tone of voice. (Body language **page 181**.)
- Neat appearance. (Get your 'ooooohhh, look at me' outfit on **page 225** or **page 237**.)
- Answers that show a degree of intelligence and questions that show a GENUINE interest. (Answers are on **page 55**. Questions on **page 79**.)
- Response to stress. (**Page 147**)

TWENTY THREE

....

TICKLE YOUR FANCY

Our brains are hard-wired to be social, but we are not born polite and refined.

Manners arrive through a series of experiences and observations, often beginning by learning to say 'please' and 'thank you.'

Seated at the interviewing table, manners are much more than just being "nice," however. Manners reflect how effective you are in a group—in other words, your level of social intelligence. Besides just knowing what is okay and not, people with high social intelligence know how to work a room, know how to mingle, network and, importantly, handle customers or coworkers who act like farm animals.

Companies, in fact, use good manners as a predictor of success.

Bad manners can be dangerous, as a single act of disrespect can escalate rapidly into brutality: from worker shoves worker, to worker shoots worker. People with this gracious goodness we call manners are less likely to become abusive and violent as adults or bullies in the workplace. By keeping civility high, companies can keep complaints, violence and lawsuits low.

But with social media friends, texting, the boards, gaming clans and VR, human contact is increasingly becoming like a novelty. Job hunters are used to talking with their thumbs not with their face. So consider this section charm school. A crash course on interviewing manners. A blueprint to help you navigate the customs inside corporate America.

Classy as f*ck. (And there's nothing I can do about it.)
Enter the building with an aura is so powerful, they can tap into it for electricity. More practically speaking, that means smile **no matter how you feel**. Smiling communicates "friend not enemy" amongst Earthlings. (And walk through the doors precisely 15 minutes early because arriving late to an interview is the worst idea in the history of ever. Being punctual is respect of time.)

As a professional, put away all of your technology and introduce yourself to the receptionist using your first *and* last name.

As soon as you see the hiring manager, everything falls back to you. It's showtime. Smile, get up off your booty (if you're seated), walk up and extend your hand. It's on YOU to initiate a handshake. (Other than the handshake, do not touch the hiring manager.) Greet the hiring manager by their last name. In a group or panel interview, acknowledge **every person** in the room and give equal "eye contact" time.

Remain standing until you're offered a chair. (You'll be more comfortable if you slightly bend your knees and shift your weight from foot to foot.) Place your belongings on your lap, chair or floor BUT not on the desk. As a good listener, lean in slightly when the hiring manager speaks, and it's okay to laugh at jokes, but do not make any jokes.

Typically the interview is finished when the hiring manager stands up. However, if you get the vibe that the interview has reached its conclusion, it is okay to stand up first and end the meeting with a dry, firm handshake. A good last impression will have as much of an impact as a good first impression.

Critical fail.
THUNK!! That would be the sound of the hiring manager's head hitting the desk. Never bring a bestie with you into a job interview. Now is not a good time to test the limits of their humor. The interview starts well before you greet the receptionist—the organization begins to evaluate you the moment you are identified, so keep your traveling companion safely out of sight. You can cuddle later. (Ahhh, the fresh smell of bromance.)

Thinking about flaking out on an interview? OH LAWD, where are your manners?! You want to get noticed—but for all the right reasons! If the commute is too long, the business feels spooky or you're feeling sluggish that week, **call ahead of time** and withdraw from the scheduled interview. Being a "no-show" to an interview stops other job hopefuls from being able to take your time slot and that's not only extremely inconsiderate, it's plain rude *and* indecent.

Once seated, avoid lonely, stone-faced yes or no answers. 'Yes-no' responses will rip the interview apart like tissue paper because you're giving off the impression you are either uncomfortable, bored or hoping they have some way to entertain you. For a hiring manager who graciously invited you in to visit, it's taken as major disrespect. Remember, they want you to be CONVINCING. It's your time to shine! A resume is a great conversation piece for an interview, but don't rely on a resume to do the selling for you.

Money-wise, the hiring manager will not exactly be open to debating the finer point of salary, vacation benefits, perks, bonuses or retirement packages until AFTER she sends an offer of employment. This bears repeating: do not bring up the topic of money at the interview unless they bring it up first.

When answering questions, few things are as powerful as honesty… unless the subject is your old boss. Bad mouthing your present-past boss or coworkers will be the **kiss of death**. Of course honesty is important, but by trashing ANYONE at the interview, you will instantly be red flagged as a person with a negative attitude towards coworkers. Remember, the hiring manager does not know any of these people, so he will assume you'll be a bad influence and infect their company with your possible issues, and this may sound shocking, but someone else will be offered job. (If you suffered a crazed, manipulative boss, **page 59** & **page 60** will show you the RIGHT way to explain things at the interview.)

Speaking of issues, remember that you're walking into an interview, NOT a therapy session. The hiring manager doesn't want to be turned into your psychologist. Keep answers short and sweet and focused on what you can contribute. Your aim is to tell the hiring manager just enough to provoke interest, but not so much that they'll wonder if they'll need duct tape and rope to shut you up during coffee breaks!

(Hey, the afterparty is on **page 169**.)

TWENTY FOUR

....

WHODAAT

Before we release you into the wild, read this section and then stop by
page 201.

Watch out, we have a bad@ss over here!
As you enter the building, keep your sunglasses on. Not to protect your
eyes from the sun, but because that's just how you roll! After you've
checked in for the interview (by yelling "DING DONG" really loud), make a quick
phone call to your BFF and drop the whole drama-bomb about last night's
party. Remember to speak loudly because you're the star of the show.
This tactic helps impress hotties also waiting to interview...they, too, will
hear you and you might score digits!

Not smooth, kiddo.

Employers see pretty quickly whether you're making an effort to act
professionally. From that they'll guess how much of an effort you would
make if they were to hire you. You have to regard that walk to the ~~inner
sanctum~~ front desk as the most important walk of your work life. Enter
lobby with all of the grace and charm you can muster, and as long as

205

you are in sight of the receptionist, the hiring manager or any company employees, carry yourself with the utmost humility. Acting like the center of the universe or saying something stupidly revealing in the reception area will **kill the relationship stone dead**.

Keep in place that high level of concentration and focus from the moment you enter the lobby to the final exit out of the building.

Son of a BIAAAaaaaaa...
You missed the bus! On the plus side, maybe you missed a bus with an ax murderer on it, like some twisted tale of divine intervention.

Whether you missed the bus, your mother-truckin' ride flaked out, or you hit serious traffic, being late is hugely frustrating and, ultimately, can be a deal-breaker because it comes off like **1** you have little respect for the hiring manager's schedule and **2** slightly self-destructive tendencies.

To be on time is to be late. To be **early** is to be on time.

But random things happen that are beyond your control, so if you find yourself running behind, make a call to the hiring manager and explain the unfortunate circumstances. Sound sincerely sorry and give a realistic estimate of your arrival time.

Although some employers couldn't give a rat's rancid rectum about why you're late, most will give you partial credit for being honest and owning up to the responsibility.

What the...Why u no ask questions?
Employers filter out mooches and look for people who want to contribute to the relationship. They want to see that you care about the job, not just the paycheck.

The fact is without asking questions at the interview, you will either look like you're only interested in a paycheck or, on the flipside, you'll seem so desperate that you'll take anything. And no employer particularly enjoys the feeling of being interchangeable with any other random employer who would have said yes. An applicant with standards is attractive. An applicant who is choosy is attractive.

Think about it: do you ask questions on a first date? Oh, and speaking of first dates, it's tacky to bring up money at your interview, unless they bring it up first. This rule does not apply if you're on a date with a cougar, your ticket into high society of retirees. You'll feel a bit gross and ashamed of a life built on lies, but if you're considering life as the wealthy toy of an aging cougar, you better have some idea of what her immaculate home and fortune is worth before you lock lips. Ask questions!

(Substitute "cougar" for "sugar daddy," if that's your flavor.)

She's ALL that.
When you walk through the door, the receptionist might give a little cattitude—girl-y attitude or, oooooooooh, girl-on-girl attitude—when it's discovered you are there for an interview. If she shoots you the stink eye, you better give her a full-on teenage eye roll right back!

(Stop. Make. Brain. Hurt. In. Head.)

Do you want to know why some companies hold interviews at restaurants? It's a trick. The hiring managers already know how you are going to treat them—with respect because you want to get the job. So, how do hiring managers quickly discover your "true" personality? **By how you treat the waiter**.

Here is the science-y reason why you should be extremely polite to everyone you interact with, especially the receptionist: 6 out of 10 hiring managers polled by world-famous Robert Half International staffing agency said that the receptionist's opinion (yup, that 19-year-old sitting at the front desk) is very influential when deciding to pick a candidate. So be courteous to *everyone* around including the 'mental issues' people meanies.

I dun wanna work at a place that can't accept me for me. Seriously. No really, stop laughing.
(Stop being such a faker-hater!)

No one is telling you to erase your personality or not be authentic. However, the word 'professional' does mean STEPPING UP your game, getting in character with the best you have to offer, and having a willingness to embrace the immediate surroundings. You're on their turf and business has its own culture and language. On top of that, companies have an image to protect. You'll be meeting at times with clients, and members of the public, and your potential new bosses will want to be assured that you'll be able to adjust, fit in and play the role. ~~If you don't learn to conduct yourself like a professional, half of the employers who want to hire you would need **"subtitles"** because they'd have no idea what you're saying or doing~~.

Begin with the basics, like a crisp and clean 20+ second introduction. (A strong first impression has a ripple effect on the whole interview. Go to **page 1**.) Then move on to practicing your answers to common interviewing questions (on **page 55**) so you that can deliver a sensational performance for the remainder of your time together. Otherwise, the hiring manager will roll her eyes, begin to tune out and start thinking of ways to conclude the interview as quickly as possible in order to move on to the next applicant on the list. In other words, turn it into a "hi…bye" interview.

"Black is what I wear on the outside because black is how I feel on the inside. DEAL WITH IT."
Ok, but sometimes how you feel is not how you look.

Some try to argue 'who cares what you look like if you're a top performer?' That's very practical, but the truth is society is very visually-based and the first thing we notice about someone is their appearance. A really well-put together outfit is going to improve the hiring manager's reaction to you. (People with the power to hire you are often forced to make snap judgments when faced with a large pool of applicants. Appearing too "different" can come across as someone who can't click with others, or worse, a troublemaker.)

But job hunters can have a really hard time dressing well, especially if they've never been taught how clothes are supposed to fit, how to match colors or how to look fantastic on a budget. The clothing section (**page 225** or **page 237**) is your go-to place and will teach you how to mix it up so that you'll look and feel astonishingly attractive, all without getting outside the lane too much.

Be sure to stay away from all overpriced, overly-complicated clothes because, once hired, you'll be given a uniform or the option to wear whatever you like as long as it's clean and respectable.

Thank you for noticing I'm awesome.
After the interview, you're audie. Hello, hello! No autographs please.

Hold on. You are not a rude person. Don't allow an interview to change that.

Take a moment to thank the hiring manager in writing (**page 281**). A thank you note shows that you don't have a self-absorbed "what's-in-it-for-me" type personality but that you're someone who can help solve THEIR problems and help them reach THEIR goals, too. Sending a thank you note right after the interview is probably your best weapon when the decision is close between you and another applicant, and a GREAT reminder of what they mean to you. **Nothing works better**.

Close your eyes. You're going to imagine the scene: A day after the interview, the hiring manager receives your thank you note. The room is tense. The hiring manager raises an eyebrow, reads the note, then blushes. "Aww, she said I'm inspirational."

The office goes wild. Brilliant! You're hired! THIS IS WHY WE PLAY THE GAME! THIS IS WHY WE PLAY THE GAME! That's how things go down in the real world. Well, sort of. Regardless, send a thank you note, as it can tip the scales and help you seal the deal.

(Extra Credit)

A cautionary tale for job hunters.
Sweet merciful Zeus!

This always happens. You enter the building, alert the front desk that you've arrived, seat yourself in the reception area and...tik-tok-tik-tok-20 minutes-30 minutes, sometimes even an hour later you find yourself trapped on a couch, without a phone, getting bored to tears. (Oh, the humanity!) But if you want the job offer, you'll put up with it. It's all part of the price of admission.

Kill this extra beat of time reading company brochures in the lobby. This demonstrates genuine interest in the company to any lookie loos and you can learn a few last-minute facts giving your answers a little more pep...assuming that you survive, of course.

....

TWENTY SIX

ALL THAT FUSS OVER EXPERIENCE

Hiring Manager: Why don't you have experience?

If you're like everyone else, you're not exactly sure what to say. You've been invited to the interview. That means you're qualified for the position. Yet the hiring manager is putting you on the spot about work experience. What gives?

While he's interested in how you answer this question, he's more interested in **how you handle this question**.

From the hiring side, if you deal with teenagers on a daily basis, this question makes a lot of sense. Noobies can be a royal pain in the @ss. They've got their head in the clouds, have no clue what they want from life and haven't held down any previous job for more than a week. They rapidly move from excitement to boredom, always feel that they are 'worth more than this' and can cost a massive amount of wasted time and productivity.

Be warned. Right now you are one of these people. You pose a flight risk. So you're answer will have to scream reassurance.

What you should do next...

We are going to make the absolute most out of your everyday life experiences.

Above and beyond anything else, the hiring manager wants to know how your hobbies, school, volunteerism—even helping out the family—have developed "transferable skills." Transferable skills can be *anything* from your personal life that is useful in the workforce like the ability to multitask, deal with people, use digital tools like computers and phones, or even a willingness to learn.

He wants you to attack this question with all of your strength and intellect. He wants to hear you say "yes, it didn't make me rich, but I've got it where it counts." HE WANTS TO HIRE YOU!

Get your mitts on one of the examples that **matches your background** first. Hopefully you are self-aware to the extent that you can figure out which example is right for you. At this point, you can decide to **1** practice the example as is or **2** take your favorite bits and stitch together your own ONE-OF-A-KIND answer.

Remember, your experience doesn't matter—it's how you package it up and explain it.

Baby sitting.
The truth is that my experience is the thing I'd like to improve upon most. This is a job that can open doors for me in the future and I've applied here so that I can work, and learn, alongside an experienced team. But I'm ready to get off to a fast start and take on responsibility thanks to my work in childcare.

Children really energize me, so I was asked to babysit my neighbor's child three days a week. You have to grow up fast because childcare is a serious responsibility. I had to be alert at all times and became great multitasker...handling all of the child's needs like bathing, dressing and fun activities.

In emergencies I became concerned, not panicked, and I always put my needs second to the needs of the child. I guess in many ways it's what good customer service is all about. What I learned is that if you're positive and highly passionate about your job, your enthusiasm rubs off on everyone around you. What I'm looking for now is gaining real valuable work experience, and I've applied here not simply for a paycheck or because I have to, but because I want to.

Helped start a small business.
This would be my first formal job, but because of my experience with a friend's business, I'm ready to get off to a fast start, roll-up-my-sleeves and begin taking on responsibility.

I was chosen as one of the three volunteers for my friend's exciting start-up. So many things went right, from putting together a business plan and collaborating as a team. Consider that in just four months as a volunteer, I helped add two thousand dollars in new business by promoting sales online. We even emailed flyers to increase awareness of our new start up.

Everything was going pretty smoothly and then we hit some rough waters. The other two employees began college and we didn't have replacements right away. This proved to be a mistake because our business plan could not work with only two people involved. Without the added help, we could not keep our orders going. It was a difficult decision, and disappointing, but we had to close down the company.

However, I learned valuable lessons like the importance of planning for 'what-if' situations and developed great customer service skills. But the biggest lesson I learned is that a growing, energetic business can never have too much talent.

Car repair.
This is a fair question and if the situation was reversed, I would probably ask the same thing. From reading between the lines, your company is looking for someone who can work well under pressure and likes to take a hands-on approach to solving problems.

Over the past year I've been running a side-business repairing and upgrading performance vehicles. I've become accustomed to a fast-paced environment and handling complicated, technical work like engine tuning and performance upgrades. My attitude is if something goes wrong, I'd like to fix it. I don't help out just for the money because I like to look at problems as an opportunity to learn. I never complain about something without offering a solution.

And whether I'm installing a cold-air intake or HID lights, I realize the importance of getting the job done, regardless of the time clock. I intend to become very active as an associate of this team because I consider this not just a job, but the start of a meaningful career. The way I see it, my real education begins here.

Community service.
I care a lot about the issue of experience and that's why I decided to volunteer for community service—to improve myself and broaden my skill set.

I happen to come across a job posting which contained a list of volunteer activities. To be honest, I had no idea what to expect, but I was excited to get a job that offers assistance to people who need it most.

To me, the real joy of life is helping people. And being a part of a team that helps solve problems for my community, and society as a whole, was extremely rewarding. As a community service volunteer I began to develop a confidence I did not know I had. My nervousness and fear changed into excitement at the prospect of meeting new people and learning new skills. The experience and pleasure was far more valuable than any amount of dollars I could have earned.

As a matter of fact, even though my work wasn't all that glamorous, I knew that I made a difference when I received a touching thank you card from one of the families I helped.

That day I realized that a career is more than just money. It's a way to learn from others and experience what the world has to offer.

Door-to-door sales.
I can understand how you would feel that way. But allow me show you how that's not quite true.

I'm a really energetic person who's a real self-starter. What I mean by self-starter is that I love taking on new projects and helping out, especially when it comes to door-to-door sales for school fund raisers.

Going door-to-door you're challenged with staying motivated, so I recruited three other students and created a small team. This was a totally winning combination. We kept each other driven, developed fresh ideas and I became a confident presenter. It was an exciting time and if you haven't had a job before, I highly recommend it. I would say that the most important lesson I learned was that people like convenience. If you can make life easier for customers, and do more listening than selling, they'll send a ton of business your way.

What I am looking for now is a new role that will challenge me, especially given my sales experience. That's why when I found out about this opening, I knew I had to apply.

Family business.
While it's true that I'm interviewing here today to start my career, practically speaking my work experience began quite some time ago helping my family's business.

My family's business was both enjoyable and challenging! Being a cashier, I was the point of contact between the family business and our customers, so in a real way, I was responsible for keeping customers happy…not easy when dealing with long-check out lines. You can always ramp things up, but you can almost never ramp things down. What I'm most proud of is my ability to handle very hectic situations and "put out fires" quickly and then move on.

I learned so much about marketing and customer service, and realize that if you want to be successful you have to work well with others and make meaningful commitments. If we determine I'm a good fit for this role, I'd like to take these skills even further as a member of your team.

Medical externship.
During my 400-hour medical externship, I coordinated appointments, authorized refill requests, obtained pre-authorization for medication, charted, faxed and handled high call volume. But the truth is that my experience is the thing I'd like to improve upon most. I've always loved the medical field…in fact, I chose this field because making connections with patients really energizes me and makes me want to begin my career as soon as possible.

I would say that years of experience can help a medical assistant understand the basics taught in school, but I learned that experience and passion are two different things.

What I'm looking for now is gaining real, valuable work experience as a health care professional. I'm very impressed with the setting you have here and if we determine I'm a good fit, ready to start contributing.

Restaurants, fast food.
While I'm a newcomer to this particular area, I would like to give you some background so that we're all on the same page. Over the past year I have been working in the fast food industry.

I consider fast food employees the heroes of the service industry. Fast food truly is a 'do whatever needs to be done' position, and when it's time to hustle and they say run, you run, and that's why organization to me is HUGE. I developed strong customer service skills by resolving problems with orders and correcting billing errors. During 'down' time, I'd mop, clean dishes and stock napkins. I've learned that if you dedicate yourself to teamwork, people notice and will even pull some strings when you're in a tough spot!

With that said, I'll put in the time needed to get up to speed as quickly as I can. I'm serious about this opportunity and ready to start at the bottom and work my way up. I believe that if you want to be successful, you have to make meaningful commitments.

TWENTY SEVEN

....

ALL UP IN THE INTERWEBZ!

Think your friends are having a tough time dealing with your internet fame, just imagine the hiring manager!

The world is changing in amazing AND disturbing ways. *Amazing* in that the unfathomably, mindbogglingly powerful internet can hand you global fame. *Disturbing* in that many employers now get instructions to scan your timeline, comments and friends list and look for evidence of moral turpitude. (In other words, dig up dirt.)

Just thinking about employers stealth-ing the web and silently killing applications gives most people the hibbie jibbies. So today you'll learn the importance of going incognito mode and start locking down your cyber life.

POLICE CANDIDATES: To help take control over web privacy, Google® the keywords '**unlist my info**' in order to find free, user-friendly services that can discover which top online sites store data about you, and get them to un-list your info.

Here's mine, show me yours.
Because job hunters actually believe they have control using "privacy" settings, they willingly divulge very personal images and opinions—broadcasting pictures, even their minute-by-minute, to the world.

"Privacy options" give people a false sense of security. Technology is not perfect. A determined company can find out anything about you in cyberspace. And if you whole life is posted online, it might be used against you.

Not even counting anything lurid or obscene, employers can discover your **sexual orientation, religion, ethnicity, hobbies, disabilities, age, political views, and activism**. So the BEST way to stay out of trouble is to not put anything in an email, instant message (IM), txt message, #blog, profile page, image hosting site that isn't okay for the whole ENTIRE world to see.

This is especially important during the job hunt, as you may come across one of those interviewers who takes their job a little too seriously. We're talking about the type of company representative who will try to blur the line between your private life and your professional life and (violating-ly) insist that you log in to your online social network during an interview. Bad-word-that-you-can't-say-that-starts-with-F THAT NOISE.

Just asking you to surrender your login and password is creepazoid-central! Refuse ~~and then laugh in their face~~. Do not log in to any of your accounts during an interview. Ever. And **never** give away your secret password, especially to some random interviewer. Exercise your right to privacy!

Shut yo bloggermouth!
People love internet lynchings, but before YOU get hyper-pugnacious and rip someone else's virtual throat out with a post or comment, know that it is risky and could ruin your professional life. It's always a bad idea.

Of course, trolling and flamewars get you a lot of online attention, but before you actually submit a textosterone-filled reply, ask yourself **1** would I be so bold if I were standing in arms reach and **2** do I really want employers to think I am a flaming troll?

LOOKS

TWENTY EIGHT

....

DON'T HATE ME BECAUSE I'M BOOTYFUL

Stop being sexy dammit!

The hiring manager will start throwing dollar bills.

> Wear your interviewing clothes *anytime* you expect face-to-face contact with an employer. And don't be afraid of interviewing because you can't afford a 'perfect' outfit or you're uncomfortable with your body—you'll miss out on a great experience!

Smelly jelly.
If you can't stand to stay in one room for fear of succumbing to your own odors, we'll have to go from sensual bath type stuff to vigorous decontamination scrubbing. Hiring managers are picky about ~~the whole feral child musk~~ cleanliness. After stepping out of the shower, dry off your provocative curves, add lotion and a bit of deodorant…deodorant really seals in the flavor.

Let's move up to onion breath. At the interview, as a good listener, you'll have to tilt forward a bit and lean towards the speaker. That'll put you within smelling distance. Carefully brush your teeth the morning of, as this will ease the exchange of ideas since halitosis will no longer be a distraction. *Speaking of distractions,* spray a very, very light mist of perfume to emit a pleasant aroma. You want the hiring manager to concentrate on your great presentation, not your honeysuckle-vanilla-peach-tropical paradise perfume.

Stop MUCKING up your outfit.
If your clothes get a grape jelly oops, give it a good spot cleaning with water and a towel. Use an iron or hair dryer to quickly dry that area. Sticky tape works wonders removing crumbs, dandruff and lint and is cheaper than a lint brush.

Clothes are guaranteed to wrinkle before your big debut, so give your outfit (and shoes) a 'once over' and check for runs in your tights, wrinkles in clothes, loose threads and rips. Going in dirty or unkept will force the question: why couldn't you tidy it up before the interview?

Tattoos.
Nice ink! Unfortunately, many hiring managers are not very fond of body-face art forms like tattoos, so this is where you should let your creativity run as wild as your personality. Think of every possible way to camouflage your visibly tatted-skin. Unless you're interviewing in a creative field such as the fashion, art or music industry, exposed tattoos still hold a degree of taboo and can hurt your job prospects, especially if the job requires a lot of face-to-face customer interaction. To complicate things more, the type of tattoo also matters. A customized shoulder with flowers and butterflies or tribal art is one thing, but gang-culture tattoos like face tears, or sexual content, or racist innuendo will be a conversation-stopper (in most fields).

Ideally, you want your qualifications to be the first thing they talk about when you walk out the door, not your unfinished half sleeves. So if you find yourself saying 'ink, please disappear,' visit **page 247** and say goodbye to your job-blocking tattoo!

Tame that frizzzeakky!
Even your poodle is giving you a WTF look!

Hairstyles should suit your face, not take over your face. Hiring managers want to make eye contact and see the lovely shape of your contours. Popular interviewing hairstyles include a low ponytail with a clip, a bun, a neat braid or half up-half down for a low maintenance, chic look. Beautifully thick, curly hair is naturally bouncy, with great volume, and generally gives you a few more choices such as bobs, tight braids and twists.

Letting your hair flow freely also looks attractive, but pull enough of your hair away so your interviewer can still see the front of your outfit. A chunk of hair that covers your face, or one eye, makes you look shady or uncomfortable.

Giving your hair a clean, natural look also means your hair tones and style should not be a **distraction** to the conversation. Highlights-streaks should match your complexion. Style should enhance what's already there. Want to rock vintage waves or a 70's post-mod British street style look? Go for it! As long as you're not swinging your hair around every four seconds and it's complimentary, you're fine.

Wet hair is unprofessional. For this reason, the crunchy or wet look is a big NO-NO. The same is true for dazzle décor like flowers, feathers, large bows, and big headbands.

Nails.
Manicured nails are a must, especially in the medical field. If you decide not to polish, keep your fingernails fresh and clean, chip-free and pretty. And stop being a biter!

Nail biting is a compulsive behavior that many people do even without realizing it. Nail biting can annihilate your fingers leaving a bloody mess that hurts like a mofo. And it's so embarrassing. Let's help you kick the habit, once and for all.

First make a new rule: stop biting one hand. Leave one hand alone. You can bite your nails, just not on that hand. Buy skin-toned, micropore medical tape, then tape off the tips of your "save" fingers to protect that hand. Now add a fingernail clipper **with a file** to your keychain. A file is mandatory. Anytime you start biting the "save" hand, clip and file the area instead. After a few days, your "save" hand fingers will look so nice, it'll all be worth it!

Once you appreciate how clean and neat your "save" hand looks, you'll snap out of it and stop biting the second. Perhaps not instantly, but with a new found awareness of your bite habits, you'll commit to "saving" 2 out of the 3 fingers on your *other* hand. Your urge to bite will steadily go down as you get used to not biting. You'll have to make a conscious effort not to chew, but in 2-8 months you'll take the final step and stop altogether. Enjoy your beautiful new nails!

Butterface: everything is good but-her-face.
Natural is attractive. Apply your interviewing makeup in such a way that people can't tell whether you're wearing any or not because we're going to trick the hiring manager into thinking that you rolled out of bed looking that hot!

Begin with a subtle foundation and light blush to the cheeks. Add a bit of eyeliner, well-blended eye shadow, mascara and a touch of lip color. Think dressy nudes (neutral colors). Do not cake on product, especially around your eyes because on hot days the makeup will run and you'll look like a melted clown. Shape your eyebrows along the natural contours of your face. You can use eyeliner, eyebrow powder or an eyebrow pencil as long as it is tasteful, but no sharpies, please, as shaved and drawn-in eyebrows will make the hiring manager completely forget what you're talking about. (If you're forced to draw in your eyebrows, define your brows with eyeshadow and pencil.)

Just keep it simple. Use the colors to enhance what is already there and what you are wearing. Turn up the color or turn down the color to give you a clean "just got out of the shower" natural look. Take a selfie and if you think you're wearing too much makeup, then you're wearing too much makeup.

One last thought before you commit to buying any cosmetics, do a glitter check of your lotion, nail polish and perfume and make sure these products contain NO glitter anything! This book is about doing something that doesn't involve bills in your g-string.

Medical-field scrubs.

If the hiring manager asks that you come-in for an interview wearing your medical scrubs, than wear them proudly. However, make sure that your scrubs are **spotless**, clean, and ironed. This bears repeating: only wear scrubs to an interview when specifically told it is okay.

Clothes.

Today, it's not just about interviewing. It's about interviewing...with style. We're going to put together a "fashion-y" ensemble beginning with well-fitting articles that flatter your body, on the cheap.

Touchy subject time: before you gently nudge into one or two sizes smaller, tight fitting stuff will increase your "visual weight." Going undersize can also make you aware of how your belly is stretching the shirt. You will feel like you're about to burst out of your clothes at any moment which can make you self-conscious and uncomfortable at the interview. Clothes can affect your self-esteem, so it's important that you feel good in them. Buttons should close properly and shirts should tuck in properly. By the same token, you don't want to wear oversized clothes. You want balance, as sloppy, loose-fitting articles will make you look bigger. Go for clothes that drape your body well and flatter YOUR silhouette, not the starving 6-foot mannequin at the store.

And hide some of your blessings! Ixnay on the micro-mini and plunging V-neck-ay. Nothing at the interview is going to be based on sex appeal and companies have an image to protect. Of course, keeping your hotness in check is practically impossible, which is what makes it so tricky!

Try this, for a typical interview, go with a cool and crisp pencil skirt, blouse and blazer. Another option is slim trousers or sheath dress, jacket and pumps. The jacket can be taken off if you feel dowdy. Wrap dresses and sleeveless tops are a bit too informal for an interview.

For a more formal interview, stick to the classics by shopping for a **2 or 3 button pants or skirt suit in neutral colors** such as navy blue, charcoal grey or black. Pants suits are popular because they retain a neat and tailored look and are low maintenance (with less worry about a run in your stockings). Pants should touch the tops of your shoes but not drape below the heels or drag on the ground. Skirts should be barely at or above the knee in length with *no runs* in your tights.

Lastly, take the sit-down hotness test. Outfits reveal different things sitting down. Skirts can ride up, buttons can gape, your bra can make a guest appearance. "Watch out! I'm so excited, I could jump right out of here!"

Trade jobs or casual settings like jobs in cowtown, the web industry, or start-ups are pretty informal, but you're still addressing a company. Dress 2-3 levels over what employees usually wear to work. If you are unsure about the dress code, swing through a few days before the interview and take mental notes of what you see. Or make a call and ask. Asking is perfectly fine and **will not be held against you**.

You: "I would like to make sure that I understand your business culture and dress appropriately. What's the dress code?"

Suit colors.
A must-have for any job is confidence.

Bold colors can demonstrate a level of confidence, but wearing a pink suit—regardless of whatever else you're wearing—will make you look like a human flamingo, so you'll have to try on different color combinations and find the line between boring-stuffy and fashion mishap. (It's a nonstop balancing act.)

To play it safe, solid black has a luxurious appeal and can be teamed up with rich vibrant colors and endless shirt options for an interview. Less-mournful colors are navy blue and charcoal grey.

Navy blue suits leave the impression of a smart and well put together woman and is perfect year round. Navy blue is a 'power' color. A charcoal grey suit is sleek traditional excellence at its best. Navy blue or charcoal grey are less severe than black, but the best way to find out is to try different colors to see what flatters your particular complexion. Do not a wear white suit.

Let's talk splashy prints and pinstripes. Subtle, thin pinstripes look bold, sophisticated and make you look taller. In moderation, floral patterns can be interview appropriate, but be careful, too much flower power can trip out the hiring manager's eyeballs.

The truth is as long as you look interview-y, factors like your introduction, hand shake and personality will have a much bigger impact on your success than the color of your outfit. In most cases, the hiring manager will snap a glance and simply think, "this candidate is wearing interviewing clothes and therefore has enough of a sense to dress appropriately to this meeting."

Tops.
A crisp white button down shirt is THE classic look.

Shirts should be long enough to cover cleavage yet short enough to still be "interesting." Light blue, French blue or pastel colored shirts calm the eye and are all great choices. Pick out a demure blouse or v-neck top for under your suit jacket. Button up the shirt with only the top button undone and spread the collar out and over the lapel.

Be mindful of low cut blouses, tops that hug too tightly, the dangerous see-through lace shirt with a black bra underneath, or anything bordering too sexy.

That's boot to the max.
Stop at nothing to find right shoes!

For a typical interview, the best way to go is with closed-toe pumps with 2, 3, or 4 inch heels that won't smash your toes. Walking around the office is often a part of the interview, so comfort is extremely important. Heel-wise, find something thicker than a 'lick my heel' stiletto, but not quite a chunky heel. With sky-high heels, wear a skirt that ends at your knees to balance things out. Use kitten heals for skirts that end right above the knee.

Color-wise black, dark grey, dark blue, taupe or any neutral color is a well-grounded, safe choice. Pink, turquoise or white shoes are too 'out there' for interviews that don't involve the music, design or fashion industry. Round tip, square tip and point boots are good to go as long as your pants cover your boots. In other words, don't stuff your pant-legs inside your boots for a traditional interview. For casual interviews, you can combine boots-skirt-leggings.

Single strap Mary-Janes are interview appropriate, but keep the style simple.

Unless you're interviewing in a creative field, be warned—NO, NO, a thousand times NO chuck taylors, uggs, thigh highs, creepers, platforms, lace-ups, open-toe, flip-flops, disco-ball, ballerina flats, prom shoes, sandals, wedges, sneakers, or biker boots. You will hurt your chances of being successful and probably get a nice visit from the interview fashion police.

Stockings & tights.
Are pantyhose required for interviewing? The answer is yes, but they should be carried in your purse and used for strangling anyone that tries to get in your way. Kidding! Times are changing and the issue of whether to wear or go bare is controversial. Stockings make you look very put together. Bare legs are sexier.

An interview is a special day, not a regular day at the office, so for conservative companies, go with stockings. Not entirely sure what to do, go with stockings. Absolutely hate wearing stocking, wear trousers. Major city creative work environment, you can skip the dreaded hose-beasts. Some companies are nitpicky, others won't notice. However, the only time to bust out your crazy pair of fishnet stockings is if you're interviewing for a trendy music, design or fashion job where it's practically required to be fashionable and hip.

Otherwise match a pair of black or dark charcoal or sheer nude stockings-pantyhose-tights to your outfit. Think a pair of black suede pumps with really sheer black stockings.

Jewelry & accessories.
Well-chosen accessories—like an oversize men's watch—aren't just fashion, they're a statement. In a pool of applicants, you'll stand out with a bold and creative accessory, but limit it to one piece. Better yet, play it safe with simple, elegant necklace such as a single strand pearl, earrings and a watch.

A watch shows your responsible and timely, but keep it simple. With a male hiring manager, a designer purse will go 'woosh,' whizzing right by him, but he'll spot a watch with gimmicky gems in a second. You want the focus on your high intelligence and qualifications, not your blingy timekeeper.

You have some leeway with other accessories, but keep in mind some "rules." Pendants should be smaller than one inch. Check necklaces in the mirror at home. Necklaces that end right above or at your cleavage act like an arrow pointing at your puppies and that's no bueno. Stick to basic piercings, one on each ear, and avoid anything dangly. Big bracelets can get in the way of a handshake, so take a pass. Bangles, baubles, chandelier earrings and hoops are wacky and loud (jewelry shouldn't make noise when you move around).

Awesome possum! Now you're fully accessorized yet still maintaining a classy, business-like aura.

Purse.
Practically speaking, a purse is just extra clutter and one more distraction from the interview. You'll fumble around when trying to shake hands, and could end up dropping things and looking flustered. Consider carrying a notebook (which has a pen holder) and placing your ID, debit card, phone and keys in your pocket. Your purse will be safely awaiting your return in the car or at home.

But some trousers have faux (fake) pockets or shallow pockets that, at best, fit a single blue-colored M&M®. If plan to wear pocketless interviewing pants, or you just love carrying a purse, don't go out of your way to buy a bag just for an interview. You'll be fine with any neutral-colored 'businesslike' bag as long as it's not OVERsize...unless you're lugging along all of your belongings because you're planning to crash on the lobby couch.

Style-wise go understated, with absofrickinlutely **no designer logos** or bold, flashy hardware. No hiring manager who pulls 20 hours of overtime every week to support her purse habit wants to see you waltz in with the same designer bag she treated herself to last month after receiving her big bonus. She'll keep eyeing your bag instead of listening to your rad presentation!

She spends money like there's no tomorrow!
ALWAYS shop at thrift stores before heading to the "regular" stores, sheesh, get with it! Thrift shops are a fashionista's dream, offering cheap, stylish and well-constructed pieces of clothes. You'll look incredible.

That said, it can be hit or miss with thrift stores, so to the clearance clothes rack at a discount fashion retailer is our next stop. A lot of the outfits and accessories in discount fashion retailers look like finds from a boutique; they won't last very long, but if they look good, who cares? Lastly, consider not spending any money at all. The truth is many clever job hunters **keep it simple and just borrow clothes**, which is probably the smartest choice. Stay away from all overpriced, overly-complicated clothes because, once hired, you'll be given the option to wear whatever you like as long as it's clean and respectable.

USE THIS SPACE TO CREATE YOUR VERY OWN CLOTHING LIST.

(Head-to-toe beauty at last! Wait! Where do you think you're going? Your interviewing answers sound clunky and forced together. Flip to **page 55**.)

TWENTY NINE

···

MANSCAPING
(NO GIRLS ALLOWED!)

~~How to be a well-dressed man~~.

~~How to look like a man-barbie~~.

How to look like a dazzling devilbeast.

The interview goes by so quickly that if you can pull a GQ, it's an incredibly powerful thing. The right clothes can earn you instant, universal respect.

But most guys have a really hard time dressing well, especially if they've never been taught how to spot the right clothes, rock colors combos, or achieve an eye-catching, tailored fit. So consider this section your single stop for the best in apparel (and grooming) to help "package" you up and make you feel like a brand new person.

> Wear your interviewing clothes *anytime* you expect face-to-face contact with an employer. And don't be afraid of interviewing because you can't afford a 'perfect' outfit or you're uncomfortable with your body—you'll miss out on a great experience!

Tame that wooly mammoth!
You're a real man's man. There's no shame in that. But it's time we face reality…they're called razors. They shave your hair. It's a brilliant invention. Give them a chance.

Angora sweaters (major body hair) and unibrows were quite stylish 40,000-60,000 years ago when stone tools and cave paintings were all the rage. But since then humanity has invented amazing ways to insulate themselves from cold weather and cover nakedness.

If you think you look like the missing link, please shave your face, pluck your ear-nose fuzz, and trim your unruly bush to achieve a winter fresh, clean-cut, capitalistic-pig look. Rest assured that it is perfectly safe to shave your body fur, too. It will not grow back sasquatchier.

Odeur.
An interview will put you within smelling distance.

The morning of, jump in the shower and go from sensual bath type stuff to vigorous decontamination scrubbing. Then pat your chiseled glutes, washboard abs, and rock-hard pectorals dry, add lotion and deodorant. Deodorant really seals in the flavor.

Now dab a tiny bit of cologne on your neck or behind the ears and wrists, or spray a small mist in the air and walk through it, or wear no scents at all. You want them to concentrate on your great presentation, not on how your cologne is fumigating the place.

And to prevent yourself from setting the hiring manager's eyebrows on fire, please brush your teeth. It's just polite.

I wish my wife was as dirty as his shirt.
You don't want your slacks to say 'dressed for success' but your shirt to say 'I'm sloppy and I like to eat a lot of grape jelly. Like a LOT of it,' do you?

Should your ~~attire~~ pimp threads get a breakfast oops, give it a good spot cleaning with water and a towel. Use an iron or hair dryer to quickly dry that area. Sticky tape works wonders removing crumbs, dandruff, and lint and it's is cheaper than buying a lint brush. Please take the time to make sure that your outfit is ironed, spotless and clean, with absofrikinlutely **no** smudges, or else the hiring manager will just sit there and stare at the grape jelly blob as he imagines the stain talking to him.

Tattoos.
Nice ink! Unfortunately, many hiring managers are not very fond of body-face art forms like tattoos, so this is where you should let your creativity run as wild as your personality. Think of every possible way to camouflage your visibly tatted-skin. Unless you're interviewing in a creative field such as the fashion, art or music industry, exposed tattoos still hold a degree of taboo and can hurt your job prospects, especially if the job requires a lot of face-to-face customer interaction. To complicate things further, the type of tattoo also matters. A customized arm with tribal art, a military emblem or anime is one thing, but gang-culture tattoos like face tears, or sexual content, or racist innuendo will be a conversation-stopper (in most fields).

Ideally, you want your qualifications to be the first thing they talk about when you walk out the door, not your unfinished half sleeves. So if you find yourself saying 'ink, please disappear,' visit **page 247** and say goodbye to your job-blocking tattoo!

Hair cut.
Gravity defying, neon-colored dreadlocks can work for a fashion or

music industry interview. However, pull your braids away from your cheeks so the hiring manager can see the shape of your face and dreamy Rastafarian, all-knowing eyes.

In other settings, you'll want a low maintenance haircut that compliments your face, not takes over your face. Swing by a 5-dollar barbershop and ask for a nice fade, or buy a set of clippers and take care of that frizzy shag, mullet mess yourself. Eye contact and seeing your facial expressions counts, and you don't want your haircut to be a distraction from the conversation.

For men with a nicely-shaped head, or bald patches, you can pull off a truly chic hairstyle with a head-hugging crew cut or total shave. Bald men are perceived as business leaders, truly poised with enduring self-assurance. But before you buzz it off, realize that bald men are either perceived as business leaders or mistaken for gang members and thugs. So, if you are formerly gang-affiliated, approach it from the right angle. Switch seats, grow out your hair and keep it trimmed and natural looking. The length could help conceal any tattoos and add a preppy richness to your appearance, showcasing the warm-approachable layer of your personality. For law enforcement interviews, a shaved head, crew or buzz cut is a GREAT choice because it will be easier to picture you in the police or sheriff's academy.

Nails.
Keep your fingernails perfectly clean, trimmed and healthy-looking. And stop being a biter!

Nail biting is a compulsive behavior that many people do even without realizing it. Nail biting can annihilate your fingers leaving a bloody mess that hurts like a mofo. And it's so embarrassing. Let's help you kick the habit, once and for all.

First make a new rule: stop biting one hand. Leave one hand alone. You can bite your nails, just not on that hand. Buy skin-toned, micropore medical tape, then tape off the tips of your "save" fingers, to protect that hand. Now add a fingernail clipper **with a file** to your keychain. A file is mandatory. Anytime you start biting the "save" hand, clip and file the area instead. After a few days, your "save" hand fingers will look so nice, it'll all be worth it!

Once you appreciate how clean and neat your "save" hand looks, you'll snap out of it and stop biting the second. Perhaps not instantly, but with a new found awareness of your bite habits, you'll commit to "saving" 2 out of the 3 fingers on your *other* hand. Your urge to bite will steadily go down as you get used to not biting. You'll have to make a conscious effort not to chew, but in 2-8 months you'll take the final step and stop altogether. Enjoy your new manly nails!

Medical-field scrubs.
If the hiring manager asks that you come-in for an interview wearing your medical scrubs, than wear them proudly. However, make sure that your scrubs are **spotless**, clean, and ironed. This bears repeating: only wear scrubs to an interview when specifically told it is okay.

Clothes.
We're going to put together a "fashion-y" ensemble beginning with well-fitting articles that flatter your silhouette, as properly-sized clothes will cost the same amount as sloppy fitting clothes.

What that means is if you're muscular or chubby—or muscly with a hint of chubby—let it speak for itself. Avoid skin tight, body hugging shirts or pants, as tight fitting stuff will increase your "visual weight." By the same token, you want to stay away from oversized clothes. You want balance, not a sagging, loose-fitting outfit because, as you can probably guess, it'll make you look pudgy.

Go for clothes that give your body just enough wiggle-room, and that means no clinging and no frumpy excess material.

We're going to hunt for a 2-piece suit (jacket and pants) if you expect to walk into a formal interview. Let's start with the jacket: it should be fitted. With your arms at your side, the jacket should end at your knuckles, and shoulder pads should end at your shoulders, not past them and flopped over. Sleeves should end halfway between your wrist and base of your thumb. Pants should fit comfortably on the hip and straight down the leg to about half-way down on back of your heal, or thereabouts.

You can pull off a three-piece suit (jacket, pants and a vest worn underneath the jacket) but know how to wear it. For a three-piece suit, your vest should wrap snuggly around your torso and touch your belt, but not dip below it.

Keep your suit jacket on during your interview! Hot or humid weather is no exception.

Trade jobs or casual settings like jobs in cowtown, the web or tech industry, or start-ups are pretty informal, but you're still addressing a company, so dress 2-3 levels over what employees usually wear to work. (That could mean a new pair of jeans, clean boots and a fresh white undershirt beneath a flannel shirt. That might mean a suit jacket and a pair of flat-front khakis and loafers. Pick your poison.) If you are unsure about the dress code, swing by a few days before the interview and take mental notes of what you see, or make a call and ask. Asking is perfectly fine and **will not be held against you.***

You: "I would like to make sure that I understand your business culture and dress appropriately. What's the dress code?"

(*Unless you know better—all hiring managers are different, after all.)

Suit colors.
You have two choices—navy blue or charcoal grey because, you know, black is too serious. Or is it?

Fashion-wise, black suits are associated with formal events like weddings and funerals. But people understand that when you are a young man you own only one suit that must fit every special occasion, so you can wear a black suit with total confidence. Most hiring managers will snap a glance and think "man in suit" not "man in English cut, black suit with notch lapels." Soften up a black suit with a light blue or pastel colored shirt and a poppy, colorful tie. The black suit-white shirt-black tie combo is out because you'll look like an undertaker or vampire's assistant.

Switching back to blues and greys, navy blue suits leave the impression of a smart and put together man and is perfect year round. Navy blue is a 'power' color. On the other hand, a charcoal grey suit is sleek traditional excellence at its best. Earth tone colors including tan, light grey and olive are considered a bit too informal.

Let's talk patterns. Subtle, thin pinstripes look bold, sophisticated and make you look taller. Thick pinstripes are for mobsters.

But pinstripes or not, earth-tone colors or not, the truth is as long as you look interview-y, factors like your introduction, hand shake and personality will have a MUCH bigger impact on your success than suit colors or patterns. In most cases, the hiring manager will snap a glance and simply think, "this candidate is wearing interviewing clothes and therefore has enough sense to dress appropriately to an interview."

Shirt.
A plain white button up shirt is THE classic look. You can also choose a solid color such as a light blue or pastel colored shirt. Light colors calm the eye and will not make you appear threatening or look like an authority figure. Patterns, graphics, or thick heavy lines on the shirt will hurt the hiring manager's eyeballs.

Make sure that the collar is snug against your neck. Your index and middle finger side-by-side should just baaaarely fit between your neck and collar. Before you buy, look for the correct collar style on the packaging of the dress shirt. "Point collars" are for men with long necks. "Spread collars" are for men with short necks. Oh, and no silk shirts!

Shoes & belt.
For formal interviews, wear a pair of all black leather dress shoes, not loafers, and a black leather belt. Lace-up or no lace doesn't matter. Brown leather will give you a little more presence, but it can be quite overwhelming trying to match brown with other colors. Black is the safest play and leaves no question marks for the interviewer about you.

Make sure your shoes are *comfortable* because it's difficult to smile while experiencing excruciating pain.

Socks.
Choose a pair of black or dark charcoal socks that are long enough to cover leg fur when seated. Patterns socks are fine unless you're already wearing attention-grabbing clothes, then the socks might be overkill. The only time to bust out your crazy pair of socks is if you're interviewing for a trendy music, design or fashion job where it's practically required to be fashionable and hip.

Jewelry.
Wear only a wedding band or perhaps a school ring. Small, conservative cufflinks look refined, but grillz might be overdoing it a little.

Briefcase.
Avoid sporting a large briefcase, backpack or bag unless you are planning on moving in. A small, leather portfolio for your notepad, pen and resumes shows you're focused and smartly put together. Buy a classy black or blue ink ballpoint pen at the 99-cent store.

Color me bad neckties.
Tie colors "send a message" to the hiring manager. Unless you are interviewing in Hawai'i or for a trade job, wear a tie because you want to avoid leaving your potential new coworkers with the impression that you received special treatment.

BLUE: This is someone we can trust. Blue signals integrity, honesty, trust, tranquility and calm.

RED: I'm where I belong. Red is a power color. Many Asian cultures consider red a symbol for good luck, wealth and prosperity. (And that's what we in the interviewing business call a clue.)

BLACK: Why yes, the beluga caviar is faaaaabulous this time of year. "Black tie" events are hoity-toity formal gatherings or parties. They are called "black tie" events because all men wear a solid black tie, and that's why a solid black tie would be a little out of place at an interview. However, patterned black ties with stripes or dots are a great way to style up your interviewing outfit.

BROWN: Brown is a down-to-earth, well-grounded, practical man's color…a man with not much else going on. Meh. A bit boring.

GREEN: On the positive side, green is the color of a newbie who is eager to learn and grow and a real team player. A green tie can give you a splash of interesting color without going over-the-top. On the negative side, green is the color of envy.

GREY: A man with a grey tie is someone who could zone out and stare at his computer screen in a meditative state for hours on end. Grey is a bit boring.

YELLOW: Yellow ties announce themselves loudly and clearly and reflect two extremes—an energetic, outgoing 'GTFO mah way' personality on one side and a jealous wimp on the other. Yellow is a risky color, so make sure you have the personality to pull it off. Or better yet, avoid this color for now.

Go online and watch a video on how to tie a tie into a *half-windsor knot*. The half-windsor knot signals honesty and trust, so that's arguably the best style to wear for an interview. Clipper and zip-on ties are not exactly selling like hotcakes nowadays, so avoid for now.

Be thrift shop-y.
ALWAYS shop at thrift stores before heading to the "regular" stores, sheesh, get with it! Thrift shops are a fashionista's dream, offering cheap, stylish and well-constructed pieces of clothes. You'll look incredible.

That said, it can be hit or miss with thrift stores, so to the clearance clothes rack at a discount fashion retailer is our next stop. A lot of the suits in discount fashion retailers look like finds from a men's boutique. The outfits may not last very long, but if they look good, who cares? Lastly, consider not spending any money at all. The truth is many clever job hunters **keep it simple and just borrow clothes**, which is probably the smartest choice. Stay away from all overpriced, overly-complicated clothes because, once hired, you'll be given the option to wear a uniform or whatever you like as long as it's clean and respectable.

(Wow, you look like you have it! Hurry, hurry and visit **page 91**! Otherwise you'll be all dressed up with no place to go. 🙁)

THIRTY

······································

THE INK ABOVE THE STINK

Are you stuck with that lazy good-for-nothing *tattoo* you married FOR LIFE?

No way! Make the switch and dump the b█████.

A message to men—the world of makeup can make some guys feel a little lost or uncomfortable. It is perfectly acceptable to ask a female family member, or friend, or someone online to assist you. Remember, this section is about covering up your tattoo, not finding your inner woman.

> POLICE CANDIDATES: If you have tattoos, you will be required to explain them.

Ewwwwwwwwww. Get AWAY from me!
Thinking about using band-aids to cover tattoos? Good luck with THAT.

Hiring manager: "So, the plan was to pretend you got cut? Are we all stupid or what? Band-aids look worse than tattoos, you beautiful fool."

Be stealthy and cover your tattoos with long sleeve shirts, tall collars, long socks, long skirts, stockings, and by growing out or styling you hair. Switch gears and use specialty tattoo makeup **for all other** itty-bitty or ginormous tattoos that may cause the hiring manager to begin hyperventilating.

Specialty makeup HOW TO.
Red light. Why risk waiting until the morning of your interview to test if your concealer lives up to its promises? Practice with your concealer ahead of time and **use specialty tattoo makeup**. Street-foundations will leave traces of makeup on the hiring manager's sleeve!

To make things easy, all of the products listed here are PERFECT for covering up tattoos. What's so special about these concealers? Unlike street-foundations, these are highly pigmented, heavy duty concealers that resist smearing all over clothes or washing off with water.

Ben Nye® Concealer Palette www.bennyemakeup.com
Covermark® www.covermark.com
Dermablend™ www.dermablend.com
Hard Candy Glamoflauge® www.hardcandy.com
Kat Von D Tattoo Concealer™ by Sephora www.sephora.com
Tatjacket™ www.tatjacket.com
Tattoocamo™ www.tattoocamo.com

Step 1—PREP
Cleanse your skin as usual to begin with a clean and dry foundation. Traces of oil, dirt and makeup can be wiped away with toner. Rinse and pat dry. Do not use moisturizer unless your product recommends it.

Step 2—CONCEAL

Products differ. Some products offer a one-step application while others require several layers. So follow the suggestions on the box.

Although many recommend using a clean, dry makeup sponge to smooth on your application, if you use clean, dry fingertips to apply small scoops of the concealer on the back of your hand, the heat from your fingers will warm the oils making it easier to apply.

Step 3—PERFECT

Apply several coats evenly allowing each coat to dry fully. One thing to remember—BLEND the edges or cover all exposed skin for an even look.

For multi-layer concealers, begin with the lightest shade of concealer on the darkest part of your tattoo first. Use a green neutralizer to cover red tattoos and a yellow neutralizer to counteract blue-color tattoos which are the most common.

Next use a shade that closely matches your skin tone.

Step 4—SET

Set it and forget it! A light dusting of translucent makeup setting powder or spray locks the makeup in place, seals in your work and removes the sheen.

Now go see how it looks!

Use both dark and BRIGHT lighting to check out your work. Bright lighting requires a heavier coat of concealer.

...MORE ▶

(Extra Credit)

Ex-gang members, wish you hadn't done it? Then READ!
You may be able to permanently remove your gang-affiliated tattoos **free of charge.**

Many local community centers are partnering up with businesses that offer gang-related (or anti-social-ish) tattoo removal either free-of-charge or in exchange for community service.

The internet is your friend. Hop online and Google® search using the keywords "free gang tattoo removal" or call your local community center representative who would be happy to put you in touch with pro's that can help. Expect to be placed on a waiting list.

Below are three **EXCELLENT** organizations that offer free tattoo removal services and in some cases much, much more. Call to schedule an appointment, or to ask for help finding organizations who offer this free service in and around your neighborhood.

Homeboy Industries™
130 Bruno Street, Los Angeles, CA 90012
Phone (323) 526-1254
www.homeboyindustries.org

Fresh Start Tattoo Removal Program, Inc.
189 East Second Street, New York, NY 10009
Phone (917) 723-4206
www.freshstarttattooremoval.org

Youth Removal
2928 Main St, Suite 100, Dallas TX 75226
Phone (214) 394-6824
www.youthremoval.org

PAPERWORK

THIRTY ONE

....

COVER LETTER, TELL ME YOUR TALE

What (the heck) is a cover letter?
A cover letter is short personal introduction in writing.

It's targeted at the person who will also be reading your resume, but provides information about your personality and work habits that's not in the resume.

A truly compelling cover letter has an intoxicating effect. It will grab a hiring manager on a human level within 3 seconds or less. That's important because hiring managers respond when they feel a real personal interest from you.

Do I include a cover letter with every resume?
No.

Many hiring managers say traditional cover letters have ZERO impact on them and add nothing to the application. On the flipside, some organizations *require* a cover letter as a part of the application process. Every employer is different and the debate over whether or not to include cover letters is as mind-numbing as homework.

To play it safe, follow this common-sense rule: if a face or phone introduction is not an option, *include a cover letter with every resume* that you plan to fire off to employers.

What makes a great cover letter, according to hiring managers?
Let's begin with what doesn't. With a stack of 283 cover letters sitting in front of them, it has reached the point where copy and paste—personality-free—cover letters are *hated* by hiring managers. It's an instant turn-off.

"To Whom It May Concern" letters are on the same level as spam and junk mail. Instead of hurting the hiring manager's brain cells, **1** address the letter to an actual real-life person, **2** be Mr. or Ms. Know-It-All about the company, and **3** keep it short while using **correct spelling**. Every word counts!

A great cover letter talks about why you're excited about the position and what impresses you about the company. You want to show a **personal** interest in working for that particular organization, but keep the cover letter bite size because it's an introduction, not your life story. Today's world is all about scanning and hiring managers have the attention span of a gnat.

If you're not sure who to address the cover letter to, make a phone call. Ask the receptionist or speak to the human resources department to **find a contact person for the cover letter**. Absolute worst case scenario, use something like 'To the office manager at [company name].' Do not use 'Dear Sir' or 'Dear Madam' or 'To Whom It May Concern' under any circumstances.

What you should do next...

Get your mitts on the short cover letter example on **page 259** and read it over a couple of times to warm up your brain.

The cover letter example serves as the basic structure of your letter. Do a quicky online search for the company that's hiring and find 1 the person you will address the letter to and 2 what the company's most proud of, or what makes it great.

Getting in the company's state of mind makes it easier for you to sound real, and the little bit of research also shows them that you want the job bad enough to tailor your letter extra for it.

To help you get your point across convincingly, you'll need to add a couple of sentences about your personality and work habits. Go to the "Tell Me About Yourself" section on **page 1** and find the example for **your particular job**. Highlight or circle the sentences that match your personality and work habits.

Now go forth and build your own ONE-OF-A-KIND cover letter. Copy the cover letter example, **personalize** it with bits and pieces from your online search to catch the hiring manager's attention, and add a couple of sentences from the "Tell Me About Yourself" section. See, it's not that complicated.

If you don't feel confident about your writing skills, or English is your second language, ask a friend or teacher to help you. People naturally like to do favors. But WAIT, before you ask, take a look at the example first. A cover letter isn't all that difficult to get right.

...CHECK OUT THE COVER LETTER SAMPLE ▶

USE THIS SPACE TO CREATE YOUR OWN VERSION OF THIS LETTER.

Dear Ms. Direction: (Address the letter to a real-life person.)

I am responding to your job posting for ███████████, which I understand may report to you.

(Add specifics details from your online search here.)
I've applied here today because I am extremely interested in working at ████, Inc. What I know about ████████, Inc. is that you ████████████████████████ and ████████████████████████, which truly shows what a great company can do with an innovative product. I'm also impressed by your inner workings, especially in terms of people and environment. In all honesty, I would love nothing more than to learn every aspect of this business, from the ground up, alongside side an experienced team such as yours.

Reading over the job description for this opening, I see my best qualities.

(Add personality and work habits from the "Tell Me About Yourself" section on **page 1** here.)
███████, Inc. is looking for a candidate with good interpersonal skills and what I'm most proud of is my ability to connect with people and talk directly to the client's needs. I am a persuasive communicator with well-developed presentation skills and love the challenge of working under pressure and facing deadlines. That's why when I found out about this opening, I knew I had to apply.

If you would like to talk with me or schedule an interview, please call me at ███████████ or email me at ████████████@████████.com. Thank you for your consideration.

Sincerely,
Beddyfear

THIRTY TWO

....

THIS IS MY RESUME. THERE ARE MANY LIKE IT BUT THIS ONE IS MINE.

How applicants *WISH* a resume works: "After I read her sexy resume, I knew I had to have her."

Please burn into your brain that the most important thing about a resume is not what's in it.

The most important thing about a resume is **how it gets to the hiring manager**.

When the hiring manager wants you, you are going to get the job offer even if your resume was scratched out on the back of a dirty napkin. Every time you read this keep that in mind no matter how great your resume looks, a phone or in-person impression is always going to be bigger and more powerful than a paper impression.

A 'resume' is a list of your accomplishments and pronounced rez-UH-may.

Here's my resume. Don't laugh at me u jerks.
This glorious creation called a resume can get you interviews, but only if you post it *fast* enough. (Often the first few qualified candidates to respond to a job ad are the only ones invited to interview.*)

That aside, even if you worked for only 5 days in your entire life, you can build a ~~bomb diggity~~ strong resume without ever having to lie, fool or deceive a fellow human being with a ~~hella~~ fake job history. The trick is to describe your *accomplishments*.

You begin by writing down YOUR contribution to school, personal or work tasks on scratch paper. Take a few hours to think about all of the projects you've participated in, but focus only on the *highlights*, as nitty gritty details are for interviews and online dating profiles. In fact, make things easy for yourself and just borrow sentences from the "Tell Me About Yourself" (**page 1**) and "No Prior Work Experience" (**page 211**) sections to fill up all of the empty spaces.

Remember, however, to list your ACCOMPLISHMENTS, not everyday responsibilities. A responsibility would read like this: "responsible for sales." Yawn! Compare that to listing an accomplishment: "increased sales by 20% in just two months." Big difference.

(*For private industry jobs, not government jobs.)

Epik phail.
Be very cautious writing under the influence of auto-correct. Spell check can change the outcome in wildly unexpected ways. For example, a typical spell-check mishap found on medical-assistant' resumes often happens when the job hopeful mixes up the words 'striper' and 'stripper.' Can you spot the difference? Both are job titles and are spelled correctly. But in this case, a 'striper' is a hospital volunteer, and a 'stripper' involves a brass pole, provocative dancing and disrobing in front of an excited crowd. Ruthlessly edit your own resume until you are absolutely, 100% sure there is not a single typo!

Alter ego.
Be warned, some creative email addresses *might* cause a hiring manger's body to twitch uncontrollably.

iaintyourdaddy@email.com
captain420@email.com
rukiddingme@email.com
momoney4mahoney@email.com
cockadoodledo@email.com
unicornbooty@email.com
2good2btru@email.com
whatsthep01nt@email.com
dontjudgeme@email.com
h8ers2daleft@email.com
divamergency@email.com
bigwanginyothang@email.com

To maintain your cyber-allure, use your original email for your online persona—or friends in your circle—and create a second down-to-earth email for your resume and job applications. Your job prospecting email can be anything as long as it's not threatening, antisocial, gang-affiliated…or containing number combos for its shock value. For example, you might think the numbers 13, 69, 187, 420, 666 look totally evil, but they will cause slight panic and brain aneurysms in superstitious, older people. Successful job hunters typically use a combination of their first and last name for their professional contacts.

I'd like to think that you two were meant for each other.
The most successful job hunters (slightly) customize their resume for each and every job ad. **You should, too**. You won't regret it. Listing the key required or recommended skills from the job posting in your resume will get a hiring manager, or scanning program, to lock-on to these particular words. Not only will this create the illusion that you are proficient in most of the job requirements, your resume will automatically *pop* out.

You'll look like the best candidate they can choose, on paper. (Once in, they want you to be CONVINCING. A resume is a great conversation piece for an interview, but don't rely on a resume to do the selling for you.)

At the top of your resume, include a few lines of basic skills that you can change up and tailor to each job posting. Copy & paste the key words or phrases from the job description into this area so that it grabs the hiring manager's attention. The beautiful part about any job titles you've held is that "official titles" tell very little about what your actual work entailed. That gives you the freedom to make creative adjustments to get in sync with the job ad.

(*A very widely used scanning program is called Taleo®. Taleo® is a 'talent acquisition' system used to scan resumes for key words.)

Damaged goods.
An amazing work or school history that's uglied up with funky font, emoticons, weird design layout or pictures won't make you "stand out." Visual clutter on a resume will just frustrate the reader, and in this case that would be the person with the power to hire you.

What's in your resume is just as important as how you package it up. People are visual creatures and judge by appearances.

The absolute best *paper* resumes will be printed on tastefully thick 24-32lb, white or subtle-off white, 100% cotton resume paper. Do not bend, fold, crinkle, crush, stain or mutilate your resume…in fact, don't even breathe on it. The day of your interview take the two resumes out of the oxygen bubble environment. At this point, you might get dust on them. That cannot be avoided and should not harm the paper in any way. Now carefully place the resumes inside a clean folder and do not spray perfume on your resume. (No flower bomb resumes, please!)

In our fast world, resume trends change at the speed of light, so follow these fast and hard rules to stay at the top of the bell curve:

Provide the facts ('increased sales by 20% in just two months') and allow the hiring manager to draw the conclusions ("ooohhh you're a keeper!"). Do not begin a resume with an objective. Use numbers to attract attention and give details. Limit the length of your resume to a single page (two page+ resumes are fine if you've really got it like that), and writing "references available upon request" at the bottom is not really necessary any longer.

My resume must suck.

Feeling left out? Want to know what happened with your resume? The truth is, being forced to read a stack of 100 resumes pushes most hiring managers into "very unhappy" mode. To many overburdened hiring managers, there's no way they're going to read all that. So, instead, they either **1** take 50% of the resumes and throw them straight in the trash, or **2** invite only the first few candidates who post or hand-deliver their resume, or **3** use recruitment agencies to sort out and narrow the pool of applicants. (There exists an ENTIRE PROFITABLE INDUSTRY devoted to screening resumes and applicants **page 93**.)

But resume or no resume, the shortest route to a new job is **direct contact**. Like back-in-the-day going from shop to shop in the mall and asking each manager for work as a clerk...or stopping by your local dining establishments for a busser or server position. This method still works today, even as your career jumps to the next level. So when you find a job posting, rather than applying online, make every attempt to get in touch with the hiring manager directly. Then apply if (and ONLY if) you sense a match. (That means you like the people a lot, or there's opportunity to grow, learn new things and build credentials, or it feels meaningful to you in some way.)

Know that job hunting is not an equipment list, it's a mindset. Resumes might get you interviews, but networking gets you jobs. (**page 172** reveals the fastest way to wiggle yourself into jobs. Go visit it!)

...(bomb-diggity) **RESUME SAMPLE ▶**

CARRIE D. AWAY

carriedaway@email.com
phone 212 555 2368

Professional | Overview

DangBro Credit Union (2017-2018)
2517 Nodowwt Terrace
Los Angeles, CA 90210
Member Service Representative

o Top new performer in 2017, earning "Rising Star" award.
o Go-to expert for explaining complex financial instruments to clients.
o Prepare submission reports tailored to key leaders.
o Solicit new accounts, exceeded new depository accounts daily and weekly quotas by 17%.
o Record of success processing treasury, tax, and loan payments in my territory.
o Cultivate strategic business relationships with local and national clients in person and by phone.
o Complete, accurate, and detailed charting of all pertinent client information.
o Cross–selling bank products including car, r/e and CD accounts, increased by 8%.
o Capture monthly productivity statistics.
o Manage cash drawers up to $25,000+.
o Strong background with 10-key, Microsoft Office™ and enterprise software.
o Recognition & Awards: **"Employee of the Month"** for 2018.

Attributes
- Conversational **Spanish** proficient
- Superb versatility
- Flexible schedule, nights & weekends
- Persuasive communicator

- Outstanding presentation delivery
- Liaison between decision makers and client
- Creative problem solver
- Readily accepts constructive criticism

Education
Epic Junior College
Associates of Arts in General Studies

Manchesthair University
Bachelors of Arts in Business Administration

Awards & Achievements
"iKindalikeyoulolsike Recipient" for 2nd quarter 2018

Volunteerism
Helped coordinate the Notkidding JK High School food drive: raised $1550 in cash donations, distributed over 725 cans of food to local soup kitchen.

Interests
Movie outings, sightseeing and learning to play musical instruments.

Profile

I have a passion for helping people put great ideas into action—any area of ▮ is a favored and welcomed challenge. Highly organized with the ability to manage multiple projects and consistently meet deadlines. Outgoing friendly person, driven by a strong work ethic.

THIRTY THREE

....

JOB APPLICATION FAQ
(FREQUENTLY AVOIDED QUESTIONS)

Today we're going to keep your application from going down in flames!

You this read wrong.
Read carefully and if you are given specific instructions, follow them!

And wait?!? Whuuut was that? You need to better representate yourself. Incorrect spelling is a job destroyer in this world, especially when combined with unfinished sentenc

Tryna check your application pacifcally for spelling if not today, tomarrow definitly. Thouse mispelled words can be a reel deal-breaker 'cause no won wants to higher a person who doesn't proof read.

(EDITED: Added typos and czarcasm lyk dis.)

Populate the boxes.
Fill in every single box in the application. If something doesn't apply to you, write either 'DNA' (as in 'Does Not Apply' not deoxyribonucleic acid) or 'N/A' (not applicable) to avoid leaving any blanks. Put down 'NMI' (no middle initial)

if you do not have a middle name. First timers with no prior job history, write 'DNA' or 'N/A' only one single time at the very top box of the work history page.

Salary box.
For the salary box, if you haven't agreed to an exact amount, you may write 'To Be Determined,' ~~or 'Infinity~~,' or 'TBD,' or 'Negotiable.'

Be very careful if the application has a "desired wage" box. The "desired wage" box is either an attempt to shame you into underpaying yourself (they're banking on an applicant with low self-esteem), or disqualify you if you happen to ask for more than what the company is willing to pay for the position. Again, write 'To Be Determined,' or 'TBD,' or 'Negotiable' on paper applications.

For online applications where you are forced to enter a number before you can go to the next screen, discover *roughly* how much your job pays per hour **in your area** (your city or county) by cold-calling local employers in your field. Avoid using www.salary.com whenever possible because the numbers are not very reliable. THE most accurate way to find out what salary the market is paying is to seek out a few local businesses, glue the phone to your face, and ask incognito-style.

You: "Hello, Citizen of Earth. I hope you're well today. I am doing career research for my school project and I'd love to talk with you about compensation. Would you be comfortable giving me a little guidance? Great! I was wondering how much dental assistants make at your office? What does the highest paid dental assistant make? And the lowest? Thanks!"

The numbers you're given are real-time data that you'll never find on the crowded web.

(Go to **page 85** if you sense that a company is trying to squeeze and lowball you out of a ~~comfortable income~~ livable wage.)

Neat freak.
Pick up or print out at least (2) application copies for each and every job opening. One copy works as a scribbled rough draft. The second copy will be your official, neatly-written form that you'll submit. Using excellent penmanship, print handwriting, and ONLY black or blue ink, take your time and complete each and every application with the utmost care.

Once finished, do not bend, fold, crinkle, crush, stain or mutilate your application…in fact, don't even breathe on it. (When the application is complete, place it down on the table and back away slowly without making any sudden moves.) Better yet, try to complete applications online. Be sure to print out a copy and keep it safely at home ~~but away from any open windows to make sure an eagle doesn't fly away with it~~ so you can keep track of where you applied and make the necessary follow up calls.

LAW ENFORCEMENT CANDIDATES: Once you submit a response in person or on paper, stick with it. Keep your story the same. Law enforcement agencies compare notes. Keep a copy of each and every application you fill out so your answers stay consistent. Inconsistent answers are considered "deceitful," even if you had no intent to lie.

Privacy isn't a crime.
Operate behind an impenetrable wall of secrecy and NEVER volunteer any information about a possible criminal record or bad conduct discharge-dishonorable discharge from the military *unless specifically asked for* in an application or required for a background check!

Shyness hurts.
Every single day job hunters, just like you, encounter confusing application questions. There's absolutely no shame in asking someone you trust or calling the employer for help because *questions will not be held against you.* Just sound happy and peachy on the phone.

You: "Hello, I'm completing an application for employment, would you mind clarifying [box number 21] for me? Thank you."

(*Unless you know better—all hiring managers are different, after all.)

After submitting your application, follow up!
Two-three days after submitting your application, make a call or send an email to see what's up.

You: "I wanted to express thanks for taking the time to review my application. I was particularly struck by the impressive team you've built and would welcome the chance to work with you! If you need additional references or information to help make your decision, please let me know.

(Waiting for a call back can be the most nerve-racking part of job hunting. If you're wondering whether your application has been shot to smithereens without you knowing, run to **page 153**.)

THIRTY FOUR

....

I'M KIND OF A BIG DEAL

Never tell ANYBODY that you've got it like that. If you've got it like that, **they'll tell you**.

From the hiring standpoint, the importance of having *other* people such as teachers, mentors, coworkers, friends and bosses "talk you up" cannot be overstated. Somebody *who has absolutely nothing to gain* by recommending you is EXTREMELY convincing, especially for a noob trying to 'get in.'

In the ever-watchful eye of a hiring manager, noobies pose a very real flight risk. A recommendation letter can help scream reassurance that you won't stick two fingers up and walk out two weeks into your new job.

And just in case you're terrified by the thought of asking for a "Letter of Recommendation," this section breaks it down and makes seeking a letter easy-breezy, especially if you're shy.

I hate asking people for favors. How should I approach this whole letter thing?
A clever email works like magic.

Comfortably strike up a conversation online by writing a letter. Why email? Because cyberspace creates a sense of distance, giving a reluctant writer a way out in case they want to decline your request. (Whether you choose to ask by mail, text, phone or face, be sure to plan out your timing, ask nice and **early**, and send a thank you note after receiving the favor!) Everything you're supposed to say in a letter asking for a recommendation is over here ▶

> HATER ALERT: Do not get a "Letter of Recommendation" from teacher, mentor or boss that you are 'not allowed to read.' A negative "letter of recommendation" can do SERIOUS damage to your application. Always proof read your recommendation letter and make sure it's a positive review **before** forwarding it to a job prospect.

Dear Mr. Fuzzy Schlong,

I hope this email finds you well. [Meaning 'I hope you are doing well and will not take too long to reply.']

Your class inspired me to begin my job search early and I have found several exciting opportunities. I am reaching out to ask a huge favor— would it be possible for you to write a recommendation letter on my behalf? [ALTERNATIVE: I am looking at a few organizations at the moment and am reaching out to ask you a huge favor—would you consider writing a recommendation letter on my behalf?] I thought you'd be a perfect person to ask as both my teacher [ALTERNATIVE: supervisor] and mentor. You challenged me to work harder than I ever thought possible and really prepared me for tomorrow's world as a student in your class [ALTERNATIVE: while working together].

But more than that, you have so much credibility as an instructor who teaches ███████, [ALTERANTIVE: But more than that, you have so much credibility as a professional who has supervised me in the field] that I believe that a recommendation letter from you could boost my future career prospects. [OPTIONAL: As you may recall, I was enrolled in your 9am-12:30pm, Monday-Wednesday English class and earned a "B+."]

I realize that it might be hard to recall the details from our time together. So to make things as simple as possible for you, I've included a draft letter that you might consider using as a template. If for any reason you don't feel like you're in a position to write a recommendation, I totally understand. But if you are willing to write a letter on my behalf, then feel free make any changes or modifications to the template that you see fit. I have tried to address my personal qualities and focus on the work habits I'm particularly proud of.

I sincerely appreciate you taking the time to consider this request. You've made a big difference in my life, and for that, I am very grateful.

If you have any questions, please call me at ███████ or email me at ██████████@████████.com.

Thank you for your support,
Willy Nilly

...CONTINUED ▶

DIY (do-it-yourself) 'Letter of Recommendation.'
Today's swamped teacher-mentor-boss-probation officer might very well ask you to write **your own** recommendation letter *for them*. (This type of arrangement is called "ghost writing.") ~~There's no reason you should take this nonsense~~.

Please do not be offended by this scenario because that's total props to you! Your reference is willing to stake their reputation on recommending you. Think of it this way: "Personally, I am too busy to write up a letter, but I trust you. I will sign the letter because I think you are *that* good." Sounds great, right?

The problem is most people are ~~shy~~ chronically introverted and cringe at the thought of having to talk about themselves. And if you're like everyone else, you're not exactly sure what to put down on paper, even if you wanted to give it a go. To help you take the weirdness out of writing about yourself, pirate bits and pieces from the glowing *recommendation letter* in the box to the right. ▶

PRO-TIP: The last thing a busy professional wants to do is spend their evenings or days stressing over a letter that you could have easily drafted on your own time with all the points that you'd like to include. The BEST approach is to provide a written draft—or even an outline or some bulletpoints—and let them roll with it. Providing a template is an **act of mercy**.

To Whom It May Concern:

I would like to make a suggestion based on my professional experience with Mack Daddy. As you know, we have many qualified applicants in the job market today and I have worked with my fair share.

Of these there is one individual who [OPTIONAL EMPHASIS: in every way so clearly] stands out that I would like to call her-his name to your attention and provide her-him with a strong recommendation [ALTERNATIVE: the strongest recommendation possible]. Mack Daddy is one of the finest young professionals I have ever worked with. She-he has an engaging personality, is extremely curious and shows a type eagerness that's well suited for today's fast-paced organizations.

I cannot too strongly emphasize the spirit of teamwork that she-he brings, as well. She's-he's first to volunteer, flexible and willing to work on any project that's assigned to her-him. Mack Daddy multitasks effectively, is dependable and eternally upbeat.

I am happy and proud to be able to call this matter to your attention, and please do not hesitate to follow up with me if I could be of further assistance.

Best regards,
Mr. Troll Trollington

(Extra Credit)

The ultimate nightmare: FALLOUT with a listed reference.

Problem: "I put my coworker-manager-teacher-bestie down as a work reference. Things happened and now she HATES me! But I already applied and they have her phone number. AM I DOOMED?!"

Solution: Call or visit each employer that has this frenemy listed as a reference and explain.

You: "Sorry but Jay Lopy has received a number of calls about me from interested employers and she is getting a little annoyed. Would you mind replacing her with this reference instead? [provide a new reference] I really appreciate that and have a wonderful afternoon!"

Should your friend-turned-serpent-tongue-enemy already have been contacted, this explanation *might* provide cover for her 'off' attitude or comments (for a little damage control). Friendly word of advice for here on out, **1** have a pow-wow with your references and ask what they will say about you **before** you list them, **2** please, please, please try to keep things cool between you and your references during your job hunt, and last but certainly not least **3** stay in touch with your references throughout the application process. "Hey there, just calling to see how you are doing... so how are your kids?"

THANKS BUT I'M COOL

EXPRESS A LITTLE GRATITUTE
AND THE OUTCOME WILL BE
FAR MORE FAVORABLE FOR YOU

THIRTY FIVE

....

THANKS BUT NO THANKS

"I totally almost got hired!"

Not that you're being told how to run your life or anything, but if you don't plan to send a thank you note to the hiring manager, you might as well tear up your resume into as many tiny pieces as you can, set it on fire and then stomp all over it.

Employers under major stress to hire new people worry not only about qualifications…but about whether the new person's going to be THE JERK WHO RUINS THE GROUP.

No one wants to put up with rude behavior.

The cool thing about thank you notes is that all it takes is a few friendly words on a card or email to prove you have OUTSTANDING manners and much, much more. (OMG fact: some employers have an unspoken rule—no thank you note, no job offer.)

You can learn this lesson now, or you can learn this lesson after paying for it with misery, time, and lost opportunity. ~~You have 3 seconds to decide~~.

What you should do next...

Look for an example that sounds like something you could write, but be sure to match your tone of voice in the thank you note to the company's culture, as you perceive it. For example, for casual jobs, use an informal-style thank you note because if a person is too formal, you couldn't imagine them fitting in, even with stellar credentials and devilish good looks. The reverse is just as true, so for upscale or "serious" type organizations, choose more refined language.

To deliver your thank you note, you have two options: snail mail or email. Each choice has a plus and minus.

SNAIL MAIL.
Buy a pack of cheap, plain 4 x 3-inch thank you cards with envelopes from a local dollar store or retailer. If you are randomly firing off resumes (without including a cover letter **page 255**), paperclip a thank you card to each and every resume that you pass out. For actual phone-face interviews, buy a stamp and mail a thank you card that same day or within 3 days at the very latest. The plus with hand-written cards is that it adds a warm, personal touch. The minus is hand-written cards take time to arrive and cost money.

EMAIL.
For resume blasting (without including a cover letter **page 255**), email a thank you note the same day or no later than 3 days to each and every employer you contact. For actual phone-face interviews, email a thank you note no later than 7 days at the very latest. (Always *hand-deliver or email* companies looking to hire **right away** because by the time post office delivers your mail, it might be too late!) The plus with emailing a thank you note is that it's free and your emailed thank you note can be forwarded to other company decision makers. The minus is that email is less personal than a hand-written note.

282

At this stage, since you're just randomly blasting off resume-thank you note combos, you won't have to include the 'To Ms. [blank]'-part. Feel free to create a knockoff thank you note from any example below that *pops* out at you, but remember, **spelling counts**.

Have a good tour! It's time to WOW the hiring manager with a juicy and delicious thank you.

Tasty example #1

My name is Sugar Bomb and I would love nothing more than to learn every aspect of this business, from the ground up, alongside side an experienced team such as yours.

If you would like to talk with me or schedule an interview, please call me at ███████ or email me at ████████████ @ ██████. Thank you for your consideration.

Sincerely,
Sugar Bomb

Tasty example #2

My name is Boom Shakalaka and I am writing to extend my thanks for taking the time to review my resume. I'm particularly interested in ████████ and would love to start in this area.

Please let me know if you need additional references or information to help make your decision.

Best Regards,
Boom Shakalaka

Tasty example #3

Reading over the job description for this opening, I see my best qualities. For this reason, I've included my resume for the position of ▮▮▮▮▮▮.

I look forward to answering any questions you may have.

Thank you so much,
Gummy Bear

Tasty example #4

My resume is a preview of what I can bring to your office, as I would very much like to join your team. If you think I have what it takes to contribute to your organization, please call me at once.

Best wishes for your continued success,
Harass Mint

Tasty example #5

My name is Q. T. Patooty and we share the same excitement for the future of the ▮▮▮▮▮▮ industry.

I believe that hard work and commitment is at the root of success and would consider joining you a real privilege.

Looking forward to hearing from you,
Q. T. Patooty

Tasty example #6

You have become a valuable resource in my job search and learning about your organization has only strengthened my desire in becoming a part of your team.

My sincerest thanks for thinking of me and making the time for introduction.

Yours truly,
Raymond Raymond bo Baymond, banana fanna fo Faymond, me my mo Maymond...RAYMOND!!!!

USE THIS SPACE TO SQUEEZE IN YOUR OWN, CUSTOMIZED THANK YOU.

...CHECK OUT THE THANK YOU NOTES FOR AFTER THE INTERVIEW ▶

"You give me an interview? BAMN, you get a thank you note!!!" Address the thank you note to the MAIN hiring manager that you interacted with during your interview. For panel interviews—or if you were introduced to several company representatives the day of—just thank each individual by name in **one** card. That will help you avoid thank you note overkill.

While on the topic, please…pretty please. With sugar on top. Do not misspell any names, titles or words! Job hunters can more or less blow it by using incorrect spelling.

Sugar-coated example #1

Dear Mr. Robot Baby,

I just wanted to thank you and your coworkers for taking the time to speak with me last week about the open position. It's great to finally put a face to the name!

I appreciate you making me feel welcome during my visit at your office. Please extend my gratitude to Mr. Deja Vu and Ms. Cliché and anyone else that I may have overlooked, as I do not have their contact information. I was particularly struck by the impressive team you've built and would welcome the chance to work with you.

~~Please enjoy all of the glitter! (****stuff the envelope with a ton of glitter****)~~

Best regards,
A. Thang

Sugar-coated example #2

To Mr. Baller,

Meeting with you, Ms. Trabajo, and the other members of your team last week made for an exciting and complete day. I was particularly struck by the enthusiasm everyone at ████ has for teamwork and customer service.

I would be thrilled to join the group you've built and put my strengths to work on your behalf. If you need additional references or information to help make your decision, please let me know. ~~I've slipped in a $20 gift certificate to speed things up a bit~~.

Sincerely,
Brew Tilly Scorched

Sugar-coated example #3

Dear Dr. Ken U. Spread,

Thank you for spending so much time with me on the 14th and fitting me into your busy schedule. It was wonderful to discover that whether it's teamwork or patient care, we both enjoy connecting with people.

If you need additional references or information to help make your decision, please let me know. I would welcome the chance to work with you.

Sincerely yours,
Pookie

Sugar-coated example #4

To Ms. Itoaduso,

I just wanted to thank you for taking the time to speak with me. I'd love to be able to help you achieve a gold star on your review next year and be a part of your work.

Feel free to reach out to me at any time if you'd like to continue the dialogue. I would welcome the chance to speak with you. ~~Studies show that 9 out of 10 employers cry three months after hiring me. They wished they hired me sooner.~~

Gratitude and best wishes,
Tom Foolery

Sugar-coated example #5

Dear Dr. Name Namerson,

During my interview today I could sense the passion that you and your team have for the company, and it made for an exciting and complete day. I'm grateful for the opportunity to meet with you and it's easy to see why your practice carries the reputation that it does in our community.

Feel free to call me at ██████████████████ or email me at ████████████@████████.com if you feel that we're a good fit. I have no qualms about setting up another meeting.

Yours truly,
Dan D. Lyons

Sugar-coated example #6

To Sgt. Barry Cade,

I wanted to take a moment to personally thank you for spending a generous amount of time with me during the interview.

Speaking with you about your experiences in the field and the importance of community-based policing has left a very strong impression with me.

Please let me know if further information or references are needed before the final decisions are made regarding this position. I look forward to servicing not just the department, but the community as a whole. ~~For f@ck$ sake, stop making excuses. Hire me already you bloody kangaroo!~~

Best regards,
Joe Mamma

USE THIS SPACE TO SQUEEZE IN YOUR OWN, CUSTOMIZED THANK YOU.

(Need to bolster up woefully saggy self-esteem? Stop by **page 147** on your way out!)

THIRTY SIX

....

DOCU-DRAMA

Let's make some assumptions (or guesses if you like). Stuff happened and your identity documents are missing, right?

Ok, enter super focus mode and dim everything else around you. Your job just got a whole lot easier as this section really cuts through all of that internet mumbo-jumbo with clear instructions on how to obtain your:

- valid ID
- social security card
- school transcripts & vocational license
- W2 tax forms
- military DD214
- passport

ID…why you always need validation?
Most jobs require a valid pictured identification card. Unlike a school ID, a **valid ID** can only be issued by a government agency like the Department of Motor Vehicles. All valid ID's must have your full name, date of birth, physical description, photograph, and be currently valid. An expired ID is not valid, even if it has been issued by the DMV. That's why your school ID, or expired DMV-issued ID, or expired driver's license would not considered valid for employment purposes.

Visit **www.dmv.org** to find the nearest Department of Motor Vehicles location and pay a visit to a DMV near your home and apply for valid ID card. Look prim and proper because the DMV will not permit you to airbrush or photoshop your headshot later. (Don't forget to pick up the driver's permit study guide while you are there!)

Social Security card.
Replacing you or your child's lost or stolen social security card is FREE and easy.

You can apply for a replacement card by completing an application for a social security card (called a Form SS-5). **A driver's license is not required**, but you will need a recently issued document that shows your identity. Call and ask your local social security office what documents are allowed to be used as proof that you are who you say you are. The social security administration will also require proof you are a United States citizen or a resident alien (as in immigrant with documents, not extraterrestrial living secretly among us ~~ALL YOUR CHILDREN ARE BELONG TO US~~).

Visit the official social security office website at www.ssa.gov to find a location near you.

Bear in mind that you are only allowed (3) replacements per year and (10) replacements during your life.

REAL LIFE WARNING: Hide your birth date and social security number like your life depends on it, especially from shady relatives, classmates, neighbors and coworkers. With your name, birth date and social security number, identity thieves can cause a serious headache or even **jail time for you!** Criminals often use other people's name-birth date-social security number to commit crimes. Then police end up arresting the poor, innocent victim whose identity was stolen.

School transcripts, diplomas, degrees, certifications, professional or vocational license.

Call and request copies of your transcript, diploma or degree from the Registrar's Office at your trade school, college or university. "Official" school transcripts are sealed (which means that the school sends it directly in a sealed enveloped) and can cost money ($) to order. "Unofficial" school transcripts can be faxed, emailed, printed from an online page, usually free of charge.

For certifications such as a Red Cross CPR or HIPAA certificate, find the school or individual that certified you and request a copy or update from them. For professional or vocational licenses, such as a pharmacy tech or contractor's license, you must contact your state's licensing board.

Remember, paperwork gets lost all of the time, so be prepared to wait longer than expected and spend more energy than you would like getting the certificate you earned physically in your hand.

PEACE OF MIND: always send applications for licenses and certificates through U.S. Post Office Certified Mail along with a return label and tracking number. The Post Office will charge a few dollars for this service, but the tracking number and return label is **legal evidence** that you submitted your application before the deadline should your application get "lost." A few buckaroos is worth peace of mind, no?

293

W2

If an employer asks you for a W2, it's a little unusual, but if your date asks you for a W2—dump this person immediately!

A W2 is a United States tax form that employers issue that states how much they paid you in that year. A W2 is used for taxes. A W2 is also used to prove that you work or worked at XYZ company, show how much you were paid, and to help you agonize, philosophize, and cry about how much money the government took out of your paycheck that particular year.

Government agencies and a very few employers (legality varies from state to state) may request your previous year's W2 to see if you ~~lied~~ *inadvertently misrepresented* your stated income on the job application or background documents.

If your W2 forms are missing or lost, you have two options: **1** you can ask the previous employer for a copy of your W2 or **2** order copies of your past W2 tax return from the IRS. (An official copy of your tax return from the IRS will contain all of the information about income you will need, if you're concerned about the original being lost.)

Employers are required to mail your W2 (for the prior year) by January 31st.

FYI: when you are hired, you will complete a W4 form so that your employer can withold the correct amount of federal income tax from your pay. You will also be asked to complete an I-9 Form, called an Employment Eligibility Verification form, to prove you are legally entitled to work in the United States. The forms are simple and easy to ~~fake~~ complete.

Military DD-214.
Prior-military members should navigate online to the following addy: www.archives.gov/veterans/military-service-records or call the National Archives and Records Administration by dailing (314) 801-0800. Once you receive the Form DD-214, sign the request and send it in.

Passport.
If your job requires travel outside of the United States, then you will need to order a passport.

Before you go through the trouble of applying, make sure that you are not on parole, probation or owe any money to child support. Your request for a passport will be declined and, as an added bonus, the government will keep your application fee.

To order a passport (Order? Yes, it costs money.), take 2 colored passport photos, fill out the application (called Form DS-11), navigate to the nearest U.S. post office location and apply inside. Call the post office ahead of time. You'll want to find out the business hours and what specific post office locations handle passport services, not all do. Also ask what you need to bring with you to order a passport (most probably a birth certificate or naturalization papers plus an ID and money for the processing fee). Some local city halls also offer passport services. Make a call and find out.

Need a passport immediately? Lost or stolen passport? Then call 1-877-487-2778 right away. You will have to fill out another application form (DS-11) and complete a statement regarding the lost or stolen passport (DS-64).

Visit **www.travel.state.gov/passport** for more information.

THIRTY SEVEN

....

I HEREBY RESIGN FROM MY
SOUL SUCKING JOB

You find yourself laying awake, staring at the ceiling at 3:00 am wondering why you took the job. Then you spent some time crossing your fingers hoping that things would change. You tried convincing yourself that this is just until something better comes along. But you realized it was time to leave when you could no longer look in the mirror and convince yourself that the money is worth it. You're a human being, and like the rest of us, have to go through the emotions, even a kind of second-guessing ritual, before finally deciding that there's too much life ahead of you to spend your time faking who you are day in, day out.

Get me out of this hellhole!
Some bosses react oddly vindictive to resignations.

Even if you've earned top marks and there's no bad blood, some sorry bosses take employee resignations personally (love hurts?) and that's when the situation can become quite grim.

One of the most important reasons to write a resignation letter is to **protect yourself** against false accusations made by a spiteful boss.

(The type who will try to drag your reputation through the mud to future job prospects by pretending you left on unimaginably horrible terms when you actually worked your @ss off.) A "Letter of Resignation" actually proves that you left on positive terms. Not only that, it's paper evidence that you gave your boss reasonable notice. And not only that, it also shows you know how to communicate effectively, in case they try to pull a "performance issues" on you afterwards. Exiting with a resignation letter is pure smarts.

Today is my last day. (At work, not on Earth!)
Three things to know *BEFORE* submitting a resignation letter.

1 Give ~~the middle finger~~ tearful hugs and goodbyes to coworkers *before* turning in resignation letter. No matter how popular you are at work, your last official ~~day~~ hour could very well be the moment you turn in your resignation letter. (Do you want to know why? Keep reading then!)

2 Print out two copies of your resignation letter. One copy will stay safely at home inside your work documents folder. One copy will be placed in your personnel file with human resources at work.

3 Get your boss to sign both copies of your resignation letter **right on the spot**. Whatever happens, do not put it off until the next day. Should your boss refuse to sign and get weirdly defensive about it, then write at the bottom of your resignation letter, "Assistant Manager Jack Schidt refused to sign my resignation letter on 04-01-2018 at approximately 4:59 PM," and gracefully exit the office and have a human resources representative sign it.

(To answer the first point as to why many organizations will not allow you to continue working after you turn in your resignation letter, it's because employees on occasion wig out and create a scene on their last day. Sparked by that fear, many companies have introduced a new rule: receive resignation, kindly escort individual from our premises as soon as possible. Today's world is all about this legal mumbo jumbo called "liabilities." Liabilities can be things like a slip and fall injury on your last day at work, or screaming 'you screwed me!' in your boss's face, or company representatives having to explain to the media what the bloodbath was all about. Although marching employees out, especially the ones leaving on good terms, appears like a ~~cruel joke~~ terrible practice, if they only single-out the office weirdos, they'll sue for discrimination.)

Your Name
Street address
City, State, Zip Code
Phone number
E-mail address

April 1, 2018

Company Name
Employer's name
Position or title
Mailing address
City, State, Zip Code

Re: Letter of Resignation

Dear Lee Departed,

Please accept this letter as my formal notification that I am resigning my position as ▮▮▮▮▮ with ▮▮▮▮▮, Inc. effective Friday, April 1, 2018.

But before I leave, I want to take this opportunity to let you know that I will always be grateful to you and can only hope that my new colleagues will be as generous and supportive as you've been. This was not an easy decision for me.

I feel duty-bound to help with the transition and will gladly extend my role for an additional two weeks, if necessary. Please let me know if you need my assistance in any other way.

Lee, what a great and distinct pleasure it has been to work as a part of your team. I wish you and ▮▮▮▮▮, Inc. much success in the future.

Sincerely,
Dain Bramaged

SPECIAL CIRCUMSTANCES

THIRTY EIGHT

....

MAN YOUR BATTLE STATION BOYS AND GIRLS

If you are reading this you have survived it all. You have survived conflict zones, traumas, devastation, heartbreak, the constant flow of mind-numbing b*llsh!t that would wear down even the most hardened rock… and yet here you are. ALIVE and unmatched by your civilian peers. Our armed forces turned you from a show pony into a war horse.

In a few moments, we're going to put your game-changing talent to use with a slowly progressing, ease-the-stick-in-your-butt guide designed to help veterans get on point.

All clear. You are good to go.

Told them I'm a vet. They looked at me like I'm some kind of mutant. (I M4 real!)
Message boards can mind-f*ck you.

Spending time on a site, 5-10-30 minutes, reading "CIVIES TUK ER JERBS" posts will make your balls shrink a bit. (Figuratively not literally and therefore applies to both sexes.) You'll read about companies or government organizations snubbing vets, dressing down vets...by the time you're finished, you'll be left thinking that America's leading employers are chemically neutering vets and probably considering career options like singing and arranging flowers.

Contrary to spirited message board postings, the scary thing about the job market is not that it's hostile to vets. The scary thing about the job market is that it's mostly indifferent.

Even if you were a medically trained doctor in the USMC, without preparation the interview will go sour right before your eyes, military experience or not. Just because you were an MP doesn't mean you can instantly become a police officer. Law enforcement agencies take interviewing-seriousness to the next level—you can feel them judge your every move—and this is where most applicants screw up. The cold, hard truth is vets who treat job hunting as an afterthought are going to struggle landing ANY job. Life is not going to be easy just because you served, even if you hold a degree. And the difference between a resume versus interviewing skills is HUGE. (Before you start gearing up for a freak out, **page 195** will get you squared away. Please sit down. Everything's under control. Situation normal.)

Remember that the Department of Defense is not a job corps program. They're in the business of defending our country. If you happened to gain future job skills while you served, then great. If you didn't, then that's perfectly fine, too. There is no set rule that you must have your career figured out by a certain age. So bounce from job-to-job until you find a spot where you are happy and set up camp, or enroll in college or trade school classes (the ones that sound the coolest) until you find what works for you! The pressure to land the "perfect" job right out the gate comes from only one place—**you**.

Military-specific headhunters.
As you may or may not know, trigger happy, online spray & pray resume blasting will not get you the results you're looking for...you need to paint your target. What we're going to do now is begin compiling a list of headhunters who specialize in transitional employment because applications, resumes and cover letters *might* get you interviews, but networking gets you jobs.

The websites below represent a tiny sampling of **specialized** recruiters—meaning they're neck deep in connections to some of America's finest companies with generous military-friendly hiring policies. Not only can they help you make the transition to the civilian workforce easier (and save you from government red tape hell), many of the reps are themselves proud veterans.

www.bradley-morris.com
www.cameron-brooks.com
www.lucasgroup.com
www.orioninternational.com

Know that headhunter services are completely FREE of charge, as recruiters are paid by the organizations who hire them (to find and screen qualified candidates). For you that typically means 1 NO minimum wage b.s. and 2 NO 100% commission and 3 thorough resume and interviewing preparation (again, often by reps with military experience). More importantly, these specialized headhunters are a part of the *inner-circle* and can make you a "connected" candidate, in with private industry businesses and civil service agencies.

To create your own list of recruiters in addition to the four shown above, Google® search using any of the following keywords: hire military grade talent, military talent, hire top quality military, military placement, military recruiting services, military placement firm, jobs for military vets. Then write or print out the contact info of the specialized recruiters you find online. Finally, make a call and schedule an appointment for a phone or face meeting and see what happens. (Any time you go kinetic, wear your interviewing clothes. This is a face-to-face meeting with a serious business contact.)

Always **ask for a referral** if a particular recruiter cannot help you!

You: "Ok, thank you anyway, ma'am-sir…so who would you suggest I call?"

HEAD'S UP: A legitimate headhunter will not charge you for connecting you to a job, *ever*. Headhunters are paid by the company that hires you. In your job search, you may encounter fraudsters that pretend to be recruiters to lure you into a scam. Some of these organizations will even host "job fairs," but it will become painfully obvious after you approach the representatives at the booth that they're just looking to make money off of veterans, not offer placement opportunities. ~~Bait-and-switch maggots~~!

Civilianize your resume.

The United States military is the largest organization OF ANY KIND on planet Earth. There is no enemy out there who will stand toe to toe with our incredible armed forces. But employers could care less unless YOU decipher how your well-honed military experience fits into civilian positions.

Most employers will look at you sideways if you come at them with military jargon like 11B, E-6, Staff Sergeant or Senior Signals Sergeant, MOS25X. Their eyes will glaze over. The only thought will be Whiskey-Tango-Foxtrot, please speak like a human being.

What you'll need is an online military-to-civilian translator—a tool that enables you generate a *civilian job description* of your duties by simply typing in your branch and MOC (military occupation classification)—to help you market your experience in everyday layman's terms and build a formidable bio.

Listed below is exactly that, three online military-to-civilian translators.

www.onetonline.org/crosswalk/MOC/
www.careerinfonet.org/moc/
www.taonline.com/mosdot

One of the most disruptive forces to veterans, especially those who recently served long deployments overseas, is the irrational fear that their skills won't translate to the civilian workplace. The above three military-to-civilian translators will help reprogram your belief system, as you have too many skills to your advantage to be worried: for one proven track record. The military sent you coast-to-coast and around the world, gaining you a level of "real-time" experience most companies struggle to find in civilian applicants, even with 4 to 8 years of corporate work behind them. Plus you've braved a work environment that would turn ordinary men and women into mice.

In fact, some accomplished vets choose to "dummy" their resume to find an 'in,' as being WAY over-qualified for an entry or mid-level opening can, ironically, push their resume to the "unqualified" pile (especially inside mammoth government bureaucracies).

Keep in mind that these overqualified Airmen, Coast Guardsmen, Marines, Sailors, and Soldiers didn't come out the womb ready to bust out interviews and job hunt, they worked at it tirelessly. Put in your share and whatever you do, never tone down or oversimplify the magnitude of your duties. Jobs aren't going to come looking for you now that you're out. You must switch to self-promoting and take credit for your military accomplishments.

Don't be afraid to be assertive. That's what hiring managers are looking for.

Veteran hiring preference? Suuuure.
According to *cynics*, here are veteran hiring benefits in a nutshell: of course you get points, dear veteran. It's just that nobody pays attention to points and there's no practical way to enforce hiring policy or do anything to management when they violate the hiring policy. But you do get points, and hiring managers really, really value them very highly. Honest. F'reals. Mm-hmm.

It's high time this was said, veteran points for civil service jobs are ten gallons of bull-f*cking-cr@p. Or are they? Breaking it down, the point system grants 5 or 10 points to veterans, which are added to a passing score on federal civil service exams. Your points are not entitlement, they are a hard earned foot-in-the-door. But the reality is that there are not enough government jobs to go around to employ every vet, and most of the .gov openings are also advertised to civilians with -0% military experience.

Like private industry jobs, that means they'll always find ways to hire the MOST qualified, educated or **connected** person (page 175). Vet or civie, when the hiring manager wants you, they'll "see to it" that you get the job, one way or another.

The true power of veteran preference comes in to play when applying for government positions under strict mandates. No civilians can apply to these openings, period. End of story. And *then* you will see how 5 or 10 points and 'veteran preference' all of a sudden matter. So don't puss out now! ~~Ninjas are trained to attack when you are at your weakest~~! Consider vet status a force multiplier, especially for jobs not open to civilians without military experience.

As you were.

THIRTY NINE

....

DON'T BE A PSYCHO-EX(TERN)

Volunteering looks just as good (if not BETTER) than a paid position because instead of using empty buzz words like "I'm a dedicated employee" you're actually practicing what you preach.

Of course, with school externship-internships, participation is mandatory. (Schools want to expose students to a real-world environment.) But *why* you contribute is not our concern here. Getting a job lined up as a brilliant volunteer is. So prepare your eyeballs, as these pages clearly lay out the answers to the most difficult problems volunteers face.

Armed with this knowledge, you will not have to find job connections. Job connections **will find you**.

Know how to win.
The higher-ups will fast-track you into a paid position if they think they can't live without you. But you must **1** be up front and tell your boss that your goal is a permanent, salaried job and **2** always look busy.

Telling your boss that you're interested in joining their team is pretty straight-forward. Looking like a busy-body to a "shoulder surfing" manager, not so much. Want to know what a busy volunteer looks like?

> *Their desk area is somewhat messy, cluttered and never perfectly organized. They walk with a purpose, and fast, and look like they know exactly where they are going—like something important is about to happen. They always carry a notebook. In their cubicle they keep a headset on. Sometimes they stare at their screen with a frustrated look and click on a pen continuously to scare away others. They ask a lot of complicated questions.*

When your work runs out, volunteer to help coworkers. When all work runs out, find a way to look busy. People almost *always* judge on the APPEARANCE of things rather than the naked facts of the matter.

Very, very wicked attitude.
Managers do not listen to what you say. They watch what you do, as one action will reveal you more than a thousand words.

The most basic task that you have to complete as a volunteer is to *get there when scheduled*. Show up on time, and if you're running late or can't make it for some reason, call ahead and provide a darn good explanation why. Volunteer work is as important as paid work, according to U.S. hiring managers, **so act like it**. And dress like it. You're on their turf and business has its own culture. That means turn off your phone, chum it up with decision makers, and take pride in your work, ESPECIALLY when it seems like there's nothing in it for you. Volunteerism fills up all of the empty space on your resume and connects you to people with the power to hire you.

Deliver on your end and you'll 'step into' your dream job without ever having to interview.

They hate me.
You might be only 10 minutes into your first shift at your site and everyone's talking sheet. You are hereby strongly advised to butt-out, duck and stay the hell out of the crossfire. The moment you begin picking sides is the moment **you** become a target.

Again, unless you are willing to sacrifice your career, piss off your coworkers, piss off your boss and irritate HR, go radio silent on ANY conversations that are hurtful to others. You can be there for a coworker that wants to talk or just needs a listening ear to vent, but stay neutral. You are a good person and volunteerism builds killer references. Don't allow your involvement in gossip or office politics to change that.

> SCHOOL EXTERNS-INTERNS: fax in time sheets BEFORE the due date each week, otherwise you'll stand a good chance of having to repeat your entire school program due to strict deadlines, which mandated by the state.

Do not kill people.
"Human beings are not on the endangered species list. What's the big deal?" Medical volunteers who do not confirm the patient's information (so that the right patients are getting the right treatment) can give toxic doses of medicine to babies, children and adults. Medicine to some is *poison* to others.

And if you're a trade job volunteer, you'll be working with dangerous tools, chemicals and in high risk environments. Regardless of your craft, now is not the time to 'figure things out.'

ASK for directions if you are not 100% sure what to do next. Human beings are people too!

You: "I don't quite know what to do here but thought that this would be the best approach. Am I on the right track?"

Coworkers are my ~~future ex's~~ colleagues.
"I'm not sure if my coworkers are getting hotter or my standards are getting lower!"

Listen, we have some crazies in our midst and your volunteer site is no exception. Be very cautious and don't be afraid to politely decline any offer to have drinks or dinner outside of work with brand new coworkers, especially the supervisors, managers or doctors, unless of course it's an official work-related activity. You don't know these people and when stuff goes down, it's always the new guy-gal that gets thrown under the bus.

You: "Thanks for the invite but I just like to relax after work."

FORTY

....

RESPECT MY AUTHORITAH!

Problems getting your foot-in-the-door because a Gatekeeper is
****blocking you from the hiring manager? This will help with the crying.
Not totally stop it, but perhaps turn it into tears of joy.

What (kind of a creature) is a Gatekeeper?
Imagine walking into a business to apply for an opening, a GATEKEEPER
is an employee that pushes your application into the garbage when you
are safely out of sight.

What motivates Gatekeepers to trash applications? Who knows, but
the most probable explanations include fear of competition (the risk of
losing their job to you), envy or just cheap laughs…hoping to offset their
unhappiness?

Regardless, Gatekeepers control access to the big boss who calls the
shots—the hiring manager—and **that is not acceptable**. These pages
clearly lay out the solution to the most difficult Gatekeeper problem that
you'll encounter in a door-to-door job hunt. Armed with this knowledge,
no Gatekeeper will dare mess with you because you'll become…
unmesswithable.

Put on your near-indestructible suit of armor.
As you enter the business to apply for a job, the brutal Gatekeeper will be distracted trying to figure out if you are a salesperson or customer, which is totally understandable since your visit is unexpected. The clever dialogue below can create the *illusion* that you're known, not a stranger. Known people are put through to the hiring manager without getting verbally beat up by the Gatekeeper. That is a fact.

You: "Hello, Kitty. If you can let the manager know that it's Mosity, Annie Mosity waiting for him, thank you."

Gatekeeper: "May I ask what this is about?"

You: "Yes, of course you can, I'm here to go over my documents with him. If you could just let him know that I'm here."

Gatekeeper: "The manager is out of the office."

You: "I understood this was the best time to come in. So the manager is not on property?"

Gatekeeper: "No, sorry."

> *Something is way wrong here. The reptilian stare is a dead giveaway.*

You: Would you mind giving this to the manager? [hand over your completed application, resume and thank you note] I'd appreciate that. May I have your company's business card?

*Anytime you sense a Gatekeeper, **ask for a business card**. When a business card is handed to you, don't just grab it and shove it down your pocket. Make the Gatekeeper feel important by taking a good 3-5 second look at the card—you might see something that could spark a conversation. Write on the back of the card the name of the Gatekeeper, the hiring manager and the date. This will be worth gold when following up with the higher-ups. Now PLACE the card in your wallet to signal their importance to you.*

You: I will give Mr. Wuttzisface [the hiring manager] a call to follow up with him. When do you expect him back in? Okay, thank you. Kitty, it was a real pleasure meeting you!

Assertive kindness is the best way to snap Gatekeepers out of their evil trance. By asking for a business card and explaining that you'll be following up with the hiring manager, you are putting the Gatekeeper on notice that any funny business with your application would be a very, very bad idea.

(Extra Credit)

It's the whole package, not just the dialogue.
You can turn a statement into an **order** (do this or else!) by using a downward inflexion in your voice. When introducing yourself, make sure your voice goes down towards the end of sentences. Most job hunters have an upward inflection on the ends of sentences. Upward inflections are perceived as questions and invites objections from the Gatekeeper. It also sounds very insecure—the opposite of authority—and more likely than not, a frazzled job applicant.

You can also transmit authority by speaking more s...l...o...w...l...y. Just think, how would a serious business contact sound like? Practice making your voice sound deeper, while still sounding polite, and try to match your tone, pitch, pauses, and emphasis with the manager's once the receptionist puts you through.

FORTY ONE

....

THUGNIFICENT

Cripwalks in (like a boss) and introduces self to the hiring manager.

Hiring manager: "Pleasure to meet you."

Homeboy: "Sup dawg, dey call me Mousy because I like to go in and out of holes."

Oh hell no…HELL NO…We're going to change the way you think, talk and act RIGHT NOW!

Menace to society.
You saw the movie? It does not end well.

Most peeps who join a gang step away within 12 months. (This is a ~~straight up~~ fact.) Gangs lure you in by promising you a form of respect, a "cause" to fight for, and easy money…**but it's a ploy**. By actually joining a gang you get the OPPOSITE. (What a ripoff!)

What you're really being sold is a fairytale…and a disaster waiting to happen.

You can't go anywhere now because it's too dangerous. Childhood friends turn into enemies. Selling drugs or stealing becomes *the only way* to make money, that is, until someone rats you out. Locked up, you watch your back not so much from your enemies, but from your own homeboys or homegirls filled with jealousy, envy and power struggles. Yes, the war is against your enemies, but most of the time you'll be greenlighting your own. And those who get sentenced to 3 years leave in 15 or never, because you just can't sit back, watch and see who could out-crazy each other. 'Don't start nothing, won't be nothing' doesn't apply in prison. YOU have to put the steel to work or it's gonna be YOU on the other side of the blade.

You see, it's a dirty game and after you're locked up and people count you out, that's when true colors show. All this time "respect" isn't what stopped homies from trying to get at your one true love, or harassing your family. Fear is what kept everyone back.

Now that you're in prison, who's going to protect your family? (You know, the people who stuck by you through thick and thin. The ones who didn't crack under pressure.)

I don't know if I can go against my peeps. What should I do?
A lot of G's say that cycle runs so deep with friends or family that, as much as they want to, they can't step away. That's called "defeatism." Defeatism is negative-self talk and **very** destructive.

Once you convince your own mind that there's nothing you can do about your life, it becomes a self-fulfilling prophecy. Repeating inside your head 'I'm powerless because of my friend's-family's involvement' is giving yourself a permission slip to do nothing about it. One indisputable lesson that history teaches is that your life can be radically changed, in any direction, *any moment you decide*. However, to achieve a result, you first need to believe you can actually achieve it. (Goals won't motivate you, dreams will.) Once you get over the negative self-talk, you'll figure out a way to "go dark" and stealth away not because you have to, but because *you want to*.

Yes, keeping in good graces with your **homeboys** or **homegirls** while stepping away isn't always easy, but believe it or not, when your *real* friends and family see your determination to change—to be somebody— and succeed in life, THEY'LL BE PROUD of you and root you on!

Of course, enemies on the streets aren't going to care that you're a changed person, so you'll still have to watch your back. But real courage means **not worrying about what people think** (including homeboys or homegirls) and doing what's best for YOU so that your name does not get added to that group of wasted talent, stuck on the shelf for the rest of their life…while the world goes on without them.

If you're reading this section, then your mind might very well be poisoned with FUD (fear, uncertainty and doubt). Let's press the pause button on all those thoughts racing through your head. Read the five sections listed below *first*, to help sort things out in your life, then circle back and continue with this section. Chin up, you are not alone.

"Always forgive your enemies—nothing annoys them so much." -Oscar Wilde
There's a time and place for everything. In prison acting hardcore puts fear in homies and enemies where ~~you're worried about being killed~~ it's a straight up death match. But OUTSIDE PRISON acting hardcore is simply known as being a douche. In society, being a douche doesn't mean you're tough. It just means you're a douche.

That's the reason why people with a cutthroat mindset do not go far in life because you'll always need to rely on people's good graces to move up. "Trust no one" might be the first rule of prison, but it's the worst rule of society. And that's also why hiring managers hold no respect for active gang members. To them, they're all violent out-of-control maniacs with no people skills.

We must get you out of your zone of trying to act hardcore and get people to see you as an adult, a human being, with real potential and talent (in other words, what you're really like when homies aren't around).

Getcho gangsta ~~on~~ turned off.
Make a habit, break a habit. We must reprogram your belief system. Here are the ten BIGGEST issues ex-G's face today and how to handle them with total confidence.

■ The stink eye. Mad dogging. The death stare. The dirty stare. The evil eye. 'Staring down' goes by many names but is best described as this glare you can just feel on the side of your face when walking by shady dudes or dudettes. The stare down is a challenge. Looking down is failing the challenge and makes you look like a limping zebra (projecting weakness) in the eyes of hungry vultures. But making aggressive eye contact back signals you're a territorial challenger. So instead, look peeps right in the eyes. Square your shoulders, keep your face blank, acknowledge them with a nod and an emotionless "hi" greeting to show respect. Walk past them with a purpose while 'scanning' your environment. ('Scanning' shows you are aware of your surroundings and not intimidated or dingy.) No smiling this time. A smile might come off as high and mighty and provoke things.

■ Advertising numbers like 13, 69, 86, 420, 666, 187 will signal TROUBLE to employers. Use the billions and billions of other number combos for your resume, email address, phone number and ~~eyelid tattoos~~.

■ ~~Dey was talking s**t so dey deserved it!~~ Keeping a cool head is one of the most valuable personality traits at work and in life. Acting out frustrations by throwing pens or slamming doors or coworkers will get you plenty of attention, but not the kind of attention you want: the popo with the fofo.

■ Hundreds of doctors, athletes, lawyers, engineers, teachers, scientists and entertainers were ~~fired~~ dismissed today. Being let go is perfectly normal and nothing to beat yourself up over. It only means there isn't a match, that's all, and most companies have a neutral referral policy anyway and generally avoid giving away details on how or why you left. (**Page 59** explains how to handle this question at an interview.)

■ Mistakes make the best stories. (Remember that time you tried to pull the gun out the cop's holster??? GOTCHA GUN PIGGY!!!!! HAHAHA-HAHAHA....oh, those were the days.)

■ Be patient with yourself. Did you get that? BE PATIENT WITH YOURSELF. Give yourself the room to adjust slowly and comfortably to the working world. You can reduce the shock of entering a brand new life and job by taking things day-by-day. In fact, soldiers who go through intense training in boot camp use this trick to make it through: don't think about what the rest of the year—or the rest of your life—is going to be like, only think about getting through today.

■ Difficulty understanding directions or reading could be a sign of a learning disability OR YOU MIGHT NEED TO STRAP ON SOME GLASSES. Smart people like to ask smarter people, like eye doctors, for help. A disability is nothing to be embarrassed about, even for a triple OG. (Do you want to know more? Flip to **page 343**.)

321

■ Rich people understand that it's not about how much money you make, it's about how much you KEEP. No amount is too small to save! Go out for coffee not dinner. Pack a lunch from home. Grab a cane and wig and ask for a senior citizen discount. Do not spend EXPECTED income or shop with credit cards. Shamelessly behave just like the rich but without the rich-y attitude.

■ People naturally like to do favors. If you want something, just ask. Most of the time, they will happily say yes. Refuse to involve yourself in theft or hoodwinking of any kind.

■ Before you start singing your guts out about everything you've ever done, coworkers are moody and enjoy switching sides to the new flavor-of-the-month. In a work setting, bragging about your hot new ghettolicious date or past misdeeds might come back to haunt you. Everybody talks. And when coworkers aren't gossiping with you, they're gossiping *about you*. Learn to keep your personal history and on-goings to yourself. When you grab a local bite to eat, act professionally, and when you go to a work party or after-work party, party professionally. One can never be too careful.

BONUS "Smile every time you make eye contact with someone *especially* if it's a person you don't like or doesn't like you. 99% of the time they will smile back. (This might not work if you have a really creepy smile.)"

~Anonymous, 2009.

FORTY TWO

....

TURN FELONIES INTO SHAMELESS SELF-PROMOTION

We have such expectations of everything. Everyone—as in all of us—make mistakes.

Own it. Own the responsibility and explain how it made you into a better person.

Bad decisions don't make you a bad person. Any normal person only needs a moment of bad judgment, or desperation, or rage to do something out of character.

Yet too many talented candidates with a prior, or multiple priors, are paralyzed by the thought of having to face the hiring manager and expose their past. Worse yet, some who have simply "had it" give up on job hunting entirely, which is especially true if they 1 suffer from rejection shock or 2 their situation is so "out there" that it seems overwhelming to try to explain it all without coming off like a crazy person.

Whether your history includes a rough and rowdy past or a one-time 'oops,' our aim here is to use a powerful, believable talking point to reveal your felony-misdemeanor to the hiring manager. Armed with the responses inside these pages, you'll go into an interview knowing

EXACTLY what to say in order to counter the hiring manager's objections and fears. You will sound like you have peace of mind about your past.

Let's kick off this section with one of the biggest questions you may be thinking about—when is it the right time to break the news about a felony-misdemeanor to the hiring manager?

> The information presented here is not listed in any particular order. All of it is important.

Judge bangs gavel Bailiff - shut that fool up!
Operate behind an impenetrable wall of secrecy and NEVER volunteer any information about your ~~criminal record~~ 'time out' unless specifically asked for in an application or required for a background check! In fact, it's not even necessary to tell the hiring manager, or headhunter, on your first phone-face interview, either. Doing so would be TMI (too much information). It's too early. Once you get the signal that they're really interested in picking you up and **a background check will be involved**, then explain your record. Right before you submit your application or background questionnaire, catch the hiring manager and indicate that you have a felony-misdemeanor. (Do not go into the details of the actual crime! That could be a conversation-stopper. Use the examples further down in this section.)

> TRUTH BOMB: There is no federal law that prohibits discrimination against job hunters with criminal records. But typically most hiring managers use common sense and take steps to ensure fairness anyways. For example, when evaluating a candidate's background, hiring managers will avoid asking if you've ever been arrested, but instead might casually ask you if you've ever been convicted of a specific type of crime that relates to the job.

Backgrounds.
Given the rise of inexpensive online background checks, many employers might dig into your personal history, even when it's totally unnecessary for that particular job.

Leaving aside how morally grotesque it is for hiring managers to scream 'security' and use it as an excuse for some Big Brother snooping, many employers today are *somewhat* caught in a bind—they can be sued if they forget to screen an employee who later harms someone. (Come lawsuit time, the first thing lawyers will want to know is if the incident could have been foreseen based on prior behavior.) Therefore, the sad reality is background checks are often more about limiting a slightly paranoid company's exposure to lawsuits than any real or imagined safety issues.

But the good news is that hiring managers and HR (human resources) often look for a "pattern of judgment."

One or two misdemeanors or a felony may not cost you the job, but with 14 arrests for 'driving under the influence' in three years, plus a possession of controlled substance (ganja) and criminal mischief…the "pattern of judgment" clearly shows someone they may not want to risk hiring for, say, a *delivery service driver*. This bears repeating: any one or two of these types of charges alone won't kill your application in *most* instances…as long as you start thinking in terms of **job matching**.

Job matching means seek out work where your crime does not present a conflict with job duties. (You'll save yourself time, misery and a desolate future void of hope.) Convicted bank-robbers should steer clear from working with cash directly. Skip out on the pharmaceutical industry if you were arrested for a drug-trafficking offense. Shy away from the trucking or transportation industry if you have multiple felony DUI's. Sex-offenders should avoid applying for work with child care or social services where background clearances will be required.

However, a former bank-robber working as an account clerk (not dealing directing with cash or purchase orders) is totally fine, and someone with a DUI may be perfectly qualified to work in nursing, or given enough time and an expunction, even squeeze into a law enforcement career with a small department.

> Background checks may include criminal history, drug screening, credit history, verification of education and training, checks with past employers, and other inquiries depending on the position.

What to write on a JOB APPLICATION about a felony-misdemeanor.
Despite your high intelligence, you may be tempted to lie on an application. The logic is that even a few days or weeks of work can alleviate an immediate financial need a pure meltdown. ("Yeah I got caught...don't care.") Lying is risky. The courts make a big deal out of things. Choosing not to disclose your arrest record to an employer may constitute a felony in some states. Not disclosing INCLUDES reversing digits on your social security number or date of birth on the background form in hopes that your background clears.

What's the best way to handle priors on a job application form, then? Besides just leaving it blank, hoping to score an interview and explaining things face-to-face, you have four basic options for divulging legal baggage. Before you pick your poison, understand that when the hiring manager wants you, you are going to get the job offer even if your criminal record has more pages than the library.

Every time you read this keep that in mind no matter how many applications you fill out, a phone or in-person impression is always going to be bigger and more powerful than a paper impression. When you find a job posting, rather than just applying online and crossing your fingers, make every attempt to get in touch with the hiring manager to introduce yourself. Then apply if (and ONLY if) you sense a match.

Don't be afraid to be assertive. That's what employers are looking for.

If you are the right candidate, the hiring manager may have the power to overlook the felony-misdemeanor on your record. The importance of being able to tell the hiring manager face-to-face that you made a mistake, you've paid for your mistake, and that you need someone to give you a second chance *cannot be stressed enough*. You are not your criminal record. Your value is not how much money you have in your bank. You deserve to become a productive member of society the same as everyone else.

Option #1 BLANK + CONFIDENTIAL LETTER

Have you ever been convicted of a Felony? _____

If yes, please explain _____

Leave it blank and attach a Confidential Envelope with a letter of explanation to your application. This strategy is uncommon, so your letter will probably be read out of sheer curiosity. The best case scenario using a confidential letter is that you may not have to address any questions about your past come interview day. On the other hand, it could put the hiring manager on the defensive because of this highly unusual approach. See the 'confidential letter of explanation' example on **page 341** so you know what to write.

Option #2 DASHES

Have you ever been convicted of a Felony? __ __ __

If yes, please explain _____

Put dashes on an application in hopes it flies under the radar and gives you the opportunity to explain yourself on interview day. Dashes means you *technically* responded to the question but in an unconventional way. The risk is that it might turn-off the hiring manager for trying to pull one over on them. The response below should be memorized if you decide to roll the dice and use this strategy.

You: "I was unsure how to handle this part of the application. I had no intent to lie but I made a mistake in the past that resulted in a felony conviction. It's rather embarrassing and since I'm not familiar with your privacy policy or the confidentiality of my application, I felt it best to explain it face-to-face and keep it between my interviewers…until a job offer is extended. I sincerely hope you can understand my position because this opportunity is so much more to me than money."

Option #3 YES

Have you ever been convicted of a Felony? __Yes__
If yes, please explain __Would like to explain at interview.__

In other words, you want the opportunity to explain this situation more fully at an interview. People naturally like to help people and may invite you in to hear your story. On the flipside, it might be assumed the situation is far worse than it really is. (Without seeing or talking to you, their imagination might run wild as to the severity of the crime.) Motivated by prejudice and fear, a percentage of employers will toss your application.

(For an offense that is clearly not pertinent or related to the occupation, you may also write "Personal reasons.")

Option #4 YES + EXPLANATION

Have you ever been convicted of a Felony? <u>Yes</u>
If yes, please explain <u>I was convicted and plead guilty</u>
<u>for DUI, went to treatment and monitored.</u>
<u>My sobriety and my career are the two most</u>
<u>important things in my life.</u>

Said another way, "My conviction was a mistake I made, but I have turned my life around, and it won't happen again." You're demonstrating mind-boggling courage and determination by coming clean on paper. If the hiring manager admires your honesty (and being a felon is not a big issue in the industry you're applying for), you'll be invited to come interview. Yes, a percentage of employers will screen you out regardless of your honesty, but you won't have to stress over the interview, live a lie, and look over your shoulder for the rest of your career.

How to explain your felony-misdemeanor to the HIRING MANAGER.
You might picture the hiring manager looking at you like there are horns growing out of your head when you mention a conviction. But the truth is your story will not rock their world. Hiring managers have heard and seen it all. OVER one out of every four American adults has some type of criminal record.

Of course, there is nothing pretty about a felony-misdemeanor conviction, but they shouldn't have to attack you with thirty different questions to know what's going on, either. You're far better off dealing with it proactively than reactively as it WILL show up if they have to run a criminal background check. Besides, hiring managers are impressed by applicants who are totally upfront. (Given the fact nearly all lives are affected by addiction, dui's, and violence, hiring managers are always happy to see the "one" who has turned their life around.)

Even so, laying bare your most private human moments to a total stranger can be a little overwhelming. You're worried that poor judgment in the past will come back to haunt you ~~and this just makes you want to cry~~. You know you would make a good employee. But you feel internal discomfort and even shame about a life you left far behind. You dread sounding like an escaped mental patient at the interview trying to explain things.

Ok, step back from the microphone for a second.

You are obviously deeply invested on a psychological and personal level in wanting to succeed. THAT IS AWESOME. We are going to carry this energy forward and make a conviction look like a giant nothing burger. Grab one of the examples that **matches your background** the most. (Please note that the "wrongfully convicted" script is at the very end.) You can customize the example or scratch out your own. Then practice your answer until you can deliver it with poise and confidence.

Remember to **1** keep it simple every chance you get **2** sound like you have peace of mind about your past (hiring manager can sense real change from lip service) and **3** look the hiring manager in the eye…don't get all reverse cowboy.

Now pick yourself up, dust yourself off and give it a go!

(Use the word "INCARCERATED" during an interview. It has a lesser degree of sting to it than saying prison or jail.)

Non-drug and non-violent offense.
You are going to find a perfectly clean record with one small exception.

I have a conviction that happened a few years ago when I was younger that was not related to drugs or violence, and *not* work related. My judgment was clouded by immaturity and I was incarcerated, required to pay a fine and court costs. I successfully completed probation with no complications and have had no other incidents since. (The state is aware of the conviction and has issued me a license to practice.)

330

I'm proud to say that I've made amends with the people involved. We've all moved on and grown up and I'm a far different person now than the confused young man-woman who strayed off the path.

I just wanted to make you aware of that so everything is up-front.

Drug offense.
When I was a teenager, I was constantly tripping over my own feet. I made some bad decisions, one which resulted in a drug-related felony. [If asked specifically what for, say it like this: 1 It was for sale of a controlled substance. 2 It was for possessing a felony amount of a controlled substance.] I realized I had made an enormous mistake right away.

As you may know, our laws are amongst the strictest in the country, and I was sentenced to 36 months but released much earlier as a result of my good behavior. (Had this incident occurred in Colorado, the charge against me would have been either dismissed or expunged.) While incarcerated, I participated in a successful treatment program and am proud to say also earned my GED. My sobriety and my career are the two most important things in my life.

The fact is I'm a far different person today and determined not to let my past interfere with my work life. It was a foolish, foolish thing I will NEVER do again.

DUI (driving while under the influence)
1 I'd like to make you aware that eight months ago I had a DUI after a party. It was a one-time occurrence and you are going to find a perfectly clean record with that one exception.

2 I would like to be totally upfront with you so that everything is out in the open. Two years ago I had a DUI and was incarcerated for this offense. This was an isolated incident and I was not 'on-call' or working when the incident took place. I got lucky. As this was my first offense, I'll be eligible

for an expunction in less than two years and my record will be clear. It was an expensive night and I'm never going to have another night like that again.

Theft.

Three years ago at the age of twenty, I plead guilty in connection with theft from an employer. I'll admit that the circumstances are a little difficult to talk about, but you have a right to know and I won't lie about my past.

I've repaid my debt in full including court costs, restitution and a fine and I'll be on probation for two more years...which I've been successfully completing with absolutely no complications. I've earned my GED and am participating in a mentorship program for at-risk youths. (I also collect donated items and provide them to shelters, churches and charities to help others from disadvantaged backgrounds.)

This monumental mistake cost me dearly and I've taken steps to ensure that this will NEVER happen again. Whatever your decision, I'd want to thank you for giving me this opportunity to explain the situation to you in person.

Violence.

Before we get started, I believe you have the right to know that I have made a mistake in my past.

In 2012, I plead guilty to felony domestic violence as a result of an extreme lapse in judgment. I'm embarrassed to admit this but at the time, my mind was clouded and I did something really stupid. I lost my freedom, the trust of my family and, most importantly, the respect in the eyes of my kids.

But it was a wake-up call for me and I used the time to turn my life around. It gave me a place where things slowed down, and today I'm a far different person than the confused woman-man who went in. Since my release, I've successfully completed my GED and I'm proud to say I'm working on an associate's degree. What I'm looking for now is gaining real, valuable work experience.

Of course, it's normal to have reservations hiring someone with a record. If the situation were reversed, I may very well feel the exact same way. But I can't change the past and there's too much life ahead of me to waste my time looking backwards.

Wrongfully convicted.
In the eyes of the general public, there is no such thing as a "wrongful conviction" and the truth is I wasn't just an innocent bystander. At the time my judgment was clouded and I was hanging around the wrong person. (Basically I was dating "one of those gals-guys" that seems wonderful in the beginning until something happens and you find out the "real" them.) In my case, we were pulled over, contraband was discovered and my girlfriend-boyfriend pinned it on me.

The only thing that was going through my mind was 'nothing.' I was so traumatized by the whole ordeal, it left me in a state of shock. It was the worst experience of my life, but luckily cooler heads prevailed at the DAs office and the charge was eventually reduced and I'm successfully completing probation…with absolutely no complications.

I have reconnected with my family and am living with my parents. They are incredibly loving and supportive…I guess if I sat around and dwelled about what happened, I would probably be angry. But it's not healthy to live in the past and there's so much life ahead of me now that this period in my life has thankfully passed. And regardless who caused the problems in my life, I'm the one who has to fix them.

…EXTRA CREDIT ▶

(Extra Credit)

Can a felony-misdemeanor be "erased" from my records?

Contrary to some rumors, conviction records or 'RAP' sheets (Record of Arrest and Prosecution) are not sealed automatically. The legal process to erase all government records of a criminal conviction for both felonies and misdemeanors is called 'expunction.'

First, you'll have to determine if your type of case qualifies for expunction. Depending on the state, certain kinds of sexual offenses or violent crimes, most felonies resulting in death or bodily injury may not be expunged under any circumstances. (Check anyways!) In many states, as long as no time was served, expunging a felony committed as an adult is possible.

Before you can expunge a criminal conviction, states typically require you wait a period of one to five years (or longer) after the date you completed your sentence or probation. Filing a petition for expunction *before* you qualify will result in your hard-earned money being wasted on a filing fee.

Once the waiting period is over, you'll file a petition for expunction. Send notice of your request to the district attorney's office that handled your case, the original law enforcement agency as well as the state agency that manages criminal histories for your state, like the Department of Public Safety.

Once all relevant parties have received the expunction request, you must now convince a judge. So the next step is to fill out a request to have a hearing with the court.

Depending on the severity of your case, the expunction process takes approximately three months to a year. In a fair amount of states, felony convictions cannot be expunged at all. The only options you'll have left if this is the case would be **1** a governor granting you a pardon or **2** request petition for non-disclosure (which means law enforcement can still see your record, but employers won't...the procedure is similar to expunction).

When mailing your application in to the governor, keep in mind governors rarely grant pardons because they don't want to appear soft on crime.

Help Wanted: not you, felon.
Keep in mind that companies may be required to get free insurance know as a 'bond' (just in case a new-hire felon goes postal). This is an extra step for companies when hiring felons vs. non-felons offered by the government. If the topic of bonds comes up, explain how easy acquiring a bond is as shown in the example right below. (While we are on the topic, companies can also receive government incentives ($) for hiring felons. The money comes from the Work Opportunity Tax Credit and might be worth researching a bit on your end.)

You: "The Federal Bonding Program offers free insurance that protects you against any financial loss. The bond reduces your risk of hiring me and signing up is easy. Would you like to know more about the Federal bonding Program?" (You sound like a TV commercial! Good job.)

To learn more about the Work Opportunity Tax Credit, go online and visit **www.doleta.gov/business/incentives/opptax**

List of felon-friendly employers.
This is a question that has been asked countless times by felons who are tired of the game, want to get a job and go straight but don't know where to start: *Is there a list somewhere of companies that hire convicted felons?*

The short answer is no.

The long answer is with 7,601,169 employers in the United States, there is no practical way to keep up with the latest hiring practices, company policy changes, or new HR laws designed to benefit ex-offenders. In addition, many companies refuse to go on the record due to "public perception."

It would be a PR disaster if, for example, one of America's largest retail chains the Men's Wearhouse® was outed as hiring people with felony records. Companies have an image to protect. (Wait. Bad example, Men's Wearhouse® is quite proud of the fact that they don't conduct any background checks and do indeed give ex-offenders a place to begin as of this writing.) Clearly the question now on your mind is 'how can one find out if a particular company hires felons?'

The answer is, first and foremost, by **applying to all job postings** as long as you have most of the qualifications (**page 171**) and through connections (**page 175**). Jobs aren't going to come looking for you now that you're out, and you're not going to find many job postings that read 'WANTED: Ex-Offenders. Training and uniforms provided. NO weirdos. 1-800-MUW-HAHA.' You must switch to self-promoting and put in your share.

Switching topics, being in and out of prison since you were 18 won't give you much of a work history. If this is the case with you, swing by **page 5** and **page 211**.

A little word of advice, when navigating the outside world, job hunters who *walk-in* to request assistance from kind strangers, such as employment-services representatives, earn BIG TIME preferential treatment over phone callers, and it's so much faster to just go in person and talk to a pretty face. Expect loooong waits if you use a phone. The reason why is that you are dealing with shamefully under-paid, under-appreciated and overworked government, corporate and social services workers. Going in person is a sign of respect and determination, and they'll do everything they can to help, even connecting you to hot job leads, offering you interview preparation and providing you with an extremely serious-looking resume. A Universal Truth is **persistence will take you further than talent**, so be extra-courteous and patient at all times (even if they don't treat you like a human being).

Alrightythen, let's start milking "the system." Create a basic list of felon-friendly potential leads by reaching out to the individuals and organizations in the gray box to the right…starting…now.

Ready. Set. Go!

And a one and a two...

What are you waiting for?! Come on! It's like you're not even trying...
go, go, go!

- Your parole officer
- Prison programs (Job Start and New Start and similar programs in your state.)
- State Employment Development Department (Ask for the person who specifically works with felons inside the EDD.)
- Labor department
- Your school's career services department
- Temporary employment agencies
- United States military (Call your local recruiter and ask about the criminal history waiver program.)
- Church-based organizations
- Non-profit organizations
- Employee contracting agencies
- **www.hirenetwork.org**
- **www.recruiting.jobcorps.gov** 1-800-733-JOBS (5627)

(You made it! You deserve a sweaty hug. Now run to **page 169**.)

...CHECK OUT THE CONFIDENTIAL LETTER SAMPLE ▶

USE THIS SPACE TO CREATE YOUR OWN VERSION OF THIS LETTER.

A Confidential Letter is a short introduction of your felony-misdemeanor in writing. You may provide a Confidential Letter if you complete a job application and plan to leave the "have you been convicted of a felony" box blank or unchecked. You may also submit your letter with your resume, bring your letter to an interview, or copy and paste your letter in the "additional comments" section, if applying online.

Keep in mind that a Confidential Letter is not a requirement and is uncommon, so it could put a hiring manager on the defensive. Look at it as one of several options to disclose a felony-misdemeanor to a hiring manager. If you think this letter will send a hiring manager into uncontrolled spasms, then do not use it. Otherwise, borrow as much as you need to from the example on the next page and build your own!

...CONFIDENTIAL LETTER SAMPLE ▶

Your Name
Street address
City, State, Zip Code
Phone number
E-mail address

April 1, 2018

Company Name
Employer's name
Position or title
Mailing address
City, State, Zip Code

Re: Application for Employment

Dear Ms. D. Bauchery: *(Address the letter to a real-life person.)*

I am responding to your job posting for ███, which I understand may report to you.

I've applied here today because I am extremely interested in working at ███, Inc. What I know about ▮▮▮, Inc. is that you ▮▮▮ and ▮▮▮, which truly shows what a great company can do with an innovative product.

This letter concerns my recent application for employment with your company. Seven years ago at the age of nineteen (19), I was convicted of possessing a felony amount of marijuana, a Schedule VI controlled substance under California law. It was a Class E felony, which is the least severe of felonies in California (Class A is the most severe) and is not classified as a violent crime. I was required by law to pay a fine and court costs, and was on probation for two (2) years, which was successfully completed with no complications.

I received the minimum possible punishment, and have fully satisfied my obligations as required by California statute. I am under no further danger of criminal prosecution based on this prior event.

I wish to openly and honesty disclose to you this unfortunate circumstance from my past. If you check my criminal record, you will note that there are no other incidences since this occurred.

If you have any questions regarding my employability, please feel free to call me directly at ▮▮▮ or email me at ▮▮▮@▮▮▮.com. I would be happy to discuss this situation with you and offer whatever insight I can. Thank you for your consideration.

Sincerely,

Jay Walker

FORTY THREE

....

NEVER DISS YOUR ABILITIES

Maybe you need to work. Maybe you don't need to work but just can't stand being in the house all day with the television.

Either way, there's a tipping point—after you've stayed jobless so long—where your mind switches from "No, don't apply. No, don't apply. No, don't apply" to "Ah, screw it. Apply, and let's see what happens." This section will address the common objections and fears about rejoining the work force *including* what will happen to your government disability benefits.

Every time you read this, know that the person you are is not the person you can become. A disability might complicate your life, but it doesn't define your life.

If you suspect you have a learning disability, you will find free advice and help by calling the Learning Disabilities Association of America at (412) 341-1515 or going online and visiting **www.ldaamerica.org**

I want to go 'out there' but I hate those looks!
The real-world fact is people are usually too worried about their OWN life and problems to even give you a second thought. Able-bodied people either avoid eye contact with physically disabled people because they **don't want to look like a snob** or seem like they are staring. They're afraid—no one wants to be the person who ruins your day.

The one thing you'll learn is that people will like you or not like you for a thousand reasons, a disability only being one. You are not your disability. Companies are not hiring a disability. Companies hiring a candidate who can do the job they want done.

How do I explain my disability?
Before we go there, you'll need to understand that a mental or physical disability is a *medical* condition. Exercise your right to privacy! You are under *no legal obligation* to reveal a medical condition to employers. However, many job hunters choose to reveal their disability for practical reasons. Early disclosure (revealing) of a disability may be necessary to ensure that there is an elevator or other accommodations for your interview. Job hunters using a walker cannot hide a disability, so addressing the issue can come as great comfort to a hiring manager who may not know if anything is needed to assist you.

Our aim here is to use a powerful, believable talking point to reveal your disability to the hiring manager, if need be. Keep your response nice and short, then move past this point and focus the interview on your qualifications.

First, choose one of the examples that **matches your condition** the closest. Second, customize the example or write your own using the example as a guide. Practice your answer until you can say it without reading it.

Disclosure—PHYSICAL

As you probably guessed when I asked about access to the building, moving around is not as simple of a proposition as I would like. That said, my impairment will not affect my day-to-day job duties.

In fact, my disability has helped me become a great problem solver and develop strong forward planning skills. I know how to think "outside the box" and actually applied for this position because I excel in the kind of collaborative working environment you've built here. I'm flexible with my schedule and can handle a high level of work intensity. From what I've seen, you definitely have the capacity for me to grow my skills.

Disclosure—MENTAL

Although it's not a requirement to disclose, I would like to make you aware that I have a medical condition. [You may broadly indicate that you have "a medical condition" or you could name the actual condition. Ask yourself 'how comfortable do I feel about it?']

I have been fortunate because my condition has not affected my performance of job-related duties. Occasionally, however, my [chronic fatigue syndrome] may interfere with my ability to [work for extended hours].

From past experience, I've learned that I work best when [I work less than four hours or I will become exhausted].

That said, I pride myself on being an effective problem solver and multitasker. My condition does not affect any of these important job duties and if you need additional references or information, please let me know.

Disclosure—AUTISM-ADD-ADHD

I would like to make you aware that I have a medical condition that is controlled with medication.

Although I receive treatment during office hours, I would be happy to adjust my schedule so I can make up the time. [ALTERNATIVE ANSWER: Although I get treated in the next town, I typically make up my time away during lunch or in the evening.]

I have been fortunate in that my condition has not interfered with my main job responsibilities. But from time to time you might see me [having trouble understanding directions]. This might affect my ability to respond quickly. So I work best when [I am given a little extra time to have directions explained to me].

I just wanted to make you aware of that so everything is out in the open.

ALTERNATE LAST SENTENCE: In fact, the number to the Job Accommodation Network is (800) 526-7234 [or doctor, employment specialist, therapist, previous employer]. They would be happy to answer any questions about my ability to handle the important job duties.

How to explain a BIG gap in your resume.
You haven't worked in YEARS. How can you possibly explain that?

Know that when the hiring manager wants you, you are going to get the job offer even if you've experienced a 10-15 year+ gap. THE most important thing about a resume is not what's in it. The most important thing about a resume is **how it gets to the hiring manager**. A phone or face introduction is always going to be bigger and more powerful than a faxed or emailed resume.

Keeping that in mind, read through the list on the right of legitimate, real-world reasons that other successful candidates use for explaining time off.

You may also use this list for filling in those resume gaps.

Volunteer work
Volunteer or freelance work includes being a caretaker-baby sitter for a family member or friend as well as internships.

Self-employment
You: "I was self-employed as a decorator and sold merchandize online." Be prepared, they may ask for proof.

Education
You: "I wished to further my education by enrolling in school. I'll be forever thankful for the opportunity my previous employer gave me." Education could mean part-time online classes, trade school, continuation school, adult education and college.

Relevant experience
Begin your work history by focusing on your prior jobs, even volunteer work, that matches the type of work you are applying to. Your work history should be entitled "Relevant Work Experience."

End with last job you had and then explain...
You: "I had to take time off due to family reasons." Don't go into it further. ~~Look sad, maybe wipe away a tear~~. No one is going to ask you to elaborate. Too awkward. Too personal.

Use whole year
Round off to the nearest whole number-year for job start and end dates. So, instead of writing "April 25, 2005-June 12, 2007," write "2005-2007." If you worked for less than one year, write "2007-2007" to keep the way you are numbering the year with a start year and an end year the same.

~~Blame marriage~~
~~I was married for four years with no time off for good behavior.~~

I will feel better if I work. Will I lose my disability benefits if I get hired?
When you are ready to ease into work, your benefits will be fully protected.

For the first **9 months** after starting your job, you can earn an unlimited amount of money without it affecting your benefits *in any way*. Income over $12,000 a year will suspend NOT cancel government disability benefits. Should your monthly income dip below $1000 a month, you are immediately eligible to receive full benefits again. Medicare coverage extends for 8.5 years after going back to work.

Is it legal for a hiring manager to ask me if I have a disability?
Well, of course, the answer is nnnyes. (This is a new word that sort-of merges a 'no' with a 'yes.') Legally, a hiring manager is not allowed to ask if you have a disability, but does it happen on occasion? Yes, but it's very unusual.

The type of question a hiring manager *is* allowed to ask is anything about job-related functions. For example, the question 'Do you have a driver's license?' is perfectly legitimate, if the job requires you to drive.

The hiring manager *may not* phrase a question like this, however: "Let's say you wanted to work here and we asked you to drive. Would you happen to have any…uh…visual <*cough, cough*> dis <*cough, cough*> abilities that would make it a problem driving?" This is a sneaky way an employer might attempt to ask illegal question!

Clearly the concern is over driving obligations. The way the above question is worded is full of all kinds of wrong, but pointing out that the question is illegal may become "off-putting." You probably won't get the job. Answer illegal questions, like this one, with a little diplomacy to avoid carrying the risk of turning things sour.

You: "I have a valid driver's license and can handle a variety of transportation needs."

Do I have to tell the truth about my disability, if asked?
Yes. Companies can fire employees for lying at their interview even if it was later found that the employer was motivated to fire the employee because of discrimination. Unless your disability can affect your job performance or you will require assistance at work, **do not bring it up.**

TOOLS

FORTY FOUR

....

MY ENTIRE LIFE IS A LIE

Security is a (ka)booming industry. Chances are if you are reading this, you're going to be scheduled for a polygraph exam with a law enforcement organization.

Let's first get you acquainted with polygraphers, the people in charge of administering the test. Polygraph examiners roll out their equipment with good intentions. They're out to protect the organization from exposure to the criminal element. A criminal in a position of power or privilege can wreak havoc. The problem is that polygraph examiners get **major props** for each and every candidate that gets rejected, including the *honest* ones, and they try their darndest to trip up, stump and derail everyone. They'll probe and look for inconsistencies in what you wrote on your application or said during the interview. Anything at all to get a DQ.

For this reason, polygraph examiners are not your friends—they're trying to find a reason to disqualify you—but some will pretend to be supporters or well-wishers to throw you off. Using deception is a part of their job. Slippery little fellahs, aren't they?

No, you lie...please be lying.
Perhaps the greatest lie ever told is that sci-fi-ey "lie detector" machines actually work.

These techno-gadgets are marketed to government purchasing agents as practically having the powers to read and decode brainwave frequencies. You are free to 'believe the hype' yourself, but the truth is polygraph exams are pretty much a scam. In fact, the scientific community considers it "junk science." So why is lie-detection still a thing? Manufacturers of the equipment, gear and gizmos are in it for the money. Polygraph examiners need to justify their existence. And faceless government agencies are caught in a bind, they require some sort of validation but have no good alternatives to the polygraph.

What all this means is that no gadget, app, digital tool or machine can detect a lie. So, breathe a sigh of relief. Anyone can fool a polygraph. (Not just your ex.)

> 'Techno-gadgets' refers to computerized polygraph machines, computer voice-stress analyzers and fMRI imaging. Not one independent, scientific study has ever been published in a respected peer-reviewed journal that proves that any technology or technique can detect a lie.

The least you should know.
A successful polygraph is about using every nonverbal signal at your disposal to show that you're certifiably honest. First impressions count, so make it positive by arriving early to your polygraph examination appointment. Big Brother is watching you from the moment you step in. Behave confident, relaxed and alert the entire time, ~~even if you can't spot the WIFI enabled micro camera hiding in the reception area~~.

The U.S. Secret Service likes to hold an all-day-polygraph-a-thon. Applicants' polygraph test will begin in morning and continue until afternoon with no break for lunch in order to wear you down mentally, so eat a large breakfast.

Now feeling a little anxiety is normal, but if you're completely panicked, do not discuss your nervousness unless the polygrapher brings it up first. Predictably, the polygrapher will proceed to explain how it won't affect the test. LOL, puhlease. The fact is being nervous means the nerve cells in your body are excited. The results, like sweating-fidgeting-increase heart rate-faster breathing, can be measured by common "lie detector" machines.

And that's the most glaring and obvious weakness of a "lie detector" machine—it can be fooled.

By maintaining the same level of panicky feelings on ALL questions thrown at you, the only thing the polygrapher will read from the machine is that you are consistently nervous, not much else. (You're effectively drowning out the machine with a constant flow of "loud" body signals. This 'white noise' strategy fogs up the results for the observer, the polygrapher, by masking your impulse response.) Since it's quite normal to experience anxiety when the stakes are so high, **being nervous by itself is not a disqualifier**.

Switching gears, when speaking to the polygrapher, it's okay to admit you're a bit nervous, but appear relaxed and *do not reference your nervousness again*. (Try to calm your mind, it's not shock therapy.) Shut the front door and do more listening than speaking at this point. People often reveal too much too soon. Case-in-point, some candidates, in the belief that it might do them some sort of good, try to establish that they are 'naturally' honest because of their religion. That will backfire. It's a big red flag. Red flags also include yawning or complaining about pain.

Moving up to the face, look the polygrapher in the eyes. Constantly looking around the room while speaking, or just sitting there, gives the impression you're either uncomfortable, hiding something or trying to escape the conversation. For a polygrapher who wants to make eye contact, it's not just a distraction, it's a red flag. Every so often, casually glance at the polygrapher's hands as he is speaking.

Common slip-ups.
In the 'pre-test' interview, don't admit anything too damaging. Little minor childhood wrongdoings are okay but anything more can snowball out of control and raise thorny questions about background.

And once you submit a response in person or on paper for any law enforcement organization, stick with it. Keep your story the same. Keep all of your answers consistent. Do not "change your story" during the time between the polygraph examination and regular interview. Do not "change your story" between a sheriff's department interview and police department interview. **Law enforcement agencies compare notes**. Any inconsistencies and polygraph examiner will raise a stink and spin statements around you faster than a snot-nosed 5th grader.

And while we're on the subject of 5th grade, if you put down on your application that you were suspended for one day in elementary school, please don't go telling the polygraph examiner a few weeks later that you were actually suspended for three days. Inconsistent answers are considered 'deceitful' even if you are innocent of wrongdoing and simply had a memory lapse. If you are unsure, begin your answers with "to my best recollection" or you can say "if I recall correctly."

Just say NO!
Saying 'no' can be complicated. The wrong 'no' can make a polygrapher suspicious that you're concealing something. The right 'no' can boost your credibility.

What separates a truthful 'no' from a deceitful 'no' in the mind of the polygrapher? Check this out ▶

(Do you want to know more? Visit **www.antipolygraph.org** for tons of info and vids on polygraph exams.)

TRUTH-SAYER

- A quizzical look, AS IF, you've got to be kidding accusing me of that 'NO'
- Speaking with conviction, a direct, no hesitation and confident 'NO'
- Unapologetically honest, 100% absolutely certain 'NO'
- Strong and borderline 'I am in charge of this polygraph exam' 'NO'

VERSUS

LIAR

- Pauses, delays, crosses legs, and shifty 'NO'
- Looks up, then to the right or closes eyes 'NO'
- Shaking head to overly-emphasizing 'NO'
- An apology that accompanies 'NO'
- Let's-get-this-over-QUICK-because-I-really *really* need-to-go-somewhere-in-a-hurry 'NO'
- Qualifies response with 'I am going to say this only once, NO'

FORTY FIVE

....

GUMMY BRAINS

Teachers punish students for being distracted. Distracted from what, exactly?

Phone calls, texts, websites, vids, and advertisements make you a better student and helps satisfy your brain's *intense* desire to learn new things. In fact, your gooey 3 pound brain does 20 million-billion calculations per second and almost instantly memorizes EVERYTHING you see and read.

But there's a catch. Memories have an expiration date. Most memories only last a split-second.

So today we're going to turn your ordinary brain into a *gummy brain* and get your 20-second introduction, answers to interview questions and much more to stick in your head for months, even years. Consider this section a personal trainer for your brain, and you're going to learn *how to study* by using the same 8 proven memorizing tricks that straight "A" students, memory champions, "geniuses" secretly use to attack a pile of study material.

You're only minutes away from unleashing your brain's full potential, but before we get started, you must first entirely give up on the notion that ANY subject in school or college is hard.

Nothing in school is hard. **It's only unfamiliar**. Drill into your head, "nothing is hard, it's only unfamiliar."

Is Alzheimer's kicking in way too early?
Intelligence can drastically change over time... in any direction.

Our goal here is to maximize your brain power, and for that you'll need **1** breaks, **2** exercise and **3** sleep. Reduce any of these three elements and your ability to learn plummets drastically. Adjust your breaks, exercise and sleep to the correct levels and watch as your brain power amplifies quite rapidly. Once you understand how your brain operates, we'll jump into the cool mind tricks, but first things, first.

1—BREAKS.
Astonishingly, schools never take a moment to teach students how to study, not even 5 minutes! And even worse, our k-12 ~~educational~~ system demands that you to shut your senses off from the world, sit perfectly still and concentrate for 1-hour blocks at a time. But that's asking the impossible. Your brain doesn't work that way. And more importantly, your brain cannot effectively learn by "working overtime."

All brains tune out after 10 minutes, even gummy brains.

Because tired brains don't learn well, only focus on your book, video-audio lecture or online study materials for **about 2-10 minutes MAX** and then take time to unplug. Breaks have restorative powers and recharge the brain. You'll notice that after chillaxing for a few minutes, you'll be switched-on, alert and good-to-go for another 2-10 minutes. Repeat this 'brain-scape' strategy for the duration of your study hours from here on out.

You'll also need a distraction free zone, so consider sneaking into an empty classroom or, better yet, using a local library. (It's a big building with books inside.)

2—EXERSIZE.
Your brain burns MASSIVE amounts of energy.

Although the human brain makes up only 2% of our total body weight, it takes 20% of all your energy! That's 10X more energy than your other organs use. (Greedy brain!) In fact, 98% of your brain remains inactive because your heart can only pump in so much glucose (brain energy) at any one time. Using more than 2% of your brain would quickly exhausts your glucose supply and make you pass out.

Exercise boosts brain power by making your heart pump more blood. Better circulation means more glucose to into your brain. That's why some suggest that the #1 brain booster is exercise.

Why do we get tired thinking furiously about some problem, even while we are sitting in a chair? Now you know.

> The urban legend that we only use 2% of our brain is technically correct. However, a small but significant distinction is that physically we use 2% of our brain **at any given point in time,** but this does not mean we only use the SAME 2% of our brain.

3—SLEEP.
You look terrible! WTF, get some sleep. The less sleep you get, the dumber you get. (This is a scientific fact.)

Sleep helps new memories stick and increases your imagination **big-time**. Of course, at this point you may be wondering how much sleep will your brain need to reach its maximum potential? Unfortunately, scientists admit that no "magical number" of hours exist for a perfect night's rest. But if you're irritable, antsy, tired, cranky and unhappy in the morning, get more sleep ~~or lay off the sugar~~!

The 8 scientifically-PROVEN memorizing tricks

Please take a seat and enjoy a nice hot cup of... brains.

Gummy brains cheat.
Ordinary brains say "don't look!" and "don't copy!" because that's cheating. It's not their fault. Ordinary brains spend 12 years in school being *socially engineered* (brainwashed). Gummy brains think differently. Gummy brains understand that great learning happens in groups.

In school it's called cheating, but in the real world it's called *collaborating*. (And online it's called the "hive" mind.)

Gummy brains solve problems by understanding how someone else would solve a problem FIRST. Gummy brains then use pattern matching to come up with lots of other possible answers to a question and many different ways to interpret a question. By copying from the EXAMPLES in this book, you take advantage of the natural way the brain learns: **imitation**. Human brains are wired to imitate.

For you, that means read the answers and dialogue in this book, and then use those examples to develop your own original answers by slightly customizing it or using the material as a guide to build your own one-of-a-kind replies. If you're not ready or able to create your own answers for any reason, then just copy the answers directly. Don't feel guilty or paranoid. No one will know what you did! (DO IT. DO IT. DO IT.)

Gummy brains act like babies.
Babies don't learn by just staring at stuff. Babies are born scientists and get their hands dirty.

A baby's brain is naturally wired to **1** observe, **2** brainstorm, **3** analyze and **4** conclude, and as a growing adult you can always go back to your roots and use the exact same process to get study materials into your cranium. For memorizing book materials, the technique is called "active reading."

Active reading simply means you begin by reading the material, taking notes along the way, and stopping at every word you don't understand, looking it up, and finally rewriting main ideas or conclusion in your own, easy to understand language. (Ideally, book pages should be tore-up with your scribbled notes, underlines and definitions.)

Let's practice it now. Construct an outline of the key points as shown in the sentence below. The sentence is purposely written using txt-style language to create a sense of difficulty so you can practice active reading.

OBSERVE (Read!)
Original text: "$0 fO d@ n3W yEarZ Ma R3zOlut!0n b3 2 FINA!Ee l00z3 8tY pOUnDz n B3 eV3n Mo B0otELiziOUz!"

BRAINSTORM (ACTIVELY fill the page with notes, underlines, circles, and drawings. Do it!)
Break it down: "$0 fO d@ n3W yEarZ Ma R3zOlut!0n b3 2 FINA!Ee l00z3 8tY pOUnDz n B3 eV3n Mo B0otELiziOUz!"

ANALYZE (Visualize the meaning inside your head.)
In your mind: "new year's rez → lose 80lb → look hot... *makes TOTAL sense!*"

CONCLUDE (REWRITE the meaning of the sentence using your own simple, understandable language on the side of the book or scratch paper.)
Handwrite your conclusion: Her New Year's resolution is to lose 80 pounds to look even more attractive.

(BONUS: Underlining and circling a word or sentence causes you to pay more attention to that word or sentence. Readers often ignore anything that's highlighted with a yellow, orange or green highlighter. And gummy brains use pens with blue ink, because red ink is harsh on the eyes and black ink is too difficult to see.)

Gummy brains repeat EVERYTHING within 15 minutes.
Ever wonder why we forget almost everything we learn in class?

Of course it's because the hottie in class looked at you and smiled for a split-second which was enough for you to blank out on everything else that happened during the next hour.

But why do we forget 90% things we learn in class when we actually pay attention? Because your brain would get information-overload if it wasn't constantly forgetting all the things you hear, see, taste, smell and touch. (Your eyes alone deliver around 20 million bits of data to your brain PER SECOND! No one expects you to know what this means, but it does sound like a humongous-ly huge number, doesn't it?) Your brain filters out almost everything and only remembers information that is **repeated** or is tied to **emotions** (because it figures that anything that gets repeated or sparks an emotion is probably important stuff). Again, typically, only repeated information and emotional situations is what's stored into memory. (How to use emotions to memorize is covered a little further down.)

Since most of the forgetting takes place in the first few hours after class, use these two strategies to dramatically increase your ability to remember newly-learned information:

■ At the end of each video lesson or class, repeat all of the things you learned **within 15 minutes**.

■ Get a hottie to eye you in every class so it won't faze you any longer. (Seriously, you don't have hotties eyeing you in every class? Gummy brains got it like that!)

Gummy brains shamelessly expose themselves daily.
The key to memory is spaced learning.

Cramming 1.5 hours the night before an interview or test gives a boost of confidence **but results in poor real world performance**. Dividing 1.5 hours into short, 10 minute study sessions over 10 days allows the brain to "get it."

Advertisers know this and expose the public to the same 30-second commercials spaced out over a day or week for the exact same reason— spaced repetition works! Most things in life get mastered by repeat practice like driving, song lyrics and using digital tools. Mastering your interviewing skills is no different.

Give it a try. Over the next 10 days, expose yourself for 10 minutes to the "Answers to Interview Questions" page at the same hour of the day. Which time, you ask? Since every brain is wired differently, find your own peak performance time. It can be any hour of the day you feel mentally sharp, even night time.

> Visit **www.supermemo.com** for more information on 'spaced repetition' and to find your own perfect time of the day to study.

Gummy brains require flash cards.
Memorizing important words, ideas and answers using flash cards is a gummy brain's hidden secret. Of course, you've probably heard about or used flash cards, but most people use them incorrectly. This is the least you should know about making flash cards work for you, starting with the basics:

Flash cards are 5-inch x 3-inch rectangular sheets of thick paper that you can buy at a local dollar store or retail outlet. Create a deck of cards with a question or new word you want to learn on one side, and the answer on the other.

Write the answer in *your own words* when possible. Now shuffle the stack of cards and begin the process of familiarizing yourself with fresh new words, answers and definitions. Say the answer outLOUD AND CLEAR first. Now, close your eyes. Think it. Say it. (Helpful hint: drawing pictures on the front of the card helps your brain recall an answer much faster.) **Do not drop the flashcards you know out of the pile**. Keep all flashcards in one large stack, but shuffle often and spend more time on the unfamiliar ones.

Gummy brains teach ~~minions~~ friends.
Until you share an idea, it remains foggy and unreal. It's not yours. You think you know, but if you wait until interview day to put your knowledge to the test, you might be in for a surprise.

Docendo discimus is an old latin phrase meaning, "by teaching, we learn." Teaching makes ideas real. Explaining an idea to friends forces you to clarify it for yourself and builds confidence in your answer. Teaching flows an idea from your brain, to your mouth, into the air, and back into your ears. Now the idea is real. *Now you own it.*

By teaching others how to interview (even if you're not done learning yourself!) your confidence will SKYROCKET at the interview because you've convinced **yourself** of the answer. That means you'll sound believable, sincere and won't be frazzled or nervously trying to recall what you're suppose to say.

Teach what you have learned about interviewing or anything else! Some people think, "Me? A teacher?" Certificates or degrees are not required to teach a friend what to say at an interview or anything else.

Gummy brains love explosive words.
Need a place to stash a really looooong answer in your head, like a 20-second introduction for the interview?

Then stop battling your brain, you brat! You are not being called a brat. Brat is an explosive word that sits inside your brain until you feel your stomach is about to burst… kah-booOOOM! "BRAT" expands into **B**anana, **R**ice, **A**pplesauce, and **T**oast; foods to eat for mild food poisoning relief.

Brat is used as a funny memory aid, an easy way to remember the acronym B.R.A.T.

Lucky for you, exploding words can be used for memorizing incredibly lengthy sentences, too.

Take this real life situation—you graduated massage therapy school and as you walk into an office for a job interview you're silently repeating, "I'm in my eye. I'm in my eye. I'm in my eye." It's not poetry or a silent prayer, and your brain's not tripping out. "I'm in my eye" expands into the full version of your 20-second introduction. Can you figure it out?

*(1) I'm Dee Vious, and (2) I recently graduated from Manchesthair College earning a Massage Therapy Diploma. (3) **In** my private practice, I have enjoyed seeing how my bodywork sessions help clients overcome stress and cruise through health obstacles with more confidence than they thought possible. (4) **My** professional experience includes deep tissue, Swedish and sports massage and am especially skilled in a fast-paced environment. (5) **I** am very interested in the opportunity for professional development as an associate in your office.*

In order to use this mind-tool, the first step is create an abbreviation using the first word of each sentence in the paragraph that you want to memorize. (In the massage therapy intro example above, you can put together the words in bold and create the weird sentence "I'm in my eye.") The funnier the sentence the better because you're tapping into emotions! Step two is memorize the abbreviated word entirely. Now for the third step, memorize the first 4-5 words of each and every sentence of your introduction. Finally, repeat all of the lines over and over just like you would with song lyrics from your favorite band. (Repeat your entire introduction 2-8 times out loud beforehand to become familiar with the sentences.) That's how it works!

"Exploding words" are actually a mind tool known as mnemonics (pronounced neh-mOn-nicks). Mnemonics takes advantage of pattern matching, the brain's favorite way to learn new ideas and recall them. Memorizing the first letter or word of each sentence is the FASTEST way to recall an introduction, answer or speech come show time.

Gummy brains tumble down the rabbit hole.
Sit down, close your eyes and get ready to tear a clean hole through what you thought was reality.

There's nothing, no, NOTHING that makes people remember more information than what's presented HERE. If you dare try it for yourself, you'll discover what memory champions, "geniuses," and brain scientists already know—**there is no such thing as a photographic memory**. Memorizing lengthy speeches or entire books of information, word-for-word, is easily accomplished by *linking* amusing, silly and vibrant images.

Linking, as a mind tool, makes memorizing random numbers such as 1870071230806 easy. Let's jump right into it and get you to quickly memorize 1870071230806. You can do it! Watch.

Step one—CHUNKING.
First, break down 187001230750 into chunks ➜ 187   007   1230
80 6

Step two—VISUALIZE.
Now create a mental picture for each chunk of numbers. 187=kill,
007=james bond, 1230=lunchtime, 806=bury someone 80 miles
away from the road, 6 feet under.

**Step three—LINK INTO BIZARRE, YET ENTERTAINING
STORY.**
*Kill James Bond at lunchtime, and bury the body 80 miles out in
the desert, and dig 6 feet under.*

Step four—TOTAL RECALL.
Kill 187 James Bond 007 at lunchtime 1230 and bury
the body 80 miles out, 6 feet under.

See?! Easy peasy!

For names, do the exact same thing. The name Jacky Rose, for example,
is broken into two chunks, Jacky + Rose. Visualize Jacky as a lumberjack
and picture a red rose in the forest. Now visualize a lumberjack axing down
a tiny, innocent little rose.

Memorizing long speeches, and even books, is just as simple.

For each sentence you need to create a visual image which relates
to a part of the line. The images can be anything that prompts you to
remember your speech and doesn't have to be exact (literal).

For memorizing a particular date such as May the fourth, try something
like "May the 4th be with you."

We learn and remember best through pictures, not spoken or written words. Vision combined with other senses like hearing, even smell, has an unusual power to bring back even distant memories. That's because the part of your brain that handles what you hear is **3%**, but the part of your brain that processes visual images is **over 30%**.

You get the picture?

(Extra Credit)

Brain dEstRUCtolD #1—BOREDOM.
Brains get all complain-y about boring stuff.

The reason why brains don't pay attention to boring things is kind of complicated. The problem is that some of the things you will have to study for work or school may put you to sleep because the brain's cells and chemicals that keep you awake remain in constant tension with cells and chemicals that try and put you to sleep which so happens to…you're not reading anymore are you?

PINCH YOURSELF AND WAKE UP!!

To ease the boredom, **1** force a friend to study with you so you two can ~~suffer together~~ test one another, **2** remind yourself that this won't go on forever, and **3** psych yourself out by *faking* interest in what you are learning.

Reward yourself with a treat every study session. To avoid feeling overwhelmed about study materials, think only about what you have to do today, not tomorrow, the next week, month or year. This prevents total brain-meltdown.

Brain dEstRUCtoID #2—STRESS.
Stress is the brain's ultimate frenemy.

Good stress is called "eustress." Preparing for an interview is a form of eustress because you're moving up towards one of your dreams. Right now, you're filled with a lot of stress because there's a lot to do in the next month. But this is the kind of stress that fills you with excitement because it means a positive change in your life.

Negative stress is called "distress." Distress is what people commonly call "stress," which is felt from time to time by almost everyone.

However, living in a hostile home or dealing with relationship, legal or money problems can bump distress up to a dangerous level called "chronic stress." Chronic stress is best described as this horrible combination of anxiety, despair and hopelessness. In other words, "My life sucks...and I don't see things getting any better." Chronic stress puts the brain in survival mode.

Survival mode is good if you're being hunted by a jaguar, but not so good if you're just trying to get out of bed.

Now, don't get stressed reading about what stress can do to your heart and brain, BUT chronic stress turns the adrenaline faucet on. Adrenaline helps you run or fight like a maniac for the few seconds you need to get out of danger. But our bodies can't handle months or years of adrenalin overload, so blood vessels become scarred which in turn may lead to heart-attacks and strokes.

Chronic stress cripples your ability to learn and remember. On the flip side, eustress (good stress) and even distress (bad stress) helps the brain form stronger memories because it taps into your emotions.

(Why does stress have to be so darn two-faced?)

Brain dEstRUCtoID #3—MULTITASKING.
Getajobpaybillsglobalwarmingneedcaffeineforeveralone.

Asking job applicants if they can multi-task is pure ridiculousness. The brain can't multi-task. At least, not in the way hiring managers would like. Multitasking is a business buzzword, one that means focusing your attention on two or more things at once, and for simple things like eating while driving it's easy…for some. But the brain has its limits. And the main one is that the brain offers only one attentional "spotlight." So focus on only one thing at a time to *memorize new things* or perform well on a complex job task.

You'll make fewer errors. You'll memorize faster. And your boss will thank you.

You'll have to play dumb at an interview now that you've read this. Should a hiring manager asks you, "Can you multitask?" respond with, "Absolutely! I see multitasking as the cornerstone of a productive work environment."

HAR…HAR…HAR.

....

FORTY SIX

PRE-EMPLOYMENT TESTS
(~~CHEATING AND BRIBERY~~)

As a safeguard against fudged resumes or credentials, and to evaluate which applicants are most likely to succeed on the job, many organizations administer pre-employment tests. (For some employers, relying on your personality just isn't enough!)

The first part of this section offers a quick description of the common pre-employment tests. If you expect to take a multiple-choice test, then find a comfortable place to sit and read the second part of this section to increase your odds of scoring higher.

Personality test.
Personality tests try to reveal the degree to which a person exhibits particular personality traits in order to assess how a person will behave in everyday settings. One common personality test asks test-takers to rate how strongly they agree or disagree using a scale of 1 ("strongly disagree") to 5 ("strongly agree") with seemingly random statements like, "I would like to be a flower shop owner."

Job tasks test.
A candidate is given samples of the job tasks and is then asked to simulate the work as if it were real in order to preview and evaluate their performance.

Emotional intelligence test.
Emotional intelligence is your ability to understand your own emotions and manage the emotions of others. A higher emotional intelligence score translates into the ability to click with others, superb impulse control, good customer service and less friction with coworkers. More and more frequently, employers are testing for emotional intelligence to reduce the risk of workplace hostility and increase morale.

Talent assessment test.
A "talent assessment" is actually just a *job matching* test to see if a particular candidate is a right fit. The goal of a talent assessment is to help predict your long-term performance. In other words, can you get the job done and be worth the salary they have budgeted for the position?

Pre-employment physical examination.
A pre-employment physical examination may be requested by some employers to determine the health, mobility and possible restrictions of a candidate for a particular job. The exam is typically conducted by a medical doctor or nurse.

Drug test.
Some employers test applicants for drug use by conducting urine drug tests (~~drink tons of water~~), hair (~~shave everything~~), saliva (~~blame it on the kiss you got right before the test~~) or sweat screening (~~rub antiperspirant everywhere and no sweat~~).

Cognitive test.
A cognitive test is a brain test. A cognitive test aims to measure reasoning, memory, perceptual speed and accuracy, as well as skills in arithmetic and reading comprehension. Cognitive tests may include knowledge of a particular function or job. ~~Sharpen your senses by staring at the flame of a candle~~.

Physical ability test.
Physical ability tests measure how strong, fast, fit and coordinated you are. For law enforcement candidates, the test might include some cardio. They'll attach a tube to your face that supplies your air and then you're made to run, and run, on a treadmill ~~until you get the sexy body you've always wanted~~ in order to measure your heart-rate and blood-oxygen levels.

Multiple-choice test cheats.

People have patterns—for example, people who take the most amount of time to finish a test tend to score the highest. Multiple-choice tests have patterns, too, and today you will learn how to draw from these patterns and spot the best answers to increase your odds at correctly guessing... using those patterns.

This section, while informative and interesting, is not 100% scientific. But it is definitely several levels above witch magic! Consider it a work in progress...

> The strategy listed here may not work on math questions or on questions that ask for the "most" correct answer.

Step 1.
To maximize your score with the clock ticking away, begin by scanning for the questions that you know the answer to. Go through the entirrrrrrrrre test and only fill in answers that you are 100% sure about at this stage. This bears repeating: do not guess at this point. Just circle the questions that you don't know the answer to, leave it blank and skip to the next question. (On computer tests where it's only one question per screen, this is not possible, so you'll have to use the tricks below to increase your odds at correctly guessing.)

Step 2.
Return to the beginning of the test and now work on guessing the correct answer to the questions you left blank, the questions you circled. (Adjust your confidence down a bit so that you are comfortable guessing.)

Step 3.
Use the process of elimination and cross out the obvious wrong answers. Be a sneakaroo about it, skip questions you don't know and look for clues to the correct answers in other questions. (Quick example: 'Who was the author of the Declaration of Independence?' and then a later question asks 'What event caused Thomas Jefferson to write the Declaration of Independence?' The answer is in the question!)

As time begins running out, take your best guess at the remaining answers from remaining questions. Do not leave any question blank.

I did not study for the multiple-choice exam. Am I doomed?
Maybe you are. Maybe you aren't. Use these tricks to increase your odds at correctly guessing.

> 1.) Confusing question about stuff that they never really covered in school.
> A.   Reasonable answer
> B.   Reasonable answer
> C.   Not sure about this answer.
> D.   All of the above.

Choose ALL OF THE ABOOOOOVVVVVVVVVVVVVVVEEEEEEEEEEE
(Questions with an "all of the above" choice is more likely to have "all of the above" as the correct answer.)

2.) What is the atomic weight of cobalt?
A. 1
B. 66
C. 58.9332
D. 23.1

Choose the LOOOOOOOOOONGEST ASWERRRRRRRRRRRRRRR
(When guessing, often the longest answer is the correct answer.)

3.) Who invented Post-It® notes?
A. Romy White & Michele Weinberger
B. Michael Sokolski & Conrad Gessner
C. Arthur Fry & Spencer Silver
D. James Pillans & Albert Stallion

Correct answer is "C".
(Contrary to urban legend, "C" is not the most common answer. That's why "C" has low self-esteem. No one trusts "C" anymore. On this type of question, you'll have to skip it and hope that you find clues in other questions and come back to it. Worse comes to worse, choose "C" if it'll make you feel better.)

4.) True or False: In the Z-Axis, you can complete a circular interpolation using NURBS curved surfaces adjusting for the flow of radiant heat and temperature fluctuations during phase change.
A. True
B. False

Choose FALSSSSSSSSSSSSSSSSSSSSSSSSSSSSSEEEEEEEEEEE
(60% of the time True/False questions are more likely to be false than true.)

> 5.) Post-It® notes were invented by which company and team members?
> A. Raytheon, Spencer Silver and Jack Kilby
> B. Boston Dynamics, Arthur Fry and Dmitri Mendeleev
> C. 3M Corporation, Harold Stephens, Nicola Tesla
> D. 3M Corporation, Arthur Fry and Spencer Silver

Choose "D".
(Questions that ask about a set of items, or the order of items, the answer with the most elements, or things, in common with the others is most probably the correct one.)

> 6.) What is an astronomical unit?
> A. An insanely large apartment.
> B. A measurement of distance.
> C. A measurement of time.
> D. A tolerance specification.

Cross out "A". Choose "B" or "C".
(Questions with three very similar answers and one way-out-there answer, you can almost always eliminate the different one. Cross the oddball answer out. Of the remaining answers, if two of the choices are very similar, chances are that one of the two is correct. In this case, the correct answer is "C.")

7.) Given the exponential rate of price/performance increases, Moore's Law stipulates that:
A. When you eliminate the impossible, whatever remains must be the truth.
B. Lex parsimoniae, the most probable answer is the likely correct one.
C. Processing speeds double every 18 months.
D. Metallic glass amorphous phase change occurs under rapid cooling.
E. Answers (A) and (B) only.

Skip this question. Circle it. Then look for hints-clues-answers in other questions or use other questions to help jog your memory or eliminate incorrect answers. (Btw, the correct answer is "C".)

I feel totally clueless. What do I do now?!
People aren't aware that 70% of the time your first guess is the most accurate, provided that you studied or were exposed to the material as some point in time. What should *you* do when you draw a blank? Choose the answer that *pops* out at you at first glance and **do not go back and change your answer** unless you feel confident that the new answer is right.

Pencils down.

That's it. This book is over! Everyone get out.

NOTES

NOTES

ONE
TELL ME ABOUT YOURSELF

3   **The initial 20-seconds of the interview may fix the overall assessment of skill, knowledge and ability by the hiring manager.** TJ Pricket & N Gada-Jain & FJ Bernieri. "First Impressions in Job Interviews." Presented at the Annual Meeting of the Midwestern Psychological Association, Chicago, IL, May, 2000.

THREE
PHONE INTERVIEWS

70   **Talk fast, don't speak perfectly, men lower pitch, women vary pitch to sound convincing.** Benki JR *et al* (2011) Effects of Speech Rate, Pitch, and Pausing on Survey Participation Decisions. AAPOR 66th Annual Conference Abstracts: 230 – 231.

SIX
NEGOTIATING SALARY

86   **Negotiating partners become psychologically fixated on the first number, and everything thereafter builds off of that initial numerical value.** Extreme and self-serving negotiators secure higher profits. Loschelder, D *et al* (2013) "The First-Mover Disadvantage: The Folly of Revealing Compatible Preferences." Psy Sci, 0956797613520168.

NINE
HATERS

117   **"Oderint dum metuant."** Latin. Purported to be a maxim of the Roman emperor Caligula, whose brief reign is marked with blood, brutality and insanity. Caligula was assassinated by his own body guards along with his wife and baby on January 24, 41 CE.

117   **"He who goes unenvied shall not be admired."** Greek. Principle that envy and "success" go together as stated by Aeschylus 525-456 BCE, Greek tradegian.

117   **Envy is hostility towards superiors, a negative feeling towards someone who is better off.** Helmut Schoeck (1969). Envy: A Theory of Social Behavior. Betty Ross, Harcourt, Brace & World, Inc. Republished (1987).

117   "Envy is resentment towards someone has a desirable object
       or quality that one does not have or can not get. Envy is the
       perverse pleasure...that is felt when a superior fails or suffers."
       Jan E. Stets & Jonathan H. Turner (Eds) (2007). Handbook of the
       Sociology of Emotions. Springer-Verlag New York, Inc. pp. 424.

                          TEN
                         RACISM

121   **Lower intelligence linked to higher levels of prejudice.** Hodson,
       G & Busseri, MA (2012) *Psychological Science* 23 (2): 187 - 195.

121   **In humans race cannot be defined as genetically discrete
       groups.** M J Bamshad & S E Olson "Does Race Exist?" Scientific
       American Nov. 10, 2003: online edition.

121   **No genetic or biological basis for "race" exists.** K Owens & MC
       King (1999) Genomic Views of Human History. Science 286 (5439):
       451 - 453.

121   **Human Genome Project, completed in June 2000, concluded
       that "race" is scientifically illegitimate, yet the concept of "race"
       continues to persist as a social construct.** McCann-Mortimer P *et
       al* (2004) 'Race' and the Human Genome Project: Constructions of
       Scientific Legitimacy Discourse & Society" 15: 409 - 432.

                         ELEVEN
                        LOVESICK

125   **Psychotic, narcissistic, Machiavellian personalities offer more
       sex appeal because they are better at dressing up and focus on
       impressing others.** Holtzman, NS & Strube, MJ (2012) People With
       Dark Personalities Tend to Create a Physically Attractive Veneer.
       Social Psychological & Personality Science.

125   **"Have you ever cheated on your SO? If so... why?"** give_me_
       the_child. Web blog post. Reddit.com. Conde Nast Publications,
       2012. Web. Nov. 7, 2013.

126   **Narcissistic personality disorder symptoms include belief that they are better than others, expressing disdain for those they feel are inferior.** Diagnostic and Statistical Manual of Mental Disorders DSM-IV-TR. 4th ed. Arlington, VA: American Psychiatric Association: 2000..

126   **Narcissistic personalities require constant praise and admiration due to fragile self-esteem.** Skodol, AE (2012) Personality disorders in DSM-5. Annu Rev Clin Psychol 8: 317 - 44.

127   hansissohot. "Hans" Def. 2. Urban Dictionary. Urban Dictionary. Feb. 10, 2009. Web. Oct 18, 2013.

128   **Narcissistic personalities have trouble keeping relationships.** Ronningstam, E (2011) Narcissistic personality disorder: A clinical perspective. Journal of Psychiatric Practice 17 : 89.

129   **Episodes that provoke jealousy undercut one's sense of self.** Ellis, C & Weinstein, E (1985) Jealousy and the Social Psychology of Emotional Experience. *Journal of Social and Personal Relationships* 3 (3): 337 - 357.

129   **The experience of jealousy results in loss of self-esteem.** Buunk, B & Bringle, RG (1987) 'Jealousy in Love Relationshipsf,' *in* D. Perlman & S. W. Duck (eds) Intimate Relationships: Development, Dynamics, and Deterioration, pp. 123-147. Beverly Hills: Sage Publications.

129   **Sexual competition causes jealousy, more in women than men.** Buunk, AP et al (2012) Intra-sexual competition at work: Sex differences in jealousy and envy in the workplace. *Revista de Psicología Social* 27(1): 85.

131   **TV romance hurts love life.** Osborn, JL (2012) When TV and Marriage Meet: A Social Exchange Analysis of the Impact of Television Viewing on Marital Satisfaction and Commitment. Mass Communication and Society 15 (5): 739.

131 **Fake images change memory and behavior.** Loftus, EF (2003) Make-Believe Memories. American Psychologist 58(11): 867 – 873.

132 **Delinquent (rebellious) behavior in young people is not caused by low self-esteem. Delinquent behavior sometimes *raises* self-esteem in those who can find no other route to "success."** McCarthy JD & Hoge DR (1984) The dynamics of self-esteem and delinquency. The American Journal of Sociology 90: 396 - 410.

132 **Study proving that reactance (rebelliousness) can be measured.** Dillard, J & Shen, L (2005) On the nature of reactance and its role in persuasive health communication. Communication Monographs 7: 144 - 168.

132 **Giving freedom to reactant (rebellious) personalities reduces reactance (rebelliousness).** Miller, CH *et al* (2007) Psychological reactance and promotional health messages: The effects of controlling language, lexical concreteness, and the restoration of freedom. Human Communication Research 33: 219 - 240.

132 **Reactant (rebellious) personalities are attracted to unobtainable objects and experience real emotional consequences if they don't get it.** Brehm, SS & Brehm JW (1981) Psychological Reactance: A Theory of Freedom and Control. Academic Press.

132 **Threatening a reactant personality's freedom causes a "boomerang effect" in which they choose the forbidden alternatives.** Silvia, PJ (2005) Deflecting reactance: The role of similarity in increasing compliance and reducing resistance. Basic and Applied Social Psychology 27: 277 - 284.

THIRTEEN
EVIL BOSS

139 **Morrissey, J. (2008).** The Art of Verbal Intimidation : Learn it and fight back!. [Blog] Jay Morrissey Online. Available at: http://jaymorrissey. com/blog/the-art-of-verbal-intimidation-learn-it-and-fight-back/ [Accessed 22 Apr. 2011.]

143 **Written self-disclosure reduces emotional distress and increases long-term well-being.** Pennebaker, JW & Beall, SK (1986) Confronting a traumatic event: Toward an understanding of inhibition and disease. Journal of Ab Psy, 95(3): 274 – 281.

143 **Written self-disclosure of trauma that uses more negative words than positive words is linked to improved health.** Pennebaker, JW (1993) Putting stress into words: Health, linguistic, and therapeutic implications, Behav Res and Therapy, 31(6): 539 – 548.

FOURTEEN
CONFIDENCE

148 **Happy people are far better at figuring out which problems can be solved and which are a waste of time.** Kuhl J *et al* (2003). Emotion and Intuition: Effects of Positive and Negative Mood on Implicit Judgments of Semantic Coherence. *Psychological Science* *14*(5): 416 – 421.

148 **Subjects concentrating on wakefulness during sleep-time can reduce stress-induced insomnia.** Broomfield, NM *et al* (2003) "Initial insomnia and paradoxical intention: An experimental investigation of putative mechanisms using subjective and actigraphic measurement of sleep." Behav Cogn Psychoth 31: 313 - 324.

148 **Effectively counter insomnia by reducing ruminations concerning wakefulness.** Morgenthaler, T *et al* (2006) "Practice Parameters for the Psychological and Behavioral Treatment of Insomnia: An Update." SLEEP 29(11):1417.

148 **Manage insomnia through 'reverse-psychology'.** Schutte-Rodin, S *et al* (2008) "Clinical Guideline for the Evaluation and Management of Chronic Insomnia in Adults." Journal of Clinical Sleep Medicine 4(5): 487 - 504.

149 Winterburn, Steven (@5tevenw) "Before you diagnose yourself with depression or low self esteem, first make sure that you are not, in fact, just surrounding yourself with assholes." 24 May 2011, 11:21 a.m. Tweet.

389

149   **The more choices people have, the likelier they will select a friend with their beliefs.** Bahns AJ *et al* (2012) Social ecology of similarity: Big schools, small schools and social relationships. *Group Processes Intergroup Relations* 15(1): 119 – 131.

150   **In more financially unequal societies, like the United States, people tend to view themselves as superior to others in contrast to more equal societies, like Germany, where people tend to view themselves more as equals.** Loughnan S *et al* (2011) Economic inequality is linked to biased self-perception. Psychological Science 22(10): 1254 – 1258.

SIXTEEN
MENTALLY BLOCKED

157   All quotations from Dr. David Viscott are transcribed directly from the videotaped television program of the following episode: "Night Talk with Dr. David Viscott" (1990).

SEVENTEEN
DEPRESSION

162   **Depressive people remain unaware negative-self talk is the root cause of anxiety as delusional ruminations feel lucid and rational.** Marano, Hara Estroff. "Depression Doing the Thinking." *Psychology Today.* Sussex Publishers, LLC 1 May 2001. Web. 18 Sep. 2013.

162   **Greater incidence of negative bias (illusion) are associated with higher depressive symptoms.** Moore, MT & Fresco, DM (2007). "Depressive realism and attributional style: implications for individuals at risk for depression." Behavior Therapy 38 (2): 144 – 154.

162   **Negative and positive illusions of social reality are associated with higher depressive symptoms.** Joiner, TE *et al* (2006). "On Seeing Clearly and Thriving: Interpersonal Perspicacity as Adaptive (Not Depressive) Realism (Or Where Three Theories Meet)." Journal of Social and Clinical Psychology 25(5): 542 – 564.

162 **Depressive people perceptions are less accurate overall especially in circumstances where they conclude to have no control when in fact they do.** Dykman, BM *et al* (1989) "Processing of ambiguous and unambiguous feedback by depressed and nondepressed college students: Schematic biases and their implications for depressive realism." Journal of Personality and Social Psychology 56(3): 431 – 445.

162 **Compared to their non-depressed peers, depressive people make less accurate real world predictions and feel overconfident about these judgments.** Dunning, D & Story AL (1991) "Depression, realism, and the overconfidence effect: are the sadder wiser when predicting future actions and events?" Journal of personality and social psychology 61(4): 521 – 532.

165 **2010 averaged 105 suicides per day and one suicide for every 25 attempted suicides.** Centers for Disease Control and Prevention, National Center for Injury Prevention and Control. Web-based Injury Statistics Query and Reporting System (WISQARS) [online]. 2010. [cited 2012 Oct 19] Available from www.cdc.gov/injury/wisqars/index.html]

EIGHTEEN
SHORTCUTS TO EMPLOYMENT

172 **Jobless applicants are not protected by anti-discrimination laws.** The unemployed need not apply. February 19, 2011 New York Times, New York Edition: p. WK9 Author Not Cited.

172 **Online job postings target currently employed workers.** Catherine Rampell (2011) The help-wanted sign comes with a frustrating asterisk. July 26. New York Times, New York Edition: p. B1.

172 **Volunteer work is as important as paid work according to 41% of U.S. hiring managers.** LinkedIn.com polled approximately 2,000 U.S. hiring managers (in 2011) and 41% stated that volunteer work is considered just as important as paid work, and 20% stated that they actually hired candidates as a direct result of their volunteer work. Of the 2,000 U.S. hiring managers surveyed, 89% percent of them had volunteer experience.

391

NINETEEN
CONNECTIONS

175   Pamela Peterson (2004) **"Eighty percent of the time people are delighted and willing to meet and to help, primarily because they recognize the value of networking as well the satisfaction that comes from being able to help someone."** Wall Street Journal, Career Journal Article.

177   Kelly Giles. "Requesting an Informational Interview." Grads in Transit. Wordpress. Apr 21, 2009. Web. Oct. 21, 2013.

TWENTY
BODY LANGUAGE

181   **Origins of human smile in human-like facial expressions of gorillas.** Waller BM & Cherry L (2012) Facilitating Play Through Communication: Significance of Teeth Exposure in the Gorilla Play Face. American Journal of Primatology 74 (2): 157 – 164.

183   **Touch influences decisions and judgments in social settings.** Ackerman, JM *et al* (2010) Incidental Haptic Sensations Influence Social Judgments and Decisions. Science 328 (5986): 1712 - 1715.

184   **Body language more important than facial expression in recognizing emotions.** Aviezer, H. *et al* (2012) Body Cues, Not Facial Expressions, Discriminate Between Intense Positive and Negative Emotions. Science 338 (6111): 1225 - 1229.

TWENTY ONE
MIND GAMES

191   Tracy JL & Beall AT (2011) **Women find happy, smiling men less attractive than proud, troubled "bad boy" men.** Happy Guys Finish Last: The Impact of Emotion Expressions on Sexual Attraction. Emotion 11(6): 1379 – 1387.

191   Christian Rudder. **Women who smile are associated with a higher level of sexual success. Men who avoid smiling or looking directly in camera are associated with a higher level of sexual success.** "The Four Big Myths of Profile Pictures." January 20, 2010 Oktrends online edition.

NOTES

TWENTY FOUR
7 WAYS TO DESTROY YOUR INTERVIEW

207 Robert Half International Inc. "Secretaries and Assistants Influence Executive Hiring Decision." Survey. www.rhi.com. IT Business Services, 28 Aug. 2009. Web.

208 **"I wear black on the outside 'cause black is how I feel on the inside."** Paraphrase from The Smiths "Unloveable" from soundtrack "The World Won't Listen." Feb 2, 1987.

TWENTY SEVEN
ONLINE SOCIAL NETWORK

221 **Vicious and degrading behavior online is associated with anti-social personality disorder (psychopathy), narcissistic and sadistic personality traits.** Buckels, E.E. *et al* (2014) "Trolls just want to have fun." Personality and Individual Differences.

TWENTY EIGHT
CLOTHING & APPEARANCE FOR WOMEN

226 SAGE Publications. "Tattoos reduce chances of getting a job." *ScienceDaily*, 4 Sep. 2013. Web. 5 Nov. 2013.

226 **Of 2675 surveyed people, 76% believe visible tattoos reduce chances of being hired.** Aaron Gouveia. "Find Out How Tattoos/Piercings Can Limit Your Career" SFGate, Jan. 2013. Web. 5 Nov. 2013.

THIRTY NINE
EXTERNSHIPS & VOLUNTEERING

309 **Volunteer work is as important as paid work according to 41% of U.S. hiring managers.** LinkedIn.com polled approximately 2,000 U.S. hiring managers (in 2011) and 41% stated that volunteer work is considered just as important as paid work, and 20% stated that they actually hired candidates as a direct result of their volunteer work. Of the 2,000 U.S. hiring managers surveyed, 89% percent of them had volunteer experience.

NOTES

FORTY ONE
GANG MEMBERS

317 **60 percent of male gang members and 78 percent of female gang members quit in less than 1 year.** Thornberry *et al* (2004) The Causes and Correlates Studies: Findings and Policy Implications National Criminal Justice Justice Journal September 1(9).

318 **Three year field study covering all aspects of gang life, depicted by gang members' own testimony, including social interaction and involvement in property crimes, theft, drug sales and drug use.** Decker SH & Van Winkle B (1996) Life in a gang: Family, friends, and violence. New York: Cambridge University Press.

318 **Principle barrier is not leaving a gang, it is rejecting friends and being welcomed into the working world.** Decker SH & Lauritsen JL (1996) Breaking the bonds of membership: Leaving the gang. In *Gangs inAmerica* (2nd ed.), ed. C. Ronald Huff. Thousand Oaks, CA: Sage.

318 **Family affiliation does not equate to gang membership, only those who claim membership are by definition gang members.** Esbensen FA *et al* (2001) Youth gangs and definitional issues: When is a gang a gang and why does it matter? Crime & Delinquency 47, January.

319 **Humble people are more helpful.** LaBouff JP *et al* (2011) Humble persons are more helpful than less humble persons: Evidence from three studies. J of Positive Psychol 1 – 14.

322 **Creepy people literally give other people the chills.** Leander NP et al (2012) You Give Me the Chills: Embodied Reactions to Inappropriate Amounts of Behavioral Mimicry. Psychological Science 23 (7): p. 772 - 779

FORTY TWO
FELONIES & MISDEMEANORS

329 Michelle Natividad Rodriguez, NM & Emsellem, M (March, 2011) **Over one out of four adults in the United States has a criminal record.** "The Case for Reforming Criminal Background Checks for Employment." National Employment Law Center.

329 Approximately half of US males have an arrest record by age 23. Robert Brame et al (Jan 6, 2014) "Demographic Patterns of Cumulative Arrest Prevalence by Ages 18 and 23." Crime & Delinquency.

335 According to the 2008 U.S. Census Bureau, 7,601,169 business establishments have a payroll. *Census*. U.S. Department of Commerce. *n.d.* Web. 09 Sep. 2013.

336 Men's Wearhouse, Inc. do not conduct criminal background checks on new hires. Hamner S & McNichol T. "Ripping up the rules of management" *CNN Money*. *n.d.* Web. 09 Sep. 2013.

FORTY THREE
DISABILITIES

348 Motoko, Rich. "Disabled, but Looking for Work." *New York Times*. 7 April 2011. Print.

FORTY FIVE
HOW TO STUDY

359 2 minute distraction makes subjects 55% better at figuring out which ideas are actually good. Ritter S *et al* (2011) Creativity: The role of unconscious processes in idea generation and idea selection. Thinking Skills and Creativity online edition: December 14.

359 Multisensory presentations make for more robust learning. Najjar, LJ (1996) The effects of multimedia and elaborative encoding on learning (GIT-GVU-96-05) Atlanta, GA: Georgia Institute of Technology, Graphics, Visualization and Usability Center.

359 Attention capture of print media advertising. Pieters, R & Wedel, M (2004) Attention capture and transfer in advertising: brand, pictorial, and text-size effects. J. of Marketing 68(2): 36 - 50.

359 3lb brain weight average. Hartmann, P *et al* (1994) Normal weight of the brain in adults in relation to age, sex, body height and weight. Pathologe. 15(3): 165-70.

359 **Walking through the door causes you to forget.** Radvansky, GA *et al* (2011) Walking through doorways causes forgetting: Further explorations. The Quarterly Journal of Experimental Psychology 64 (8): 1632 - 1645.

359 **Human brain speed 20 million billion calculation.** Raymond Kurzweil (1999). The Age of Spiritual Machines. Penguin Books, Ltd. pp. 103 - 105.

360 **People misjudge their own intelligence.** Bjork, RA (1999) Assessing our own competence: Heuristics and illusions. Attention and performance XVII: Cognitive regulation of performance: Interaction of theory and application Cambridge, MA: MIT Press pp. 435-459.

360 **Study time.** Son, LK & Kornell N. (2008). Research on the allocation of study time: Key studies from 1890 to the present (and beyond). In Dunlosky J & Bjork RA (Eds). A handbook of memory and metamemory. Hillsdale, NJ: Psychology Press pp. 333-351.

360 **10 Minute Rule**. Hartley J & Davies IK (1978) Note-taking: a critical review. Innovations in Education & Training International 15(3): 207 – 224.

361 **Roots of the "we only use 10% brainpower" myth.** Kalat JW (1998) Biological Psychology, sixth edition, Pacific Grove: Brooks-Cole Publishing Co: p. 43.

361 **Overall energy requirements of the brain and carbohydrate effects.** Bourre JM (2006) Effects of nutrients in food on the structure and function of the nervous system: update on dietary requirements for brain. Part 2: macronutrients. Journal of Nutrition, Health & Aging 10(5): 386 – 399.

361 **Exercise may increase blood flow to brain and increase academic outcome for school aged populations.** Singh A *et al* (2012) Physical Activity and Performance at School: A Systematic Review of the Literature Including a Methodological Quality Assessment. Arch Pediatr Adolesc Med 166: 49 – 55.

361 **Effects of exercise on school aged population's brains and their academic outcomes.** Strong WB *et al* (2005) Evidence based physical activity for school-age youth. J. Pediatrics 146(6): 732 – 737.

361 **Incubation (sleep) increases creative output (imagination).** Wagner U, et al (2004) Sleep inspires insight. Nature 427(6972): 352 – 355.

361 **Less sleep, the dumber you get by 30 to 40% first night, 60% the next night.** Angus, R G., Heslegrave R J (1985) Effects of sleep loss on sustained cognitive performance during a command and control simulation. Behavior Research Methods17(1): 55 - 67.

362 **Learning is best in groups.** Lave J (1996) Teaching, as learning, in practice, Jean Lave. Mind, Culture, and Activity 3(3): 149 - 164.

362 **School environment does not reflect real world training.** Bjork RA (1994) Memory and metamemory considerations in the training of human beings. In J. Metcalfe, & A. Shimamura (Eds.). Metacognition: Knowing about knowing.   Cambridge MA: MIT Press pp. 185 -205.

362 **Copying from examples aids memory.** Michelene TH (1989) *et al* Self-explanations: How students study and use examples in learning to solve problems. Cog Sci 13(2): 145 – 182.

363 **Blue makes us more creative and receptive to new ideas, red can trigger drop IQ and trigger avoidance.** Mehta R & Zhu J (2009) Blue or Red? Exploring the Effect of Color on Cognitive Task Performances. Science 324(5915): 1226 - 1229.

363 **Children learn like scientists.** Gopnik A (1996) The scientist as child. Phi of Sci 63(4): 485-514.

363 **Babies are scientists.** Gopnik A *et al* (2000) The Scientist in the Crib. What early learning tells us about the child. William Morrow pp. 60 – 75 & pp. 85 - 91.

364 **Ebbinghuas' forgetting curves: 90% of newly learned information forgotten within 30 days.** Ebbinghaus H (1964) Uber das Gedachtnis Untersuchungun Zure Experimentatellen Psychologie. H.A. Ruger & C.E. Bussenius, Trans. New York: Dover.

364 **Brain forgets 90% of learned information within 30 days.** Wozniak RH (1999) Introduction to memory: Hermann Ebbinghaus (1885/1913). Bristol, UK: Thoemmes Press.

364 **An ECS is the best processed information of any type (better encoded, better recalled).** LaBar KS & Cabeza R (2006) Cognitive neuroscience of emotional memory. Nature Reviews Neuroscience 7: 54 - 64.

364 **ECS helps recall even without repetition.** Harris CR *et al* (2005) Enhanced Memory for Negatively Emotionally Charged Pictures Without Selective Rumination. Emotion5(2): 191-199.

364 **Retina sends 1.25mb/second to brain.** Koch K et al (2006) How *Much* the Eye Tells the Brain. Current Biology 16(14): 1428 - 1434.

364 **Brains switch attention to emotionally charged cues.** Stormark KM et al (1995) Attentional shifts to emotionally charged cues: Behavioural and erp data. Cog & Em 9(5).

364 **Evidence for "chronotypes" and genetic predisposition to being an "early bird" or "late bird."** Schmidt C *et al* (2012) Circadian Preference Modulates the Neural Substrate of Conflict Processing across the Day. PLoS ONE 7(1): e29658.

365 **Spaced repetition in advertisements.** Appleton-Knapp S et al (2005) Examining the spacing effect in advertising: Encoding variability, retrieval processes and their interaction. J Consumer Res 32: 266 - 276.

365 **Spaced repetition.** Benjamin AS & Bird R (2006) Metacognitive control of the spacing of study repetitions. J Mem & Lan 55: 126 - 137.

365 **Flashcards help school-age children learn words quickly, accurately with greater comprehension, but educators are not aware of this.** Tan A & Nicholson T (1997) Flashcards revisited: Training poor readers to read words faster improves their comprehension of text. J Ed Psychol 89(2): 276 - 288.

365 **Studying one large stack of flashcards is better than dividing flashcards in many small stacks.** Kornell, N (2009) Optimising learning using flashcards: Spacing is more effective than cramming. Applied Cog Psychol 23: 1297 – 1317.

366 **Dropping flashcards out of the pile has a negative impact on learning.** Nate K & Bjork R (2008) Optimising self-regulated study: The benefits—and costs—of dropping flashcards. Memory 16(2): 125 - 136.

366 **Vocalization leads to best retention.** Gathercole S & Conway M (1988) Exploring long-term modality effects: Vocalization leads to best retention. Mem & Cog 16(2): 110 – 119.

366 **Chunking and paired groups mnemonics makes learning more enjoyable and effective.** Beitz, J (1997) Unleashing the Power of Memory: The Mighty Mnemonic. Nurse Educator: 22(2): 25 – 29.

368 **Photographic memory is a myth.** Pring L (2005) Savant talent. Developmental Medicine & Child Neurology 47: 500 – 503.

368 **Mnemonics helps students memorize and recall information.** Carney R *et al* (2000) Mnemonic instruct, with a focus on transfer. Journal of Ed Psychol 92(4): 783 – 790.

368 **Mnemonics used to by ancient Romans and Greeks to memorize historical archive: before books were printed and populations became literate.** Rachal J (1988) Gutenberg, Literacy, and the Ancient Arts of Memory. Adult Education Quartely 38(3) 125 -135.

370 **Memory boost twice as much with smell.** Maylor EA *et al* (2002) Preserved olfactory cuing of autobiographical memories in old age. Journals of Gerontology B Psychol Sci Soc Sci 57(1): 41 – 46.

370   **Brains don't like to pay attention to boring stuff.** Norris CE & Colman AM (1993) Context effects on memory for television advertisements. Social Behavior and Personality 21(4): 279 - 296.

371   **The stress of a hostile home and marital problems.** Bryner C (2001) Children of divorce. Journal of the American Board of Family Medicine 14(3): 201 – 210.

371   **Brain evolved for short-term stress not long term.** Sterling P (2003) Principles of allostasis: optimal design, predictive regulation, pathophysiology and rational therapeutics. In *Allostasis, Homeostasis, and the Costs of Adaptation*. J. Schulkin MIT Press.

371   **Stress can help form stronger memories.** Cahill L *et al (2003)* Enhanced Human Memory Consolidation With Post-Learning Stress: Interaction With the Degree of Arousal at Encoding. *Learning & Memory 10: 270 – 274.*

371   **How chronic stress can lead to heart disease.** Henry JP (1986) Mechanisms by which stress can lead to coronary heart disease. Postgrad Med J 62: 687-693.

371   **Stress causes stroke.** May M *et al* (2002) Does Psychological Distress Predict the Risk of Ischemic Stroke and Transient Ischemic Attack? Stoke 33: 7 – 12.

372   **Multitasking is slower than performing two tasks separately.** Just MA *et al* (2001) Interdependence of non-overlapping cortical systems in dual cognitive tasks. NeuroImage 14: 417 - 426.

FORTY SIX
JOB TESTING

375   **If you want to increase accuracy, slow down what you're doing.** Starns JJ et al (2012). Evaluating the unequal-variance and dual-process explanations of zROC slopes with response time data and the diffusion model. Cog Psychol 64: 1 – 2.

377   Mike McClenathan. "'The most common answer on the SAT is C.' No, not really." Blog.pwnthesat.com. March 2011. Web. June 13, 2013.